Cinema India

ENVISIONING ASIA

Series Editors: Homi Bhabha, Norman Bryson, Wu Hung

CINEMA INDIA

The Visual Culture of Hindi Film

RACHEL DWYER and DIVIA PATEL

REAKTION BOOKS

DEDICATIONS

Rachel: For my Bombay homegivers, Imtiaz, Maithili, Rekhi, Udita and Shaad

Divia: To my grandfather, Bhanabhai S. Patel

Published by Reaktion Books Ltd
79 Farringdon Road
London EC1M 3JU, UK

www.reaktionbooks.co.uk

First published 2002

This work is published with the support of the Society for South Asian Studies

Series design by Ron Costley

Printed in Hong Kong

British Library Cataloguing in Publishing Data
Dwyer, Rachel
    Cinema India: the visual culture of Hindi film. – (Envisioning
    Asia)
    1.Motion pictures – India – History
    I. Title II. Patel, Divia
    791.4'3'0954
    ISBN 1 86189 124 5

Contents

Preface

This book is the result of a collaboration of two authors who have, over the last decade, witnessed the rising interest in Indian cinema and the visual culture of India. The authors' aim is to provide a unique insight into aspects of this field of study, which hitherto has not been researched or written on in any great depth. It brings together Rachel Dwyer's extensive knowledge of Indian cinema and Divia Patel's expertise in Indian art and design. Thus, in chapters One and Two, Rachel Dwyer has written an overview of the history of Indian cinema, followed by an in-depth study of the visual style of films as created through sets and costumes. In chapters Three and Four Divia Patel examines the visual culture of film advertising, first from an historical perspective and then by means of a study of the greater meaning of these cinematic images and their use in a wider field. The Introduction and Conclusion are jointly written.

Many Indian cities have changed their names in recent years. For this book the authors have preferred to use Bombay (for Mumbai), Poona (for Pune), Calcutta (for Kolkatta), Madras (for Chennai) and Baroda (for Vadodara).

Introduction

'One of the most significant phenomena of our time has been the development of the cinema from a turn-of-the-century mechanical toy into the century's most potent and versatile art form. In its early chameleon-like phase the cinema was used variously as an extension of photography, as a substitute for the theatre and the music hall, and as part of the magician's paraphernalia ... Today the cinema commands the respect accorded to any other form of creative expression. In the immense complexity of its creative process, it combines in various measures the functions of poetry, music, painting, drama, architecture and a host of other arts, major and minor.'[1]

So wrote Satyajit Ray in 1948. Less then ten years later he was to become India's first internationally acclaimed film director. Ray's words, however, were not an accolade to the Indian film industry, rather they were an observation of the cinemas of Italy, France, Germany and the Soviet Union. For, according to Ray, India had failed to produce anything that could match their quality. He felt that the Indian film industry needed 'a style, an idiom, a sort of iconography of cinema, which would be uniquely and recognizably Indian.' Influenced by these other cinemas he made his first film, *Pather Panchali*, for which he won an award at the Cannes Film Festival in 1956. Since then Ray's distinct 'art-house' films, made in black and white, with their simple linear narratives conveying realism and emotional truth, have come to define, and be regarded in the west as synonymous with, Indian cinema.

Yet this is not the only cinema of India. Today, more than fifty years later, India has developed many cinemas, each with its own film styles, each with its own combination of 'poetry, music, painting ... and a host of other arts', and of those many cinemas it is the distinctive style of the Hindi commercial cinema that is the focus of this book. Its films are criticized for their excessive length, their complicated plots within plots, their song and dance sequences, their colourful costumes, and their incongruous locations. In 1948 Ray believed that a 'truly Indian film should steer clear of such inconsistencies and look for its material in the most basic aspects of Indian life, where habit and speech, dress and manners, background and foreground, blend into a harmonious whole'.[2] It is precisely these inconsistencies, however, that have since come to define the style of the Hindi cinema.

Hindi cinema's style is unique and recognizably Indian. It is determined by the film sets, locations and costumes seen within the film (as well as the cinematography) and is projected beyond the screens and cinema halls through the film's advertising and promotional material. These components constitute the visual culture of the Hindi film. Considered vulgar and kitsch by some and glamorous and trendsetting by others, this 'filmi' style, as it is known, permeates every aspect of Indian and Indian diasporic culture. Its ubiquitous nature is made apparent through the music that is played in people's homes, through the clothes worn on the streets, at weddings, in nightclubs and social gatherings, as well as the profusion of cinematic images visible across the landscape, on hoardings and posters in the streets, on magazines, on television and on the Internet. Thus, rather than *reflect* the 'harmonious whole' that is an observation of everyday Indian life as envisioned by Ray, Hindi commercial cinema has become *part* of everyday life, part of its 'habit and speech, dress and manners, background and foreground'. This all-pervasive visual culture is an integral part of the complexity that comprises Indian cinema and any study of it. It is the aim of this book to explore that visual culture, its production and reception, and its cultural, historic and aesthetic significance.

The Hindi Commercial Cinema: Local/Global Culture

Spoken largely in northern India, Hindi is the government's designated national language and as such has become the most widely understood language across the country. The Hindi commercial cinema, although produced in Bombay, is considered to be the national cinema of India, in part because of the language in which it is produced. As such it is a prominent form of mass entertainment and is therefore distinguished from the other cinemas of India.

There are, however, many other regionally defined commercial cinemas, of which the most notable and largest in terms of production are the Telugu- and Tamil-language cinemas of South India. It is here that the cinema halls are concentrated and the largest cinema-going public is to be found. These films are rarely shown outside of their heartlands, except where Tamil and Telugu speakers have settled elsewhere in India or overseas. Similarly, the 'art-house' cinema, which includes avant-garde and experimental films, is also regionally defined. Here it is the Bengali cinema that has achieved a prominent position, largely because of Satyajit Ray, but this is followed closely by the Malayalam-language cinema of Kerala, South India. While these cinemas are internationally acclaimed, primarily because they fall into a recognized school of film making, within India their appeal is restricted to a relatively small, intellectually defined audience, with their success attributed to the popular belief of the intellectual superiority of the Bengalis and the high literacy rates of Kerala. The other major languages of 'art-house' films are Hindi and more recently, English. Despite these other cinemas, however, it is the Bombay-produced, Hindi-language cinema that is not only screened across India but is also dubbed into local languages.

Thus, as India's national cinema, this is a primary form of Indian public culture. Here the term 'public culture' is seen to address the complex and fluid interaction that exists between the categories of high/elite and low/mass culture in India (whereas the term 'popular culture' implies a more rigid distinction between the two).[3] The need to study public culture as a source of information about the society in which it is produced has long been acknowledged. The very nature of its close engagement with the people of a nation makes the Hindi cinema a primary source of such information. Studies of it thus far have informed us of the cultural specificity of certain defining features of this cinema, such as the narrative structure, the lack of realism and the multiplicity of emotional content.[4] These studies also point to the more powerful personal levels of association that the public have with specific male/female roles, and the familiar subject matter of family, marriage, social order and morality.[5] Here social background is seen to affect the manner in which these roles and themes are evaluated and identified with. It has been suggested that, during the early development of cinema, genres of the 1920s such as historical, mythological and stunt films were 'lower class' films primarily because they offered visual spectacle. With the advent of sound in the 1950s, the new genres were seen as more 'middle class' since they placed greater emphasis on the narrative and focused on social concerns.[6] Class identifications continued to shift with the emergence of new genres, which themselves reflected political, ideological, economic and social changes within Indian society, thereby making Hindi film a key to India's national culture. Furthermore, as this cinema is the most widely distributed overseas among the Indian diaspora in the UK, USA, Canada and elsewhere, and has over the years attracted large audiences in Russia, Indonesia and the Middle East, it is also an insight into India's global culture.

Cinema India

Since its inception much has been written about the Hindi cinema: from books that chart its historical development[7] to encyclopaedias,[8] from numerous monographs on actors and directors through to more in-depth studies regarding aspects of production, technology, reception and ideology.9 However, having established the primacy of Hindi cinema as both a national and global culture, it is surprising that little has been written about one of its most striking elements: its visual culture. This evolved from the rapidly developing urban environment of nineteenth-century India, where the colonial encounter saw the dynamic interaction of new technologies with indigenous practices. This was a period when Western theatre companies travelled through the urban centres, when the exciting new medium of photography was introduced, when the European aesthetic practice of realism became the favoured form of representation, and when the advancement of printing technology changed forever the depiction of Indian deities. This was also a time when the political structure of India was changing, when power transferred from the East India Company to the British government and when Indian nationalism began to take shape. Being born of such circumstances, and of such diversity, the visual culture of the Hindi cinema encompasses an inherent hybridity, constantly adapting to changes and adopting new forms. This hybridity has over time incorporated the influence of Hollywood, the European film industry, theatre and international art movements, and is currently absorbing and responding to the infinite range of imagery offered through global technologies such as satellite television and the Internet. This book presents a unique insight into that visual culture.

Cinema India is split into two distinct halves: the first identifies and explores the visual components that constitute the very structure of Hindi film, while the second investigates the visual culture that extends beyond the films themselves – the advertising.

Chapter One contextualizes our subject by giving a brief account of the history of the Indian cinema, examining its antecedents in both Western and Sanskrit theatre before outlining the major steps in its development. It then looks at the factors that form and define Hindi film. These include the financing and production of a film; the narrative structure and the interplay of melodrama and realism; the film star and the cultural practice of *darshan*, which constructs the star image; the song and dance sequences, where the primacy of music distinguishes Hindi film from all other cinemas, and the influence on that music from a wide variety of other sources.

Of these factors, two not only form the structure but also construct the 'look' of the film: the settings and costumes. Their importance is such that they are explored in depth in chapter Two. They are both major components of the *mise-en-scène* of the film and it is their function as projectors of meaning that is examined here. Thus, we see the representation of the State through the use of the courtroom or the police station; the people–nation through street scenes and bazaars; the family through domestic interiors, and such structures as the grand staircase as liminal spaces. Also explored are the use of outdoor locations; the representation of paradise through the use of Kashmir, Switzerland and Scotland; the changing depictions of the city and village; and the Utopias of consumption as seen in designer shops and shopping arcades, where modern romance is tied to lifestyle opportunities and consumerism.

Alongside sets and locations, meaning is also created through costume, hairstyles and makeup. These factors are examined in the context of the representation of the body and the changing notions of beauty, sexuality and consumerism. Clothing is seen as a means of highlighting issues of caste, class, region and religion and is represented through the differentiation of ethnicity and Westernization, the former seen in the wearing of the veil, sari and *salwar-khamees*, and the latter through the wearing of dresses, suits and the products of Western designers such as DKNY. The chapter then looks at the issues of nudity, exhibitionism, narcissism, fetishism, cross-dressing and androgyny, concluding with a look at the 1990s and the way in which the rise of the new middle classes, the explosion of new media such as cable and satellite television, and the flourishing of the magazine industry, advertising and 'sex 'n' shopping' novels, have presented new ideals of the body and fashion, which are then reflected in film.

The visual culture of Hindi film is not confined to what is presented on the cinema screen. Equally important and often the first reference point to the cinema is the film advertising and promotional material seen on the cinema fronts, in the streets, in magazines and elsewhere, and it is this material that is studied in the following two chapters. Chapter Three gives a detailed historical account of the development of film advertising over a period of a hundred years from the early text-based newspaper notices to the colourful hoardings, posters, booklets, lobby cards, magazines and Web sites that are today used to promote film. Hoardings with their large-scale vibrant images and bright colours have been identified as the most distinct feature of film advertising. They are also the most ephemeral, however, as they are destroyed once a film finishes its run in a cinema. Since there is little surviving evidence of the type of imagery depicted on early hoardings, this study is based primarily upon handbills, posters and booklets, which, despite their fragility, have survived. It seeks to document the aesthetic evolution of these forms of advertising, to position them within India's visual vocabulary and to establish their significance as sources of information about the society in which they were produced. Here shifts in style and design, which range from the Western Art Deco movement to indigenous chromolithographs, are seen as a reflection of social, economic and political changes in Indian society, and this chapter shows how a study of this visual culture is able to inform us of those changes.

Chapter Four looks more specifically at the film poster, examining the components that typically constitute a poster design, such as the star portrait and recurring male and female images, and shows how they are multi-layered in terms of the meanings that can be read from them. It breaks down these components and distinguishes between meanings that are universally understood and those that are culturally specific. Following on from chapter One, this study expands the analysis on the construction of a star image and serves to establish the importance of advertising and promotional material in this process. It gives an in-depth examination of the star portrait and shows how it is loaded with many different meanings acquired through the historical and modern processes and techniques involved in producing it. Following this, the cultural specificity of a poster is assessed through an examination of character 'types'. This chapter concludes with a look at how the dynamic nature of Hindi film, and its cultural significance, is currently being acknowledged by 'fine' artists. It observes how these artists use film imagery in their own work, both as a critique and as a homage to the industry, and how they not only give meaning to their creations but project new meanings onto the images themselves.

1 Indian Cinema

Origins and Beginnings

Cinema in India dates from around the time of its very origins in the West.[1] The first cinematograph films of the Lumière brothers were shown in Bombay on 7 July 1896, where they attracted large audiences. Several Indians collaborated in making films of a largely documentary nature, but it was not until 1913 that D. G. Phalke produced the first entirely Indian film, a 'mythological' called *Raja Harishchandra* (illus. 1).[2] Phalke was a remarkable person, who trained in many of the new industrial arts before travelling to London to obtain equipment and seek training in the skills of film making. Most of his films were based on Hindu mythology, creating a new film genre, the mythological, although he also made documentary films. He continued the trend of the stage mythological in using special effects to depict miracles, which deeply impressed his contemporary audiences.

Other film companies were founded following Phalke's example, including Baburao Painter's Maharashtra Film Company in Kohlapur (1918–32), financed by the Maharaja of Kohlapur, which made mostly historical films and introduced new talent such as V. Shantaram. The Kohinoor Film Company[3] (1919–32) of Bombay launched the careers of such great stars of the silent screen as Sulochana and Gohar.

Indian cinema has very strong links with indigenous performing traditions, but there has been much over-interpretation of these connections by some writers, trying to find an essential 'Indianness' that was transmitted to cinema. Rather, as Partha Chatterjee argues,[4] when modernity was first introduced into traditional societies they responded by using modern forms to reform themselves, resulting in what Ashish Rajadhyaksha calls a neo-tradition.[5] Much of Indian cinema is thus the product of a new public culture that arose during the nineteenth century, the hybridity of which is inherent to its very nature, as it brings together traditional Indian images with industrial technology.[6]

Among these new forms of public culture, the new urban theatre was one of the most important antecedents of cinema. Indian cinema is often given a misattributed genealogy from Sanskrit drama, a form (restricted to a small élite) that had died out several centuries earlier, being revived only in the nineteenth century. In the colonial period

1 The famous bathing scene from the first 'Indian' film, D. G. Phalke's *Raja Harishchandra*, 1913.

both local British amateur dramatic societies and touring theatre companies brought many of the features of Western theatre to India, including commercial features such as advertising and tickets.[7] As early as the eighteenth century British playhouses were built in India, such as the Bombay Amateur Theatre, which opened in the city in 1776, bringing the proscenium arch, the curtain, sets and a new relationship between audience and actors.[8] This form of theatre spread from the presidency cities to the whole country and beyond to Singapore in the latter half of the nineteenth century, largely through the efforts of Parsi theatre companies,[9] who were major contributors in establishing this new urban theatre. It remained popular until it was largely superseded by cinema in the twentieth century.

These theatres were certainly eclectic: the repertoire was drawn from Shakespeare, modern versions of Sanskrit classics and original works; the languages in Bombay included English, Hindi, Urdu, Gujarati and Marathi, while Bengali theatre flourished in Calcutta and beyond.[10] The plays included songs and dance set between long dialogues and displayed many features that we later find in Hindi films, notably the presentation of a series of attractions (see below), such as miracles, which interrupted the narrative, and the use of song and dance.[11]

The song and dance tradition seems to have been one of the most important legacies of the folk theatre to Indian cinema, other connections between these two forms being more tenuous. The folk theatres in India were largely religious and performed in specific ritual contexts, whereas this urban theatre is part of the new urban, public or mass culture, of which cinema is a part. While the early films were silent, music performance by live musicians was an important part of the cinematic event.

The Silent Film

As early as the 1920s three major genres had emerged in Indian cinema: the mythological, the historical and the stunt. While these proved popular, Hollywood, whose films could be rented at lower prices owing to their larger market, was a serious competitor, since around 85 per cent of films shown in India were foreign in origin, including those from Europe and the USSR. Although the European national cinemas had evolved their own distinctive styles, Hollywood's classical way of film making and its codes of continuity and editing were taken up by many Indian film makers, although some resisted. In total, 1313 silent films were made in India.[12]

Indian film makers often had a more direct involvement with Western cinema. Himansu Rai, who began acting when a lawyer in London in the 1920s, appeared in several films produced by a company he formed with German producers, including *Prem Sanyas* (*Light of Asia*, 1925). In 1929 he married Devika Rani, who had an élite European education that included studying at RADA and training as an architect. She worked as an assistant on several films, including Marlene Dietrich's *Der Blaue Engel* (*The Blue Angel*, directed by Josef von Sternberg, 1930), before starring in Rai's first talkie, *Karma* (1933), made in English after their return to India. Rai and Rani continued to work with German personnel after they founded their own company (see below),[13] with Rani becoming a major star. Also educated in Europe was Dhiren Ganguly, whose *Bilet Pherat* (*England Returned*, 1921; illus. 2) was a send-up of the 'brown sahib'.

India's first major distributing company was Madan Theatres, founded by Jamshedji Madan, an actor from the Parsi theatre, who moved to Calcutta in 1902. The company later expanded into film exhibition and distribution, having 172 cinemas at its peak across India, Ceylon and Burma. These cinemas screened mostly imported films aimed at a European audience until the First World War but then they began to import Hollywood films. In 1917 Madan Theatres began film production, mostly of filmed plays, before collapsing in the 1930s largely due to the costs of converting their theatres to sound.

2 Dhirendranath Ganguly in the satire on colonial culture, *Bilet Pherat*, 1921.

The Coming of Sound and the Studio Period

The first talkies in India were made in 1931, establishing another major feature of the Hindi cinema, namely the importance of song. A studio system similar to that of Hollywood operated, with each employing its own directors, stars and music directors on the same salaried basis as their other staff. The history of these studios is intricate and complex since many were offshoots of other studios, so here I will touch on just some of the major ones.

The silent film could reach a wide audience in India, undifferentiated by language. Once sound came, the issue of language had to be addressed by the film makers. The most widely understood language in India was that from the area around Delhi, which was labelled as Hindi when written in the Devanagari script, with Sanskrit words in the formal registers, and as Urdu when written in the Perso-Arabic script, with Persian and Arabic words in its formal registers. Urdu had a rich lyric tradition and was the main language used by the Parsi theatre, so film tended towards its registers, although at a colloquial

3 The singing star K. L. Saigal as Devdas and Jamuna as Paro, in their childhood idyll in the New Theatres' Hindi version of *Devdas*, 1935.

level, and as a spoken language there was little distinction between the two languages.

Most of the cinema produced in Bombay was made in Hindi-Urdu, but the regional studios either made films in their local languages (such as Bengali, Marathi or Punjabi) or they made two versions of their films simultaneously, one in their local language and one in Hindi-Urdu. South Indian films were often made outside their language area but were rarely made simultaneously in Hindi-Urdu.

One of the most important regional studios was New Theatres (1931–55) of Calcutta, which was characterized by its élite members and whose productions drew heavily on theatre and literature. Their main language was Bengali but they also made dual-language versions of many of their most famous films. Founded by B. N. Sircar, who was later joined by Debaki Bose, Dhiren Ganguly and P. C. Barua, the studio's major stars included K. L. Saigal (illus. 3) and Barua, who played the title role in the separate Hindi and Bengali versions, respectively, of New Theatres' most famous film, *Devdas* (directed by P. C. Barua, 1935). Several key figures central to the Hindi film industry from the 1950s, including Bimal Roy, Nitin Bose and Hrishikesh Mukherjee, began their careers at New Theatres.

The founders of the Prabhat Film Company (1929–53), based initially in Kohlapur and then later in Poona, included V. Shantaram, Vishnupant

Damle and Sheikh Fattelal. Their concerns were less literary than New Theatres', concentrating on social films by Shantaram and devotional films by Damle and Fattelal, all of which were renowned for their music and created such major stars as Master Vinayak and Shanta Apte. One of Damle and Fattelal's productions, *Sant Tukaram* (1936), is regarded as one of the greatest films made in India.

Devika Rani and Himansu Rai founded Bombay Talkies (1934–54), which also nurtured major talents, including Gyan Mukherjee, Sadat Hasan Manto, Ashok Kumar, Dev Anand, Kamal Amrohi and Dilip Kumar. Most of its films were socials, including Franz Osten's *Achhyut Kanya* (*Untouchable Girl*, 1936) and *Kangan* (*Bangle*, 1939) and *Kismet* (*Fate*, directed by Gyan Mukherjee, 1943).

The other studios included Ardeshir Irani's Imperial Films Company (1926–38), which made the first talkie; the Sagar Film Company (1930–39), which made films in many languages other than Hindi and introduced Sulochana;[14] and Ranjit Movietone, which was formed by Chandulal Shah and the great star Gohar. Several companies made films in specific genres including stunt films, starring 'Fearless Nadia', at Wadia Movietone (from 1933), while historicals were the speciality of Sohrab Modi's Minerva Movietone (1936–53).

During this period the coming of sound precipitated the development of new genres, which attracted audiences from particular classes. Vasudevan argues that the three major genres of the 1920s – the historical, the mythological and the stunt – were seen as 'lower class' since they offered mainly spectacle. In the 1930s, as the talkies introduced sound and music, new genres emerged that were more narrative driven, including the social, the Muslim social and the devotional. These were seen as middle-class films, offering a critique of Indian society.[15]

The social, which is an omnibus term loosely describing a film with a contemporary setting, also encompassed the social reform film. Both types were closely associated with contemporary literary movements, which were themselves preoccupied with social questions. The Muslim social, the origins of which may lie in the silent era, is similarly set in the contemporary period, but its characters exist in an almost exclusively Muslim society. Kesavan analyses the 'Islamicate'[16] features of this genre, such as that of the woman concealed by the veil, a glimpse of whom makes the hero fall in love but also gives rise to mistaken identity. The genre also uses flowery (Urdu) language and the imagery of the Urdu lyric (*ghazal*), with a particularly Islamicate *mise-en-scène*.

The devotional genre narrates the often miraculous lives of India's many medieval singer-saints, who are associated with the traditions of *bhakti* or 'loving devotion', where the devotee's deeply personal and emotional relation to the deity is often expressed in song. The singer-saints composed many of the most popular songs of India, so providing the film makers with ready-made songs and stories. Nearly every 'regional' language of India has a strong saint tradition, and although Hindi, the future national language, is too late for this tradition there are key texts in its variants, such as Braj Bhasha and Avadhi. The films historicize *bhakti* as the religion of the people, emphasizing its origins outside Brahminical religion, through its introduction of vernacular languages and its inclusion of low castes and women, rather than the Sanskritized forms that later developed.

Independence and After

Bombay became the centre of the Hindi-Urdu film after the coming of sound in 1931, even though it lies outside the Hindi-Urdu speaking area of north India, because Urdu was one of the major languages of the city, largely owing to its sizeable Muslim population. However, once Hindi was promoted as the national language of India and the Bombay film industry came to be seen as the national film industry, the language of its cinema became somewhat inaccurately called Hindi. Urdu, which became the national language of Pakistan, had come to be regarded as the language of Muslims. Until independence, however, Urdu was the language of culture of Punjabi Hindus and Muslims, hence the high proportion of personnel from these communities employed in the film industry with the coming of sound. Their language skills were in demand particularly as writers of dialogues and lyrics, and as actors whose accents would be acceptable in north India. This further developed the cinema's hybrid nature, allowing it to evolve a style that would be seen as national, while India's other cinemas began to be regarded as local or regional. Although the Partition of 1947 resulted in a decline of the Muslim population of Bombay, it saw the arrival of a number of displaced Punjabis, some of whom had worked in the Lahore film industry. The majority of these Punjabi refugees settled in Delhi, which replaced Lahore as their cultural capital, although their nostalgia for their homeland of Punjab never waned. Their north Indian style of culture is of critical importance, for the Punjabis have continued to dominate the industry as producers, directors and male actors, inscribing Punjabi culture as the national public culture of India.

The collapse of the studio system in the 1940s was due for the most part to the economic boom, in particular that of the 'black' economy of the war years. The independent producers who emerged at this

4 Raj Kapoor as Raj, the urban migrant, in *Shri 420*, 1955.

time were often Punjabi, mostly migrants or refugees from Lahore. They saw stars as the critical box-office factor and began to woo them assiduously for their movies. The stars represented idealized forms of masculinity and femininity, whose images circulated in film, photographs, gossip magazines, advertising and movie publicity to become national icons. The operation of a star system was further reinforced by the films' specific requirements for their heroes and heroines to appear as ideals, rather than as natural, psychologically plausible characters.

The norm of the film's characters is that of the urban, upper-caste, north Indian Hindu. Characters from other religions, regions and castes are portrayed as 'others', and their style of speech, attitudes and clothes seen as humorous or exotic. It is not surprising then that most of the male stars have been Punjabis, whose height and fair skin approximate north Indian ideals of physical beauty, an association reinforced by the British who created a myth of Punjabis as a martial race, notable for their 'masculine' qualities. The great stars of the 1950s were Dilip Kumar (Pathan), Dev Anand and Raj Kapoor (the last two both Punjabi). All three were tall, light-skinned (Raj Kapoor even having blue eyes), slim and lightly built; their bodies, which were barely shown, were not particularly muscular or athletic.

The 1940s and '50s are usually regarded as the Golden Age of Indian cinema, perhaps because the new system of independent production allowed more flexibility than the studio system, although the producers often sought to minimize risk by using the 'formula' ingredients, such as stars, music and dance. This period saw the emergence of some of the most highly regarded directors, including Raj Kapoor, Mehboob Khan, Guru Dutt and Bimal Roy; the emergence of playback singing and the advent of the 'nightingale of India', Lata Mangeshkar; and the rise to super-stardom of Nargis, Madhubala, Dilip Kumar, Raj Kapoor (illus. 4) and Dev Anand.

Meanwhile, Satyajit Ray, who made his first film, *Pather Panchali* (*Song of the Road*, 1955), with help from the West Bengal government, established himself as one of the world's great *auteurs*. Although Ray's narratives are often taken from Bengali literature and have specifically Bengali locales and cultural milieux, his films belong to the traditions of international art cinema and never established a national popularity except among the art-house film viewers.

In the 1950s the new nation's media debated the creation of a national cinema and the government's role in its development.[17] Although Nehru was not fond of cinema, he realized the political advantages of Raj Kapoor's popularity in the Soviet Union and elsewhere, and maintained good relations with the film world. Government enquiries into the rapidly expanding industry, however, resulted in its censorship and heavy taxation, but yielded few benefits to the film makers. In fact, the government's negative views led to a boycott of All India Radio by film music producers[18] and the resentment of the industry, which thought it was viewed as a major source of tax rather than a cultural resource. During this period the government established national academies of dance, literature and theatre but not of cinema. In 1960, however, it set up the Film Finance Corporation (which merged with the Motion Picture Export Association in 1980 to form the National Film Development Corporation, for financing and exporting films) and in 1961 established the Film Institute in Poona in the old Prabhat studios (soon augmented by the National Film Archive and later extended to cover television). For the first time students could learn about film making in an academic environment, and many art film personnel as well as a few of the Hindi film personnel were trained there. In 1973 the government established the Directorate of Film Festivals, whose brief was to organize an annual International Film Festival, which to this day remains one of the few places for the Indian public to see art and other international films.

This period marks a deeper separation of categories of film in India than we saw earlier with the generic changes in the 1930s. Madhava Prasad argues that the Hindi film's omnibus genre of the social, with its underlying theme of the feudal family romance,[19] which long resisted generic differentiation, was segmented in the early 1970s. He sees this as part of a wider change in ideology, as the fragmentation of the national consensus brought about political mobilization, challenging the aesthetic conventions and mode of production of the film industry.[20] This resulted in the emergence of three major forms of the Hindi cinema: developmentalist state realism; identification-orientated realism of the middle-class arena; and the aesthetic of mobilization.[21] This model situates these changes in terms of wider issues of politics and ideology and shows how all these types of cinema to some extent drew on existing practices of narrative codes and signification.

During the 1980s the Hindi commercial cinema produced mostly films derived from the 'aesthetic of mobilization', where violence was the major attraction. While having roots in wider political and social trends of the 1970s, this phenomenon is also connected to changes in the composition of the cinema audience caused by the introduction of colour television in 1982, followed by the increasing availability of the VCR. Thus the middle-class audience began watching the new television soaps and viewing films on video at home, while the cinema halls became run down and regarded as suitable only for lower-class men.

Despite the advent of cable and satellite television in India in 1991, the middle class returned to the cinema halls during this decade, largely as the result of improved marketing and the vastly improved cinema facilities. Middle-class audiences will pay Rs 100 to see a film in a fully equipped luxurious cinema, compared to the Rs 10 in the cinemas in lower-class districts. Commercial cinema caters knowingly to different audiences, screening different genres in different theatres in different parts of the country. These include the action film, which is screened in the cheaper movie halls, and the comedy, largely a one-man genre centred on Govinda, who is very popular among the lower classes, but whose talents have recently found a growing audience among the middle classes.[22] The major hits of the 1990s, which have broken most previous box office records, are the big budget, plushy, romantic films, which, I argue, mark the dominance of the values of the new middle classes and uphold them to the pleasure of a socially mixed audience both in India and overseas.[23] These films revive a form of the feudal family romance in a new, stylish, yet unmistakably Hindu, patriarchal structure, which is connected to the (largely indirect) part they play in the resurgence of Hindutva politics in the 1980s and '90s.[24]

Southern Indian cinema had a huge impact on the Hindi cinema in the early to mid-1990s as the films of Mani Ratnam and other directors, dubbed in Hindi, became great successes. Several Tamil films were also remade in Hindi. Their indirect influence, by introducing the music of A. R. Rehman and improved technical standards, has been greater than their own box office performance.

At the time of writing (2002) the Bombay cinema industry perceives itself to be in the midst of a major crisis. Although it gained recognition as an industry from the government and is making inroads in the west, the Hindi film world faces serious problems. In 2000 only two or three films were hits, a few did average business, while others lost considerable amounts of money. One of the chief film financiers, Bharat Shah, was arrested and is awaiting trial, while rumours of his connection with the underworld circulate. Rakesh Roshan, director and producer of one of the biggest hits of 2000, *Kaho na pyaar hai* (*Say that it's Love*), narrowly escaped an assassination attempt, supposedly because he refused to pay protection money, and other producers and stars are aware that these threats are real. One young star was arrested in connection with cocaine and rumours of widespread drug abuse in the industry have further damaged its reputation. While the film industry has always seen itself on the brink of a crisis, it seems that this time drastic measures are needed in terms of organization and output. Before I discuss some of the major features of the Hindi film, it is important to look briefly at the conditions under which films are made.

Film Finance, Production, Distribution and Marketing

The only non-economic analysis of production in the Hindi film industry appears in the second chapter, entitled 'The economics of ideology: popular film form and mode of production', of Madhav Prasad's path-breaking book.[25] In this he discusses 'the nature of the nexus between economic, ideological and political forces that shape the conditions of possibility of cultural production in India',[26] and goes on to conclude, firstly:

As regards the production sector, I will argue that the mode of production in the Hindi film industry is characterized by fragmentation of the production apparatus, subordination of the production process to a moment of the self-valorization of merchant capital, the consequent externality of capital to the production process, the resistance of the entire class of exhibitors to the expansionist drive of the logic of the market, and the functional centrality of the distributor–financier to the entire process of film-making.[27]

Secondly, Prasad argues, the Hindi film is produced by a heterogeneous form of manufacture, rather than the serial or organic form seen in Hollywood. In other words, the various elements of the film are produced by specialists and then assembled rather than focusing on the development of a central material, which he argues affects the status of the 'story' in the Hindi film. Thirdly, he identifies a struggle in the industry between India's state-controlled capitalist development, which aims at producing a national culture, and pre-capitalist ideologies. He argues that this tension has precipitated demand for certain types of state-intervention, 'a campaign for realism and melodrama', and attempts to set up an independent production sector.[28] This is true of some sections of the industry, but the top banners (production houses), such as Yash Chopra's Yash Raj Films, are aiming at a homogeneous or serial form of production, where they control all means of production and extend their interests into all aspects of film making from finance to production and distribution.

In order to seek funding most producers have to approach financiers, who may impose certain restrictions on the film. While most financiers are respectable figures, there is a long-acknowledged relationship between film financing and the laundering of black money. Since the average ratio of a movie's success to failure is very poor, financing a film is a high–risk business, unlikely to appeal to the cautious investor, but the opportunity to launder money and associate with the industry's glamour proves an irresistible combination to some of Bombay's richest inhabitants. The implications of this association with the underworld are unclear, but there has been talk of several unpleasant incidents in the industry being linked to the mafia underworld of Bombay and the Gulf States. In addition to these risks for the producer, the financiers charge a very high rate of interest, said to reach as much as 60 per cent by the time the film is finally made.

The producer often uses distributors as a major source of funding. In brief, for the purposes of film distribution India is divided into five major territories. These are sold by the producer to the distributor at different rates according to the film's predicted market value (based on a conjunction of the choice of director, stars etc.), with the most expensive being Bombay for some genres or stars and Delhi/Uttar Pradesh for others. In recent years the overseas market has become more important than any of the domestic territories, with the UK being the most profitable, followed by the US. These two territories have come to form independent territories, while the remainder of the overseas circuit is not usually subdivided.

Distribution rights are sold in three major ways in the Hindi film industry, according to the status of the producer and the predicted box office success of the movie. The producer may sell the film on a profit-only basis, where the distributor pays an advance to the producer, paying a pre-arranged percentage of profits once this money and extra fees for the cost of prints (Rs 80,000 per print) and publicity have been covered. The producer has the advantage of advance funding and a reduced risk if the film fails, for the distributor bears the loss. The second option is a percentage-only sale, when the distributor and producer agree in advance the percentage share of box office receipts. The third is an outright sale, where the distributor buys the film at a fixed price and keeps the profits for himself, although he also may have to shoulder the losses. The distributor in turn sells the film to exhibitors, hence spreading his risks still further. The distributor and producer then negotiate the number of prints to be released. Rajshri (the Barjatyas' company) is the only distributor to have a national network, all the others being local concerns.

The marketing of films became increasingly important in the early 1990s, reaching beyond the use of lobby cards, posters and songbooks seen previously. Yash Raj Films has been at the forefront of film marketing in India, along with Rajshri Films. Sooraj Barjatya marketed his *Hum aapke hain kaun ...! (What am I to You?*, 1994) in an innovative manner that brought about important changes in film viewing practices as well as marketing. Indian cinema had perceived itself to be under threat from the video-cassette in the 1980s and from the newly arrived cable and satellite television in the 1990s. Those who could afford a VCR or the cheaper cable link stayed away from the cinema, and cinema halls became run-down, catering to a male, lower-class audience. Barjatya astutely observed that the new media could provide useful marketing tools, and he sold a programme on the making of his film to one of the new channels. The music for the film was a great hit, but rather than show the 'picturization' of the songs, he put together a montage of short clips from the film to the song's music, thus whetting the audience's appetite to see the song in its entirety. He instituted the practice of 'video-holdback' (videos had been released along with cinema prints, largely in an attempt by the producer to avoid piracy), then released an increasing but still limited number of prints of the film, beginning with a single print released in Bombay's prestigious Liberty Cinema, redecorated for the release and embellished with stage lights surrounding the screen, which were lit sequentially to accompany the big songs of the film. Yash Raj Films followed these innovations with various 'Making of ...' television programmes, showing montages, and taking their video-holdback to the stage where *Dilwale Dulhania Le Jayenge* (*The Brave Heart Will Take the Bride*, directed by Aditya Chopra, 1995) was not released until 2002.

The large banners began to use the Internet in the late 1990s. Yash Raj Films set up its own Web site in 1998, largely co-ordinated by Uday Chopra (http://www.yashrajfilms.com). The site is similar to those of the other major production houses, having information on current productions and releases in theatres and on DVD/video, alongside a special feature on a particular film, with interviews, reviews, stills and music excerpts. Other sites provide information about Yash Chopra's life and career, there is an archive featuring stills, video clips and music from the major films, and other locations offer email cards, screensavers and interactive fan sites. This allows the company to project its own media image and marketing, albeit to the limited section of the audience that has Internet access and reads English (see below for more on the audience).

Making a film in India remains an exacting process given the harsh conditions under which the industry operates. In spite of the film industry's association with wealth and glamour, the reality is quite different. Industry finances are very small indeed compared to those of Hollywood. It is almost impossible to obtain any hard facts about finance, but one hears figures of around Rs 20 crore for a big budget film, then rumours that the sets for the current remake of *Devdas* by Sanjay Leela Bhansali cost Rs 16 crore (approximately £3 million). Given that the star's fee is said to account for over half the cost of the film, and *Devdas* has three top stars (Shahrukh Khan, Aishwarya Rai and Madhuri Dixit), the eventual budget must be an all-time record. However, this is still probably only the cost of making a trailer in Hollywood.

Although cinema ticket prices have increased dramatically in recent years, box office returns are finite, for even with the possibility of large audiences, given India's enormous population, it remains a very poor country despite the high visibility of a wealthy minority. This means that the producer has to allocate his budget very carefully to cover the expenses of the star, the music director, the sets and the costs of taking the units on an outdoor schedule, particularly if it is overseas.

Although the film industry, like other sections of the Indian workforce, has great technical skills, the equipment used has been of poor quality – until recently. Yash Chopra says that foreign film makers have told him they would not use his equipment even for a documentary. The top film makers, who have made considerable profits in recent years as they reached into overseas markets and sold their music at previously unheard-of prices, are now buying more sophisticated equipment. Studios such as Manmohan Shetty's Adlabs in Film City now have digital facilities and sound-recording equipment as good as anywhere in the world.

Working conditions on the studio floors where films are shot remain almost unbearable. It is hard to believe, when looking at the sophisticated style of the song 'Le gai' ('Took away') from *Dil to Pagal Hai* (*The Heart is Crazy*, directed by Yash Chopra, 1997), that it was filmed in a studio without air-conditioning, with no fans and sealed doors, and under a corrugated iron roof, while outside temperatures were approaching forty degrees Celsius (illus. 5). Air-conditioned studios are rare, and outside sets and locations can also be unbearably hot or require heroines to wear light chiffon clothes in freezing temperatures. The stars may have air-conditioned vans, but the rest of the team makes do with very basic dressing rooms and other studio facilities.

Stars usually have a very limited career span in Indian cinema, rarely exceeding ten years. They are keen to exploit their success and often sign for several films simultaneously, working on more than one shift a day. This leads to tensions between producers and stars, as the former claim the latter are unprofessional and under-committed. While some stars are known for their slapdash approach, the top stars who have the highest budgets, such as Amitabh Bachchan and Shahrukh Khan, are renowned for their professionalism and dedication, working even when extremely ill.

5 The glamour of the sets shown on this publicity for *Dil to Pagal Hai*, 1997, belies the actual conditions of the Bombay film studios.

Recent events in the industry, in particular the likely exposé of underworld connections following the arrests of key figures and several assassination attempts, have increased the desire of major producers to restructure the industry. In 1998 fifteen top producers (including Yash Chopra, Subash Ghai, Vidhu Vinod Chopra, J. P. Dutta, F. C. Mehra, the Nadiadwalas, the Barjatyas, Rakesh Roshan and J. Om Prakash) formed the United Producers' Forum, a super-league of producers that is the most expensive and the hardest to join, given that all members must approve a new entry. The Forum meets regularly to discuss crucial issues and is active in promoting producers' interests, such as the negotiations, led by Yash Chopra, resulting in Government recognition of the movie business as an industry, thus allowing such benefits as access to bank finance and insurance.[29] This latter achievement shows the movie industry's determination to portray itself as a professional, organized business capable of negotiating with the government. These top production houses are keen to work towards a corporate style of management, which seems unlikely to be achieved within the immediate future given their present somewhat feudal style of operation as family businesses. The seriousness of this desire, however, was indicated in March 2001 by a high-profile meeting of the Federation of the Indian Chamber of Commerce and Industry (FICCI) in Bombay, attended by key figures in the industry and in government, as well as by banks and other financial institutions.

Melodrama and Realism

Many critics wish to find an indigenous or native aesthetic for the study of the Hindi film, so they import *rasa* theory, the study of emotion, from the 'golden age of Indian civilization'. However, the so-called applications of the ill-defined *rasa* theory and the transmission of an aesthetic of classical courtly literature in urban public culture in the nineteenth century remain unconvincing.[30]

Indian cinema uses a certain type of realism, largely drawn from literary and middle-class sensibilities that are heavily influenced by Western culture. In the Indian film industry it operates in a melodramatic mode, a form often found in societies where the pre-modern is giving way to the modern.[31] While some Hindi films are made in a more realistic mode, such as those influenced closely by the social concern novel and the Indian People's Theatre Association movement (for example the films of Bimal Roy, which also drew on Italian neo-realism), others are more melodramatic.

Melodrama is used to describe cultural genres that stir up emotions, drawing on a 'tragic structure of feeling'.[32] It is often seen as cheap sentimental trash, provoking ridicule for its failed, mundane tragedy, its straining for effect, its exaggeration of plot and characters, and its dominance of emotion over other considerations.[33] In melodrama the emphasis is not on the psychology and lifestyle of a unique individual but on the functioning of characters in situations that push their emotions to extremes. Melodrama needs to be read metaphorically to understand its typical focus on the family, the suffering of the power-less good (especially through illness, family break-up, misunderstand-ing and doomed love), often at the hands of a villain who is known to the family. There are situations that can be resolved only through convenient deaths, chance meetings and implausible happy endings. Stephen Neale argues that the pleasure of melodrama or the pleasure of being made to cry is a fantasy of love rather than sex (in psychoanalytic terms, it is a narcissistic fantasy), hence the involvement of other family members, the community or, even, the nation.[34] In these plea-sures the audience can overcome the meaninglessness of everyday existence and find reassurance for their fractured lives.

Melodrama foregrounds language, as it makes all feelings exterior, with the characters verbalizing their feelings and creating discourses on their emotions. In the Hindi movie one of the key places for an outpour-ing of feeling is the song lyric, where visuals and language are simulta-neously foregrounded. This also applies to the dialogues, which are often delivered, rather than spoken, in a grand theatrical manner, rang-ing from such formulaic expressions or already interpreted speech[35] as 'yeh shaadi ho nahi sakti' ('this wedding cannot take place') or 'main teraa khun piungaa' ('I shall drink your blood')[36] to the realistic in films where realism dominates.[37] The dialogues are a major pleasure for movie fans, who relish these grandiloquent statements, frequently learning chunks by heart so they can recite them in subsequent repeat viewings. Cassettes and CDs of the dialogues are also available for repeat hearings. (Manil Suri's *The Death of Vishnu* has a dying woman's last wish to be entered in the *Guinness Book of Records* as the first person to memorize an entire Hindi film script. She fails.[38])

Melodrama also affects the image as it uses close-ups to increase the effect of emotional depth, and heightens the role of the star (see below) and the viewers' interaction with the image. The star must appear as a star, not as a character playing a role. Barry King[39] suggests there are two forms of acting: impersonation, where the actor transforms his or her body and voice, and personification, where the actor's persona retains significant similarities in different performances. The latter form, found most often in Hindi cinema, creates and maintains the star's text, restricting the way in which an image can be presented.

The exterior display of emotions is heightened through the use of such features as storms, remote places and other symbolic representations of a character's interior feelings. Such melodramatic features change the whole look of the film. Yash Chopra has identified 'glamorous realism' as a style he uses in his films where reality is glossed over to make it more attractive.

A Cinema of Attractions?

Ravi Vasudevan argues that in Indian cinema the 'relationship between narrative, performance sequence and action spectacle is loosely structured in the fashion of a cinema of attractions.'[40] Gunning and Gaudreault[41] coined this term to describe a cinema in which popular traditions such as the fairground and carnival meet an avant-garde subversion. It is seen most notably in the work of Sergei Eisenstein, where 'a montage of attractions intensified this popular energy into an aesthetic subversion to undermine the conventions of bourgeois realism.'[42] This is an exhibitionist cinema in which linear narrative, driven by characters and the logic of the narrative itself, and the realist illusion of film are interrupted by spectacle and other 'attractions'. Vasudevan points out that attractions appeared in certain genres of early Indian cinema, such as the lower-class stunt and the mythological, but by the 1950s were included in the previously middle-class 'social', which expanded to become a very loose omnibus category.[43]

The main 'attractions' of Hindi cinema include the sets and costumes, action sequences ('thrills'), presentation of the stars, grandiloquent dialogues, song and dance sequences, comedy interludes and special effects.[44] These attractions are part of the problem that has held back the Hindi film industry from gaining recognition as a form of cultural capital.[45] The term *filmi* ('belonging to or associated with film') is seen as derogatory, suggesting something cheap and trashy. As mentioned earlier, the films of the 1920s were seen as lower-class genres, while the more literary genres that emerged in the 1930s were associated with sound. The independent producers were keen to incorporate attractions into their films since they thought this would improve their chances of success, although several directors working within the conventions of the popular film, such as Guru Dutt and Bimal Roy, tried to incorporate them into a more tightly woven narrative structure and a more realistic style. Prasad's model of segmentation in the 1970s may be considered in the light of attractions. State-sponsored realism largely eschewed the attractions of the commercial cinema, while middle-class cinema continued to incorporate them along the lines followed by some of the directors of the

6 One of the 'items' in *Naseeb*, 1981. The denouement takes place during and after a song as a revolving restaurant catches fire, with the couples of the multi-star cast dressed as Cossacks, Chaplin and Hepburn and a matador and a flamenco dancer.

1950s. The cinema based on the aesthetic of mobilization, by contrast, deployed the attractions to the full. The star persona of Amitabh Bachchan, the song and dance routines and the use of comedy and stunts, in particular fight sequences, reached a state of parody in the films of Manmohan Desai, who subordinated the narrative to these 'items' (as he called the attractions), piling item on item, for example in *Amar Akbar Anthony* (1977) and *Naseeb* (*Fate*, 1981; illus. 6), with characters making knowing direct address to camera. (I do not imply this as criticism, since Desai's films are some of the most entertaining movies I have ever seen.) The plushy romances, typified by those of Yash Chopra, have negotiated the attractions skilfully, deploying the star and song and dance, while subordinating them to the drive of the narrative. Shyam Benegal, the exemplar of state-sponsored realism, recently shocked many people by making *Zubeidaa* (2001), a 'commercial' film employing stars and song and dance items. I would argue that this film is in the tradition of the middle-class cinema discussed above, suggesting that the present upheavals in the industry may bring about some very exciting realignment of the cinema of attractions and realistic cinema in the near future.

Leaving aside for the next chapter a detailed study of the attractions of sets and costume, the remainder of this chapter looks briefly at some of the other major attractions of the Hindi film.[46]

Attraction: the Star

Richard Dyer's work on stardom has brought the study of the star phenomenon to the fore in Western film studies.[47] He argues that an individual is said to be charismatic when he or she is the centre of attraction who seems to embody what, at a given time, is taken to be a central feature of human existence. This figure offers value and stability as the focus of the dominant cultural and historical concerns, thus creating interest in the life of the star and his/her whole off-screen existence.[48] Dyer's notion of the star text is an amalgam of the real person, the characters played in films and the persona created by the media,[49] which has an economic and institutional base. In short, the star is important for the way we think about ourselves and others – as Christine Gledhill argues, stars 'signify as condensors of moral, social and ideological values'.[50]

Mechanisms of involvement with the star are a central part of the pleasure of cinema. Murray Smith examines the spectators' emotional responses to cinema, arguing that 'identification' glosses over the relations between spectator and character. He sets up a model of character engagement (recognition, alignment and allegiance), while avoiding using psychoanalysis. He acknowledges the importance of the star system and his/her charisma,[51] but does not explore this in detail. In her classic study of scopophilia (the viewer's pleasure in sight in the cinema),[52] Laura Mulvey describes how in cinema viewing the mechanisms of fetishism and voyeurism operate to make a denial of difference between the viewer and the star.

The emotions the viewer feels for the star exist outside the cinematic experience. Jackie Stacey explores the question of the identification the female viewer may have with a star of the same sex,[53] bringing feminist arguments to her study of the female audience of Hollywood cinema. She finds that the viewer adopts different attitudes to the star, ranging from an emotional tie to some perception of a common quality.

It seems that there is little difference between the creation of the star in a Hindi film and in a Hollywood film. While south Indian stars are closely connected with politics (again a phenomenon found in many countries from the USA to the Philippines),[54] Hindi film stars seem to fit Dyer's highly influential, in fact predominant, theory of the star, which has barely been challenged in twenty years.

In Hindi cinema the star text is created within the films themselves, mostly melodramas that are vehicles for star performances rather than realistic dramas. The film draws on images of the star in other films and in other media to give them roles as national icons of beauty and desire, presenting them as Utopian beings. This is also encouraged by viewing practices in India, where repeat viewing is the norm and the audience has an incredibly detailed knowledge of the life of the star and other personnel involved in the film.

Madhava Prasad, who is keen to avoid orientalizing discussions of the cultural specificity of the Hindi film, is unable to avoid discussion of the practice of *darshan(a)*. This term is used for a structure of spectation found in Hindu religious practice[55] (and also in some social and political practices), in which the image authorizes the look (rather than merely being its object), thereby benefiting the beholder. In other words, *darshan* is a two-way look, the beholder takes *darshan* (*darshan lena*) and the object gives *darshan* (*darshan dena*), in which the image rather than the person looking has power. Ravi Vasudevan argues that *darshan* can have enabling as well as authoritative functions. He argued in an earlier article that the use of stasis and tableaux permits this hierarchical *darshan*,[56] a contention I find persuasive. The star frequently appears in tableau scenes that seem to invite *darshan*, thus hierarchizing the look and giving the star associations with the traditional granters of *darshan*, notably kings and gods. I will return to this much disputed topic of *darshan* in chapter Two, but suggest that, while it may operate within the film to produce the star, I cannot otherwise see any culturally specific ways in which the star is produced.

Wider social practices concerning the creation of the star manifest more localized practices. The star needs other media not only to maintain visibility beyond the brief moment of performance but also to allow the creation of a star persona. Indian television is an ideal medium for this, screening the star's earlier films, video clips of film songs and interviews with the star. The other major area of circulation of the star's image is in the film and lifestyle magazines that tell of their off-screen exploits. Dating back to the early days of cinema, film magazines remain the key place to find out about the stars' off-screen personae, although unofficial gossip, such as that documented by Gandhy and Thomas, has always circulated.[57] A radical change in the 1970s saw the appearance of gossip film magazines, the central concern of which was the creation of a readership tied together by the circulation of gossip, largely of a sexual nature. Here the star's story is told in a way that provides an arena for debates around sexuality, in particular female sexuality. These magazines are closely bound with the emergence in India in the 1970s of new social groups and the availability of wider consumer pleasures and lifestyles, and have continued as such until the present.[58]

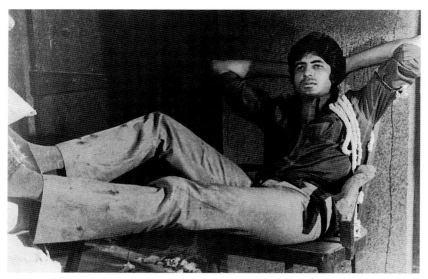

7 Amitabh Bachchan as Vijay, the angry young man, before a fight in the docks in *Deewaar*, 1975.

The major star of Hindi cinema is undoubtedly Amitabh Bachchan, who, although one of the most famous men in the world and a major international icon, is hardly known in Europe and North America outside the South Asian communities. He emerged as India's undisputed top star from the early 1970s, subsequently winning popularity polls as the star of the year, even in years when he did not have a film released. Born into an élite family and a childhood friend of the Nehru-Gandhis, Amitabh's first major successes were in middle-class cinema where he established himself as a fine actor. His greatest role was one he played in many films of the 1970s, that of the angry young man or 'industrial hero',[59] introducing a new physicality and style to Hindi cinema, using his tall, long-limbed body and deep voice to great effect. A typical version of this role appears in *Deewaar* (*The Wall*, directed by Yash Chopra, 1975; illus. 7). When Vijay (Amitabh) is a child his family is wronged by society and, after the father deserts them, they come to the city. As an outsider he finds that he can support his mother and educate his younger brother by taking to crime. When they discover the source of his money, they argue that he must uphold the law, embodied in the film by his younger brother, now a policeman, who ultimately has to kill him in a shootout. Vijay dies in his mother's arms in front of a temple.

Clearly this character has the makings of a folk hero, supporting traditional values relating to religion and, in particular, to the family. Often an orphan, he criticizes the 'system' or the state, fighting for righteous causes from outside its sphere of operation. There is no doubt that he is on the side of Right, but these values conflict with those of the state and to resolve these he has to die, adding martyrdom to his cause. The attraction of violence deserves a separate study, and in his movies Amitabh Bachchan is often not actually violent, but angry. Madhava Prasad connects the popularity of the angry young man with the political violence in India at that time,[60] arguing that *Deewaar* shows an unofficial history, played out in private, where the Law (of the father and of the state) has broken down.[61] According to Javed, one of the two scriptwriters who created this character:

Vijay, the hero of *Zanjeer*, reflected the thinking of the time. Two years later, the same Vijay was seen again in *Deewaar*. By then he had left the police force, he had crossed that final line and become a smuggler. He wages war against the injustice he had to endure and he emerges the winner. You can see that the hero who had developed between 1973–75 – the Emergency was declared in India in 1975 – reflected those times.[62]

After several years of unsuccessful films, he re-emerged as a celebrity in 2000 as the television presenter of 'Kaun banega crorepati', the phenomenally popular Indian version of 'Who Wants to be a Millionaire?' Later the same year *Mohabbatein* (*Loves*, directed by Aditya Chopra), with Amitabh playing a major role as a headmaster and made with his old director/producer Yash Chopra, was one of the two major hit films of the year. His crowning moment was at the Filmfare Awards in Bombay in February 2001, when his waxwork from Madame Tussaud's was the chief guest while the real Amitabh won Best Actor in a supporting role!

Attraction: Song and Dance

As Irving Berlin was said to 'be' American popular music, so Hindi film music is (north) Indian popular music. However, I must contest the absurd claim that in some way music is more important in India than elsewhere. Perhaps there is some confusion with the decline of participation in making music in the West, for music remains omnipresent there too.

   Sound was introduced to the Hindi cinema at around the same time as the advent of radio. Before the audio cassette, reproduction of popular music in India was very limited as few people could afford gramophones, even though cheap imports from Japan were available. People heard the songs in the film, but most importantly they heard them on the radio and people sang them themselves. There was no sheet music market, as there was in the West for the Hollywood musical, but hired performers sang songs in the street as part of the cinema's publicity campaign.

Indian film music has a complicated relationship with classical Indian music, which has never been part of popular consumption, as Western classical music has been at many levels. Indian classical music was associated with the royal courts, with religion, and with the *kotha* or houses of courtesans, only reaching out to wider, albeit still musically trained, audiences as part of performance arts well into the twentieth century. Many music directors and singers of Indian cinema, however, are trained in the classical tradition. They rarely use this music, although some music directors use *raga*-based compositions, preferring a light classical to a popular style.

Film music is famously hybrid: indeed this was one of the terms with which it was castigated by many, including Dr Keskar, who banned it from All India Radio during the 1950s. It draws on a wide range of musical sources, including Western popular music, changing styles frequently. While a few Indians have pursued Western classical music, it is Western popular music that has been most successful in India. Western-style orchestras seem to date back at least a hundred years. It is unclear where most of these musicians trained, many of them seeming to have picked it up by ear, but some may have been trained for colonial bands who played on the bandstands and at parties in Victorian India, while others may have been recruited to the military bands that were a feature of cantonment culture. Backing music is nearly always Western orchestral music, which, it is argued, gives a wider range of emotions than is afforded by other forms of music, but once again shows the dominance of a Hollywood style.

Early film music was largely in a light classical style and was not orchestrated in a harmonic style, even when multiple instruments are playing. Much of it seems to be sung in the so-called *mehfil* ('assembly') style associated with courtesans. Film music was revolutionized in the 1940s with the introduction of playback singing, where actors began to mime to professional singers.

The musical lost its dominance as a genre in the West in the late 1950s, largely due to the advent of pop music and rock. India saw no such change, even with the arrival of MTV and the growth of Indian pop music. Music is what has preserved the Hindi film industry, marking it apart from Hollywood. It is hugely important in economic terms: the sale of music rights can cover much of the film's budget, and pre-release songs and trailers publicize the film. Here, however, I will only

8 Elaborate sets and choreographed shapes in *Taal*, 1998.

consider its function as an attraction within the film.

Song sequences are one of the most striking features of the Hindi film (illus. 8). They are often used to denigrate it ('running around trees', 'bursting into song at the most unlikely opportunities'), yet, paradoxically, this is the element in the film most celebrated by its fans. As in the Hollywood musical, directors have worked in different ways to incorporate the song into their narrative. Sometimes the song is diegetically part of the film, when the character is a singer, a dancer, a courtesan and so on. The song may be a set in a stage show, a film or it may be a folk song. Other song situations include the 'dream sequence', the lovers' fantasy that may take the form of a stage show. Some directors have experimented with other ways of incorporating song: Guru Dutt's films, for example, often move from dialogue into song and dance so smoothly that the transition is barely perceptible, like the moment at which Fred Astaire stops walking and starts dancing. Many other songs do not pretend to have a purpose within the logic of the narrative, but function to allow an expression of feeling that cannot be articulated otherwise – notably the declaration of love. Eroticism in the movies is largely contained within the song, which also contains other breaks in continuity such as numerous costume changes and a whole different range of gesture and movement.

While the songs involve different personnel such as composers, dance directors, troupes of dancers and special dancing stars, they may even be shot by a different director, since the songs in Vidhu Vinod Chopra's *1942: A Love Story* (1994) were directed by Sanjay Leela Bhansali. The stars rarely sing the songs themselves but instead mime to a playback-singer, drawn from a small pool of professional singers employed in the film industry whose voices are instantly identifiable. The director may choose different singers to sing for the same star in the same movie, although *Mohabbatein* (2000) used a major singing star, Udit Narayan, to sing for the main hero, Shahrukh Khan, while six new singers sang for six other actors.

There is often a break in continuity regarding location since the song may start in India but move to Switzerland or some other such paradise, without any reference to moving in space, although holidays or dreams are sometimes used as an excuse. Real time is again suspended as the heroine may change her costume frequently during the sequence. Love may be expressed in the song but not necessarily acknowledged in the narrative. A good example of this is the song 'Dholna' ('Sweetheart') in *Dil to Pagal Hai* (*The Heart is Crazy*, directed by Yash Chopra, 1997), which begins when the hero and hero-ine embrace at a wedding in Bombay. There is then a cut to Germany, where they sing verses of the song with frequent changes of location around this German setting and numerous changes of costume. Special, elaborate sets may be designed for the songs in order to heighten the spectacle further. The meaning of these shifts in time and place will be discussed below under settings and costume.

Asha Kasbekar argues that song and dance sequences allow erotic digressions from the main plot in the film, sanctioning 'areas of height-ened transgressive pleasure'.[63] She points out that the audience is able to disavow the pleasures of its own voyeurism by the use of 'bad' char-acters such as the vamp, who is often billed as a special feature of the film, notably the most popular of all vamps/dancers, Helen. The song also violates other conventions, such as refracting the exchange of looks between the performer and the audience through the presence of an on-screen audience, onto whom the feeling of voyeurism may be transferred.

The music has a life separate from the rest of the film as the sound-track goes on sale on audio cassette and CD around two months ahead of the release of the film. At this time the images and the songs are also shown on television, although some producers make a montage of images and sequences rather than show the actual song 'picturization'. This means that the music may have two entirely separate audiences apart from the cinema audience – that of the listener (audio cassette, CD, radio, background music) and the television audience. The music is crucially important to the producer since its sale to a record company may cover around half the budget of a film, but it also acts as a marketing device shortly before the film's release, together with posters, trailers and television programmes about the making of the film. Thus the film audience is already familiar with one of the major attractions in advance, allowing it the pleasure of seeing already known material integrated into the wider film narrative.

Other Attractions

Finally, there is a loose group of 'other attractions', of which the most important are the comedy, the stunt and the special effect. Although some hero-actors are adept at comedy, for example Amitabh Bachchan and Govinda, there are also specialist comic actors, such as Johnnie Walker, a great comic of the 1950s who acted in many of Guru Dutt's films, Johar, Ajit and Mehmood. Johnny Lever is undoubtedly the most successful of the many contemporary comics. These performers, often playing such roles as the heroine's brother or the servant, provide comedy through their use of language and speech, sometimes dressed in ridiculous clothes and performing various slapstick acts, usually to loud sound effects. Their style of acting is usually different from that of the actors, eschewing any idea of realism for a more theatrical or loud style that addresses the audience directly in a fashion that seems to belong to a lower class altogether. The comics are all male, although occasionally a woman such as Archana Puran Singh will play a comic role, usually as a sexually predatory vamp.

While stunt and action ('thrills') provide important attractions in most films, some films may even be said to constitute a separate genre, with a special group of action men heroes. These films foreground maleness, presenting the male body as a major spectacle, often wounded and suffering in a somewhat masochistic style. They are said to be more popular in cinemas attracting a lower-class male audience and they seldom do well in the overseas market. The rarer genre of war and patriotic films may be included loosely in this category. Once again these are films with a very male content, although the emphasis is on heroism within the requirements of the state, whereas the action films often have the hero taking the law into his own hands. The larger budget films may involve the armed forces in their making. Other attractions featuring in these films may include top stars, grand locations and stirring songs, as well as romantic songs in connection with absence from one's family. It is surprising, given the number of times the modern state of India has been at war in its short history, that this genre has not been more popular.

Lastly there is the special effect, which has only recently returned to film in a major way. Practitioners of early Indian cinema were keen to exploit the magical possibilities that the film medium was able to offer, greatly extending the already considerable repertoire of special effects that the Parsi theatre was able to offer. Phalke combined his interest in magic with his desire to see Indian gods and goddesses on screen by showing miraculous events such as Krishna's rising from the Yamuna on Kaliya or Kamsa's imagining of Krishna decapitating him in *Shri Krishna janma* (*Birth of Lord Krishna*, 1918). Sean Cubbitt has written on the special effects of Phalke's films:

Phalke's effects are not only beautifully achieved, but seem far more integrated with a cultural formation which is already antipathetic to colonialism. Here magic functions not as the unconscious, but as an entirely legible code which not only evades colonial censorship but delights the unwitting coloniser.[64]

In Phalke, however, one has the sense that the narrative, however fragmented by the vagaries of preservation and transmission, occupies a sovereign position, but as metonymic, almost holographic shards of the Hindu epic tradition.[65]

Other makers of mythological films used special effects to great acclaim, but the rise of the social film in the 1930s meant that special effects were of little importance. Special effects are always needed for mythological films, so they are used in the *nagin* or snake-goddess films and *Jai Santoshi Maa* (directed by Vijay Sharma, 1975), as well as in the television religious soaps that became popular in the late 1980s, such as Ramanand Sagar's *Ramayana* and B. R. Chopra's *Mahabharata*. Other genres dependent on special effects, such as the sci-fi movie or the thriller, which have been so popular in Hollywood (*Star Wars, Jaws, E.T. the Extra-Terrestrial* and *Jurassic Park* being some of the top-grossing films), are extremely rare in Hindi cinema. This may be due to the costs, the inability to compete with the Hollywood films during the 1970s and '80s, or simply that the producers felt their main audience was not interested in such films. In recent years, however, as this technology has allowed Hollywood to return to genres that had become too costly, such as the historical film, so India has taken advantage of advances in digital computerized technology and has even exported experts to the USA. Indian film makers, however, have begun to use this technology only for details and not on the scale of projects dependent on special effects, such as *The Matrix* or *Independence Day*. Recent examples of these special effects have included generating cloud movements showing the arrival or not of the rains that could end the drought in *Lagaan* (*Once upon a Time in India*, directed by Ashutosh Gowariker, 2001), and the maple leaves that link the scenes of *Mohabbatein* (*Loves*, directed by Aditya Chopra, 2000), and for the battle scenes in historical films such as *Asoka* (directed by Santosh Shivan, 2001).

Many of the attractions described above are organized around the pleasures of looking (scopophilia). Yet despite this centrality, little has been written about the visuality of cinema. The following chapters do not aim to trace the history of the look or the gaze in India[66] but to observe the image and its artistic deployment in the film – in location, sets and costume – and, beyond the film, in the film poster and other publicity produced for the audience.

2 Film Style: Settings and Costume

Components of Film Style in India

'Film style', a term with wide currency in film studies, consists of four major components.[1] The first is the *mise-en-scène* or the 'staging of the event', which covers everything in front of the camera, notably the setting, lighting, costume and the performance. The second is the shot itself or the cinematography, including the size and shape of the image, its framing, the use of monochrome or type of colour, the camera (depth, angle, level, height and movement), speed and perspective. Editing, the third component, is concerned with how the shots are put together or connected, as well as principles of continuity, while finally sound deals with the way sound functions with the image, its technical forms (such as stereo and digital), the use of dubbing and so on. These four elements are used together to give a film its own style or formal system, whereas a study of style across films gives a history of a particular cinema's style.[2]

Among the many key works on Hindi film, little has been written about how the film actually looks or, more accurately, on film style. While several writers have discussed some of the more technical aspects of film style, notably Vasudevan's outstanding pieces on cinematography and editing,[3] there is no extended study on the lines of Bordwell's authoritative *On the History of Film Style*.[4] Nor have these pieces come together to form a narrative of film style on the lines of what Bordwell calls 'the Standard Version' of film style, let alone its questioning by major critics such as Bazin and Burch. Moreover, the two major elements on which this chapter focuses, namely location and costume, have been almost ignored.

While it may seem self-evident that Indian cinema[5] has its own unique style, it has never been identified.[6] Major questions need to be asked, such as: Is there a critical body of films? Are there groups of styles? Does Indian cinema have a coherent aesthetic? Does Bombay cinema just follow Hollywood or has it evolved its own original or distinctive style? Is this a national style? What are its origins? This chapter can barely begin to answer these questions, but it makes a few brief suggestions and comments about some aspects of film style, before turning to look at two aspects of *mise-en-scène*, namely the setting and the costume.

The Image and Ways of Looking

A new visuality was created in colonial nineteenth-century India, distinct from that seen in traditional art forms such as miniatures and religious sculpture. New forms of painting emerged, including 'bazaar art', the 'Company' style (Indian artists working for British clients) in presidency cities, and oil painting associated with Ravi Varma.[7] Industrial arts grew rapidly, including photography, which arrived in India in the 1840s,[8] along with the opportunities offered by the new printing techniques of the chromolithograph,[9] the woodcut print and the news sheet. This led to the creation of a new inter-ocular field[10] among these new images in a range of media. Chris Pinney argues that:

It is as a result of the *conversation between* or the semiosis between the idioms of chromolithography, theatre and photography – together with strategic alliances between these representational forms and the realms of religious authority and nascent ideas of the 'nation' – that 'realism' was able to triumph among certain sections of the Indian population in the late nineteenth century.[11]

These three forms – photography, chromolithography and theatre[12] – show many clear connections, with designs on chromolithographs featuring curtains draped on proscenium arches, while theatrical sets and gestures show the influence of the other arts.[13] They also positioned the spectator and introduced a form of perspective, imposed by the proscenium arch and carried over into the more direct forms of photography and cinema. These, along with other new industrial arts, such as the printing of bills to advertise performances and ticketing, were then taken into cinema,[14] which was to develop its own art forms, such as backdrops and, later, sets, to create a whole *mise-en-scène*, the origins of which are interwoven with the earlier industrial art forms.

Cinema, with the additional complexity of the moving image, had other issues to address in developing its own visuality. The Hollywood 'classic' codes of continuity, which became established in the 1930s, are so widely accepted that they are taken to be 'transparent' and realistic and have become universal. While very much part of Hindi cinema, they are often used in a seemingly random way,[15] for example by being suspended during the 'attractions', such as the song and dance or the presentation of the star (see chapter One), or even disregarded, inviting other looks in the cinema.

Ashish Rajadhyaksha and Geeta Kapur have argued that iconicity is often deployed in films, hardly surprising given that 'all Indian art

9 Vishnupant Pagnis as *Sant Tukaram*, 1936.

traditionally places an iconic articulation as central to it'.[16] Kapur
does not use iconicity in the Peircean sense of a relation of resemblance, but as a meaningful condensation of symbolic meanings into
one static image, which is not necessarily religious or mythological.[17]
Kapur also identifies a formal category of 'frontality' in the Indian
popular arts including 'the word, the image, the design and the perfor-
mative act',[18] the last named category including cinema. Frontality
here means not just filming from a right-angle plane or direct address
to camera but also through the spectator's knowledge of such aspects
as narrative and *mise-en-scène*.[19]

   Phalke drew on the iconic image of early photography, the frontality
of which in turn had developed from conventions of miniature painting where the subject is 'always a type or even archetype',[20] via works
in the Company style and those of Ravi Varma. Kapur argues that in
Sant Tukaram (directed by Damle and Fattelal, 1936; illus. 9) religious
iconicity is mediated to secular effect through shots of the devotee
mediating between god and the viewer, and through the direct address
of the saint. She further argues that the style of representation and
performance of Vishnupant Pagnis as Tukaram is such that his face is
privileged as sign, allowing it to be not only iconic but also indexical,
of both actor and character.

10 Friends, now devotees, worship Krishna as he rises victorious from the River Jamuna after overcoming the serpent Kaliya. *Shri Krishna janma*, 1918.

Frontality may also be seen in film as a freezing of space, and sometimes of time, in a tableau to give an iconic representation and to position characters and objects in relation to one another.[21] This feature is used in melodrama (see below) to give the 'spectator the opportunity to see meaning represented, emotions and moral states rendered in clear visible signs.'[22]

This is further complicated by the manifestation of local ways of looking in the cinema, notably that of *darshan* ('seeing'), mentioned in chapter One. This term is used most often in the context of religious worship, where it is a two-way look between the devotee and the deity that establishes religious authority (illus. 10),[23] although it may also be applied to social and political authority. It is a look that establishes an authoritative figure or icon and the space around him or her, assigning positions in a hierarchy that may be open to negotiation and change. Vasudevan argues:

Instead of seeing the discourse of *darsana* [*darshan*] framing cinematic narration, we need to think of *darsana* as being enframed and reconstructed by it. Here, the localised deployment of filmic techniques in the micro-narration of a scene – editing, shot-distance and angle, camera movement, lighting, sound elements – alert us to how characters and spectators are being cinematically positioned in relation to the *darsanic*. The *darsanic* is not static, and generates new sources of authority from it, and in ways not entirely comprehensible in terms of established conventions ... The cinematic process of iconic reconstruction may in fact deploy and subordinate modern methods of subject construction modelled on Hollywood narration. By convention, the continuity system, and especially its point-of-view editing, is associated with the drives and perception of individuated characters. However, it is quite common in popular Hindi cinema to observe the yoking of such views to the bearer of *darsanic* authority. But the emergence of such enshrining views is tied to the dynamic of reconstruction, and is mobilised to the end of a patriarchal transformation.[24]

The narration invites *darshan* by its use of tableaux,[25] a feature that has long been seen in such forms of worship as the *jhanki* or tableau of the gods, which devotees view in the north Indian *raslila* and the *Ramlila*. Vasudevan also shows how *darshan* may be invited even when there is not an iconic frontality but when continuity codes, notably the shot/reverse-shot, are used. He analyses the devotional song sequence from *Pyaasa* (*Thirst*, directed by Guru Dutt, 1957), where 'the relation between devotional voice, devotee and object of devotion determines the space of [the] scene'.[26] He points out that, in this complicated structure of spectatorship and address, the song frames the composition since the object of devotion – the hero – does not return the *darshanic* look, thereby breaking the circuit of *darshan* and authority, albeit temporarily since it is reinstated later in the film.

Mixed codes exist side by side in cinema as they have done for decades in other mass arts. Anuradha Kapur has noted that the Parsi theatre mixed 'pre-colonial audience relations with bourgeois realism', with the iconic and realistic existing in a state of tension.[27] However, most of these studies on iconicity, frontality, the tableau and *darshan* draw on early films and those from the 1950s and do not trace more recent changes in styles of looking.[28] While these codes may be less striking nowadays than in older films, their endurance may be seen in the use of spectacle, in particular the depiction of the star (see chapter One).

It is clear to the untrained eye that Hindi film style has changed rapidly in recent years, notably in such instantly striking ways as the editing, which has become much more rapid, perhaps a style copied from the music video popularized by MTV. It is not clear if there is a particular film style of camera work, although many people sought to find a particularly Indian style in Shekhar Kapur's *Elizabeth* (1999). Kapur himself has alternated his own views on this, but the film is clearly a modern version of the Western popular historical style.

Individual directors and their cameramen have certainly established an individual style, such as that shown in the dramatic black and white films of Guru Dutt and his cameraman, V. K. Murthy. Certain genres have a clear style of camerawork, such as the glossy romantic film of the 1990s, which has made great use of the trolley, especially from mid-shot to an extreme close-up for emotional sequences, using panning to present exotic scenery during song sequences. Rather than digress to a much deeper and precise exploration of the history of Indian film style, however, I turn now to my two major concerns in this chapter, the use of setting and of clothing, which have been chosen for their importance not only within the film but also in the wider context of the Hindi film in society.

Setting

Indian films have used both locations and sets from their very beginnings. The early films were largely shot on location, due to limited lighting technology, with Phalke famously shooting *Raja Harishchandra* in Dadar, a suburb of Bombay. Several heads of princely states, including the Maharajah of Jaipur and the Nizam of Hyderabad, were interested in film and allowed units to shoot on their land, sometimes offering the use of their palaces, armies and other facilities.

With the coming of sound in the 1930s sets were favoured, since they allowed more controlled conditions both for sound and for new lighting technology, and by the 1950s indoor sets were the norm for films with some outdoor sequences. The static microphone and the recording of simultaneous sound in the early days restricted movement, while by the late 1940s playback singing allowed new forms of song picturization and more natural delivery of dialogue. During the 1960s, as colour films became the norm, producers returned to location shoots, seeking new and ever more exotic locations as major attractions in a film. Raj Kapoor's first colour film, *Sangam* (*Union*, 1964; illus. 11), for example, has many sequences shot in Europe. Shooting on outdoor locations in India was also increasingly popular, whether in the idyllic landscapes of Kashmir or, in the 1970s, adding the gritty realism of street scenes, mostly of Bombay. Sets became more and more infrequent during the 1980s, as producers used urban locations and rented large houses ('bungalows') to be used as the homes of the film's characters. These bungalows still appear in the 1990s, but they are most frequently used just for the exteriors, as directors prefer the freedom of the set for interiors, which allows more dynamic camera movement. Recent years have seen the return of simultaneous sound recording, for example in *Lagaan* (*Once upon a Time in India*, directed

11 The first film to use European locations. The cover of the publicity booklet of *Sangam*, 1964.

by Ashutosh Gowariker, 2001), which creates a more 'realistic' use of sound than that provided by present dubbing practices, even though it requires more careful control of the shooting environment.

In recent years big budget sets have been used for films including the construction of whole villages and towns, such as the recreation of

Simla for 'Mall Road' in *Mohabbatein* (*Loves*; directed by Aditya Chopra, 2000). This film also used Longleat House, a stately home in Wiltshire, England, for the exterior of the school in which much of the action occurs; the interiors were all sets in Bombay studios. Although the action of the film takes place entirely in India, the English exteriors, with winter landscapes, were not seen as disrupting continuity.[29] Budgets have rocketed as art designers concoct more and more elaborate sets. Sanjay Leela Bhansali, for his remake of *Devdas* (scheduled for release in June 2002), decided to build *havelis* (mansion houses) to recreate the historical look of the characters' homes, and these are said to bring the budget for Nitin Desai's sets to Rs 16 crore (approx. £3 million), more than the budget of most Hindi films.

Songs have continued to violate the usual norms of a film, employing spectacular sets and exotic locales that may have little or no connection with space and time in the rest of the film. The cost of these sets and taking a unit to a foreign location is enormous, but producers feel this is justified as the song acts as an attraction in all senses of the word and becomes part of the marketing of the film (see below).

Although much could be said about the creation and design of sets, this chapter focuses on the meaning of sets and locations within the films themselves. Although some producers hired designers to build elaborate sets, notably M. R. Achrekar, who was responsible for some of the most memorable sets of the 1950s including the dream sequence in Raj Kapoor's *Awāra* (*The Vagabond*, 1951) and the deserts and palaces of Mehboob Khan's *Aan* (*Savage Princess*, 1952; illus. 12), most films were made in a more *ad hoc* manner. One of the key films for the changing depiction of wealth is said to be *Waqt* (*Time*, directed by Yash Chopra, 1965).[30] At a time when designers were still a rarity, Yash Chopra and his assistant, Mahen Vakil, bought Western magazines and pulled out the pictures of any details they liked. They then went to the shops themselves to buy the materials (using, for example, red velvet instead of carpet for the flooring) that were put together by artisans. (Mahen Vakil also bought the men's clothes for this stylish film, while the women had their own dressers.)[31]

Many people are involved in choosing locations and designing sets, including art directors, set directors, location scouts, cameramen and carpenters, but they come under the control of the director and ultimately the producers who decide on the overall look of the film, assisted by the technical specialists. Although Indian filmgoers are highly knowledgeable about the various personnel who have contributed to films, the production designers come way down the list

12 Publicity for Mehboob Khan's swashbuckling *Aan*, 1952.

after the stars, producer, director, music composers and script writers. Technical and other personnel have long been undervalued within the industry itself, which views them as craftsmen. Lata Mangeshkar, for example, fought for recognition of her contribution as a singer in the 1940s, while Salim-Javed established the importance of screenplay and dialogue writers in the 1970s by insisting on having their names on publicity material. As the cost of technical staff, in particular the art director and costume designer, has multiplied for the producer, so has the market value of the film created in part by these people. Belated recognition came with the introduction of the art direction category at the 1955 Filmfare Awards, the Indian 'Oscars', while some figures have now become celebrities with recognizably distinctive styles. In recent years the sets of Sharmishta Roy,[32] including those for *Dil to Pagal Hai* (*The Heart is Crazy*, directed by Yash Chopra, 1997), *Taal* (*Rhythm*, directed by Subhash Ghai, 1998) and *Mohabbatein*, have become celebrated as bringing a new urban chic into Hindi cinema, while Nitin Desai is known for the enormous sets of *1942: A Love Story* (directed by Vidhu Vinod Chopra, 1994) and *Hum dil de chuke sanam* (*My Heart's Already Given*, directed by Sanjay Leela Bhansali, 1999). The two work very differently: Roy draws up detailed designs

13 Mehboob Khan and Mehboob Studios, in the booklet *Mother India*, 1957.

and drawings, which she uses in discussions with her producers and directors, while Desai makes sketches and models.

These sets are built for the period of filming and are then demolished. Even Film City, built by the government in the Goregaon district of Bombay during the 1970s, has only one or two standing sets, such as the courtroom, although there is space to allow the construction of outdoor sets in addition to the sound stages. The studios, as we saw in chapter One above, largely disappeared in the 1940s although a few remain, such as Mehboob Khan's Mehboob Studios (illus. 13), V. Shantaram's Rajkamal, Raj Kapoor's RK Studios and Kamal Amrohi's Kamalistan. They are rented out to producers on a daily rate rather than being part of an integrated production unit. They comprise several hangar-like buildings with sound stages, rather than having Hollywood's traditional huge backlots and standing sets. They also lack many facilities that would be regarded as basic, such as air-conditioning, green rooms, dressing-rooms, and even clean bathrooms. Yash Chopra is one major producer now planning to build integrated studios, with offices for his production company, two studios for film and television along with offices, equipment and other production necessities, as well as facilities for the artistes.

The primary purpose of film settings – sets and locales – is to create a fictional space for characters and narratives and thus fulfil a number of functions within a film. They set the place and time of the character action, and within them the characters are spaced relative to one another. The settings may be narrative, as they help guide our attention to understand what we see and allow us to infer further information about the story and the characters. This can range from simple information as to a character's social status to a form of making the characters' state of mind external, following the melodramatic style of exteriority.[33]

Hindi films are often said to be unrealistic (see chapter One), but to a certain extent the lifestyles of the characters and the sets and locations draw on the 'real world'. The sets have also influenced many film and other interior designs, notably those of B. R. Chopra, whose galleried hall is modelled on that designed for the heroine of *Waqt* (1965), but in the Hindi film this world is constructed and stylized rather than 'real' and 'authentic'.

Indian interior design was previously the preserve of the wealthy and upper middle classes. Ancient texts such as the *Kamasutra* describe the style of the urbane man's house. The Mughals built extravagant palaces, as did more modern maharajas who often employed Western architects[34] and had them furnished in the latest styles from Europe. Wealthy merchants furnished their *havelis* or mansions with finely crafted pieces[35] and often a whole range of religious art and *objets d'art* connected with the *haveli* temples of Krishna.[36] Many older films show these palatial interiors, with the rich living an approximation of the princely lifestyle. In the 1940s and '50s the houses of the wealthy are shown along Western lines, often in a baronial style with sweeping staircases, grand pianos and stuffed animal heads on the wall (illus. 14; see below for more on these features).

While village style appears in a sanitized form in films, along the lines of the 'Indian arts and crafts' style promoted by the government and tourist industries, there are fewer depictions of the interiors of the urban middle classes. Interior design arrived late for this group, for whom the standard interiors under 'permit Raj' were pistachio-green paint, strip lights and brown plastic seat covers. Their increased spending power and the rise of consumer choice from the 1970s allowed them to enjoy new forms of consumption and lifestyle opportunities.[37] Interiors are now often furnished from shops ranging from designer boutiques to government emporia, which provide a choice of styles from ethnic chic to high tech. The films and 'real life' continue to interact with each other in fashions for interior design.

Locations are also important for showing the social status of characters. This has been further complicated by the creation of a consumerist society in India, as the urban middle classes begin to define themselves by patterns of consumption rather than work or birth. The rise of the new middle classes in urban India in recent years[38] has made romance and consumption-leisure-pleasure integral to a middle-class lifestyle, created by and reflected in the mass media

14 The sets, especially the piano and clothes, emphasize the modern and sophisticated lifestyle of the characters in *Andaz*, 1949, starring Nargis, Raj Kapoor and Dilip Kumar.

through a wide range of practices including advertising, cinema and photography.[39] A new middle-class Utopia has been defined for the enjoyment of love, wealth and equality where the family has become the location for intimacy and sexuality. Much romance is now located in the liminal spaces of leisure, travel/tourism and nature. These new middle classes enjoy a range of consumerist and leisure practices including travel, beauty, fashion, health and fitness, with their aesthetics based on the commodity and their sentiments expressed in spectacle. Hence commodities and consumption are not opposed to romance but form a key part of it, its preferred romantic situations being sites of consumption whether gastronomic, cultural or touristic. Eva Illouz argues further that modern love is comprised of three major elements: the sexual, the ritual-consumerist and the rational-economic. Film settings reflect and create these aspirations as they include ever more extravagant sets and exotic locales, providing a further attraction of spectacle (illus. 15).

Settings also divide the scenes, as a change of setting indicates a change of time or place. This can be realistic in the sense that a character is seen to be 'real' and living in a particular time and space that are

15 The clothes and sets of *Waqt*, 1965, created a new image of the glam-ourous lifestyles of the wealthy emulated by subsequent films and in real life. Raaj Kumar and Sadhana.

made clear and in part define the character. In *Ghulam* (*Slave*, directed by Vikram Bhatt, 1998), for example, Aamir Khan is shown to live in a typical Bombay street (actually a Film City set), albeit slightly glamor-ized by its roof terrace and its state of upkeep.

The films can also violate conventional continuity of time and place, being idealistic, rather than realistic. In such instances empirical real-ism is suspended and place and time are subordinated to such require-ments as the display of wealth or Indianness. As we have noted, conventions of time and space are suspended in the film song, which moves freely from space to space, with the characters changing their clothes, hairstyles and other features. For example, during a song in *Darr* (*Fear*, directed by Yash Chopra, 1993) the engaged couple's flat can suddenly appear fully furnished, they may give every appearance of having been long married and the walls open out onto a Swiss meadow. In the case of the mythologicals and similar genres, on the other hand, the film is largely set outside any mundane understanding of time and place, in divine time and space inspired by the work of Ravi Varma.

Certain characters only appear in certain scenes as they mark out different domains (see below). Sets are by and large contemporary, except when efforts are made in historicals, which have often provided huge spectacles: the enormous budget for the Shish Mahel sets in

16 The servant Anarkali (Madhubala) dances for the Mughal emperor in the famously expensive set of the Shish Mahel in *Mughal-e Azam*, 1960.

Mughal-e Azam (*The Great Mughal*, directed by K. Asif, 1960) is still legendary and the results continue to dazzle viewers (illus. 16). Most films have no stylistic reference to the passing of time: a film covering a hero's life story, for example, may show characters wearing contemporary fashions within sets of similar design when the hero is a child and when he is an adult. Some period films, however, such as Shyam Benegal's *Zubeidaa* (2001) or Aamir Khan's *Lagaan* (*Once upon a Time in India*, directed by Ashutosh Gowariker, 2001), take pains to show this passage of time in fashion.

The sets and locations can be very historically or socially vague, as there is said to be little awareness of architectural history. The audience does not seem to mind if characters live in unlikely places or well-known public buildings or hotels. In *Taal* (*Rhythm*, directed by Subhash Ghai, 1998), not only was a hotel lobby used as the sitting room in the hero's house, but little effort was made to cover up any of the signs and indications of its nature. The former Town Hall, now the home of the Asiatic Society of Bombay, is a frequent location, its Doric columns and vast stairs presented as courts of justice or any other public building the director may require.[40] Frequent jumps in location, such as cuts between Switzerland and India, do not seem to disturb the audience at all since the purpose of the setting is to create a structure of feelings and looks, not necessarily to be realistic.

Props used in films have acquired their own symbolic meanings: pianos are icons of modern bourgeois style in the 1950s and '60s, while high-tech goods, such as mobile phones, video cameras and computers, are shown in the 1990s and continue the display of icons expressing modern life. Different forms of transport have their own symbolism: the tonga, or horse and cart, represents the rural or the historical; the horse may represent the artistocrat or untameable nature; the train is a major icon of modernity; the bicycle indicates youth and freedom; the car allows a display of a wide range of wealth; while the autorickshaw and the taxi tie together middle-class and proletarian city dwellers.

Sets

The close visual connection between the arts and the theatre has been mentioned above and the early links between cinema and theatre were discussed in chapter One. One of the areas in which direct connections between these art forms may be seen is in early stage sets. In the nineteenth-century urban theatre a wide variety of scenic types was used, including flats and box sets, while props and mechanical devices were deployed extensively.[41] The sets were painted by artists following Western ideas on perspective and drew on the visuality created in the chromolithograph and the photograph.[42] Phalke was trained in European art techniques at the Sir Jamsetji Jeejibhoy School of Art in Bombay and at Kala Bhavan in Baroda, as well as being a practitioner of chromolithography,[43] so it is not surprising that his sets and costumes are similar to the images created in these fields. Other early cinema makers with strong backgrounds in art include Baburao Painter, whose very name shows his profession, and V. Shantaram, who began his work in cinema as a painter, while Dhiren Ganguly studied at Shantiniketan and the Government School of Art in Calcutta, and was an art teacher at Nizam's College, Hyderabad. Just as these new forms of visuality were products of an interaction between colonial and indigenous cultures, so cinema was also massively influenced by Western cinema, in particular by Hollywood, the most popular form of early cinema. Phalke himself talks about the inspiration of seeing the film *The Life of Christ* and he received his film training in London.[44]

Of the thousand-plus silent films made in India, very few remain, so it is almost impossible to trace a history of the style of sets. It may be that certain genres produced certain styles as their audiences were divided along class lines, as seen earlier. Historicals, for example, can be seen to show the clear influence of not only the Hollywood historical and biblical films but also the Indian calendar art depictions of heroes and deities. Recent studies of stills from this period indicate that an 'Islamicate'[45] style was very popular.[46] We should also expect to see much in the way of regional influences as early film makers were from particular communities, such as the Parsis (Ardeshir Irani, Sohrab Modi), while many were Gujaratis (including Chandulal Shah). Prabhat Studios in Pune, which made simultaneous Hindi and Marathi versions of its films, changed the style of dress and décor used in its modern 'socials' to show a north Indian style for the Hindi films and a Maharasthrian style for the Marathi films.[47] Many of the personnel at Bombay Talkies were Bengali and a clear Bengali influence permeated Bombay after the demise of New Theatres in the early 1950s. Many of the Bengali personnel in the industry were from highly Westernized élite or even princely backgrounds and several, including Devika Rani, were educated in the United Kingdom. In the 1940s the industry underwent a 'Punjabification' (see chapter Two) that remains dominant even six decades later.

The marketing of music by releasing the songs as advance publicity several weeks ahead of the film has also encouraged the use of exotic locations and grand sets for the song sequences. In some earlier films, such as *Chaudhvin ka Chand* (*Full Moon*, directed by M. Sadiq, 1960) and *Mughal-e Azam* (1960), song sequences were shot in colour while the rest of the film was made in black and white. Audiences showed a marked preference for colour, and black-and-white publicity for Mehboob Khan's *Mother India* (1957) was withdrawn lest the audience think the film was in black and white.[48]

Colour has had further implications for the *mise-en-scène* as the emphasis has shifted from texture and light contrast to the use of colour co-ordination and filters as major features. Colour only became standard during the 1960s, with Mehboob Khan alone using it regularly in the 1950s. In the 1990s a particular image of colour saturation, using filters and carefully colour co-ordinated costumes, typified by the Tamil films of Mani Ratnam, has been much emulated, although there is nostalgia for the rich textures of black and white among film buffs.

Theatre continued to influence cinema as many actors, directors and writers were connected with the left-wing Indian People's Theatre Association (IPTA), which developed in the 1930s and, like the Indian Progressive Writers Association (of which many scriptwriters were members), promoted social issues and social realism in the arts. While IPTA influenced 'art' film more closely, such as that of Ritwik Ghatak and Mrinal Sen, it entered the mainstream with such artists as K. A. Abbas, whose scripts included Raj Kapoor's *Awāra* (1951) and *Shri 420*

(*Mr 420/The Fraudster*, 1955); Bimal Roy, whose IPTA influenced films included *Do bigha zameen* (*Two Acres of Land*, 1955), starring Balraj Sahni with music by Salil Choudhury, both IPTA members; and members of Navketan films, including Chetan, Vijay and Dev Anand, who also employed Guru Dutt.[49]

Until 1991 Indian state television (Doordarshan) had only two channels. Its most successful television programmes were soaps, which first introduced commercial funding, including the phenomenally popular religio-soaps of India's two great epics, the *Ramayana* and the *Mahabharata*. These gave new life to India's oldest film genre, the mythological, on which they drew, while creating a new style of presentation of religious and epic characters that has become standard in television. The introduction of cable and satellite television in 1991, bringing a choice of around sixty channels in urban areas, has had a profound impact on the Indian media. Television has changed the circulation of publicity for Indian cinema, transmitting a large number of programmes using material from films, notably the film song, and screening old films, star interviews and other film-related journalism. The interaction between film and television style seems to be in both directions as personnel move from film to television, while film has noted the youth programmes and style of MTV and Channel [V]. The latter have had an enormous influence on the picturization of the film song, as well as on fashion, and have introduced a style of rapid editing.

The increasingly consumerist lifestyle of India's élites in the 1990s is seen in films that now feature a mix of Indian and Western designers in their clothes, furnishings and so on. As noted above, this may be said to have begun with *Waqt* (1965), which depicted the new lifestyle of the urban rich in a manner that has since been much emulated. Films of the 1990s have shown hugely extravagant interiors that many believe are not found in India, but they share many of the lifestyle values of the rich people in the film industry themselves.

Locations

Indian cinema has certain specific chronotopes of romance, associated with remote or even fantastic places, accessed in dream sequences or without diegetic explanation. Sometimes the chronotope is more closely linked with a defined place such as Kashmir (illus. 17), and by extension Switzerland and other mountainous areas, and with such motifs as the log cabin where the couple seek refuge in a storm;[50] with the earthly paradises of parks and gardens in full bloom; with waterfalls and rivers marking the eroticism of water; and with the tropical paradise beach.

17 Sharmila Tagore in the paradisal setting of Kashmir. Publicity still for
Kashmir ki kali, 1964.

These places constitute some sort of privacy for the romantic couple,
a private space in the public domain, where they are away from the
surveillance of the family that prevents, encourages and controls
romance, love and marriage. The couple can dance in these spaces, not
only because of the beauty of the backdrop (the spectacle of which
undoubtedly appeals to the audience), but also because this is beyond
the time and space of their normal, everyday lives.

Overseas locations were first used in films in the 1960s, as colour
film encouraged the use of landscape as spectacle. The 'great show-
man' Raj Kapoor was one of the first to benefit from these opportunities in *Sangam* (1964), and he was quickly followed by other directors
offering such titles as *Love in Tokyo* (directed by Pramod Chakraborty,
1966) and *An Evening in Paris* (directed by Shakti Samanta, 1967). In
these films travel represented the exotic and Utopias of consumption
for a range of lifestyle opportunities and consumerist behaviour, not
least owing to the prohibitive cost of foreign travel and problems of
gaining foreign exchange. The link between travel and romance as
consumerist activities in Western culture is also seen in Hindi films,
where travel inspires associations ranging from shopping in airports'

duty-free shops, eating and drinking out, and medical treatment in Swiss clinics, to expensive sports such as sailing and skiing. The films also allow for a new range of costumes, cars and specific references that associate travel with romance. Films may present these locations diegetically as the characters travel as part of the narrative, or they may be used in dream sequences or simply to represent part of India.

Since the economic liberalization of the 1990s an ever-increasing number of Indians have travelled abroad, in part to visit their overseas family now that belonging to a transnational family is almost a hall-mark of being middle-class in India. This Indian diaspora represents an increasingly important part of the market to the producer. For them, the attraction of exotic locales may not be so important, but the films also give meaning to locations in India. This is particularly true of the so-called 'diaspora films' such as *Lamhe* (*Moments*, directed by Yash Chopra, 1992), *Dilwale Dulhania Le Jayenge* (*The Brave Heart Will Take the Bride*, directed by Aditya Chopra, 1995), popularly referred to as *DDLJ*, or *Pardes* (*Overseas*, directed by Subhash Ghai, 1997; illus. 18). *Lamhe* portrays Rajasthan, long India's most popular destination for overseas tourists, as a place for love and romance for the NRI (non-resident Indian). *DDLJ* is addressed to the Punjabi diaspora, showing 'Punjabi' locations in London, such as Southall, romance in Switzerland and the final denouement among the family in the Punjab village. In other films, such as *Dil to Pagal Hai* (1997), overseas space is not only a holiday destination, but also an economic space, somewhere one travels to find work and money, whether in Germany or Japan, with India projected as a Manhattan cityscape or as a country resort for a dance school.

The chronotope may sometimes be more closely associated with time, in particular seasonal or annual time. Although snowscapes are often seen in romance, this is more because of the association with travel, remoteness and the opportunity to wear a different range of clothing. The usual seasons for romance are spring and the rainy season, which are employed as settings for two different types of romance: spring for love in union and the rainy season for love in separation. These two categories of love are found in Sanskrit theories of aesthetics and throughout Sanskrit literature, where love in union is celebrated in spring, while the category of separation is closely associated with the rainy season. Spring is also the season of Holi, an important carnival in north India at which coloured powder and water are thrown and which is associated with intoxication and sexual license rather than with the erotic. The rainy season is associated with the happy return of the traveller or with his absence, which creates the

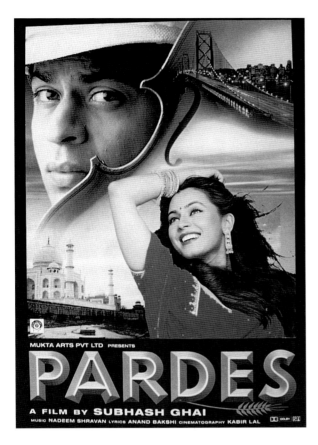

18 The relationship between the Indian diaspora and India is explored in *Pardes*, 1997.

mode of love in separation. These associations are found not only in Sanskrit literature but throughout many medieval traditions and modern folk songs, while a range of *ragas* (loosely translated as 'melodies') is specifically linked to the rainy season.[51]

The Hindi film song, however, while drawing on this imagery for its use of the rainy season, is also part of the tradition of Urdu lyric poetry, whereas many songs also draw on the folk songs of Hindi and its dialects. Urdu literature, drawing on Persian literary traditions, has an entirely different imagery of romance and eroticism, the season for love being spring, the location gardens with the cypress, the nightingale and the tulip. The traditional paradise of Urdu literature is associated with that of Kashmir, which was first used as a film location in Raj Kapoor's *Barsaat* (*Rain*, 1949). Kashmir featured as a location for romance for several decades, until the political situation made shooting there almost impossible. Other areas have stood in for Kashmir as

19 The famous drum-dance from *Chandralekha*, 1948.

the location of romance, such as Kulu Manali and Wellington in *Roja* (directed by Mani Ratnam, 1992); it featured again as the location for a combination of love and terrorism in *Mission Kashmir* (directed by Vidhu Vinod Chopra, 2000). It was only in the 1970s that this Kashmir came to be displaced by Europe, above all by Switzerland, with Scotland gaining popularity in recent years, together with new locations in Germany, North America and New Zealand.

Ravi Varma largely invented a mythological landscape in his oil paintings and later chromolithography, drawing on existing images but bringing in elements of colonial culture, notably Western Romanticism (both painting and literature[52]), photography and the other arts. Following painters of the picturesque, Victorian photographers in India were inspired by a mixture of Kant's and Schiller's ideas of nature as spectacle and Turner's views of the sublime to create a Romantic landscape of picturesque scenes of India.[53] This view of nature is very different from that of the parks and gardens of Hindu and Muslim traditions of paradise, but existed comfortably alongside them in photography and film, as well as in literature.

The range of locales and sets is so great that it would be impossible to cover them all. Leaving aside some particularly spectacular sets, such as that of the drum dance in *Chandralekha* (directed by S. S. Vasan, 1948; illus. 19), I wish to highlight some of the major settings crucial to the character of the Hindi film, including those that not only appear as an attraction but also contribute to the melodramatic features of the film. The most important of these is provided by the contrast between city and village. Whereas the village film almost died out in the commercial cinema, although it remains very popular in the art movie, the depiction of the city, almost exclusively Bombay, continues to change. I will then show how various settings have particular connotations for romance, both in its relation to post-modern consumerism and for transgressive romances. Finally I will discuss some specific sets and locations seen with great regularity in Hindi films.

The City and the Village

The opposition between the city and the village is frequently made in Hindi films. The contrast depicted in the films is not between the 'real India' of villages, as Gandhi called it, and the problems of the increasingly over-burdened Indian cities, but is more to do with a contrast between the pre-modern or timeless village and the city as an icon of modernity.[54] The nature of the city has changed over the century of Hindi cinema. While it is not possible to document this fully in the present context, some major trends may be identified.

Early films were often taken from literary sources and the village was presented as the place from which the hero had to leave. One of the most enduring subjects is the story of Devdas, taken from Saratchandra Chatterjee's Bengali novel of the same name, published in 1927. Its most popular versions include the New Theatres' versions made in Bengali and Hindi in 1935[55] and Bimal Roy's Hindi film of 1955, while Sanjay Leela Bhansali's version is scheduled for release in 2002. As children, Devdas and Paro live in an idyll reminiscent of the childhood of Krishna. Devdas's patriarchal father, however, forbids him to marry Paro. Too scared to elope as Paro suggests, Devdas goes to the modern city of Calcutta where he is caught up in alcoholism and begins visiting prostitutes. Paro meanwhile marries and lives as an orthodox Hindu wife. Devdas undertakes a journey around India by train, returning to Paro's house to die outside her gate. Neither the city nor the village is valorized at the expense of the other: while the village feudal system prevents the couple from marrying and the patriarchal father emasculates Devdas, the city and its temptations continue to destroy him. Although he cherishes his dream of being with Paro, he cannot survive in the village.

Mehboob Khan, a major director of the 1940s and '50s who had grown up in a village, made one of the greatest Hindi films to date,

Mother India (1957), which is set in a village: the only mention of the city appears in a song where the heroine seeks her husband who has deserted the family after he becomes dependent on them. This film presents a romantic version of the village in the early days, with farm workers singing and romancing in the fields in Soviet-style images, before showing the problems that beset the villagers, such as moneylending, humans labouring as beasts of burden, illiteracy and natural disaster. Nehruvian modernity is promoted as the solution to the village's problems, symbolized by the opening and closing images of the inauguration of the dam designed to prevent the villagers suffering from floods and water shortages. This contrasts with the image of the village presented in B. R. Chopra's *Naya Daur* (*New Era*), released the same year, in which the villain brings modern technology to a village already beset by pre-modern problems of caste and religion. The main drama lies in a race between a *tonga* (horse-drawn carriage) and a bus, which proves that traditional technology is as good as the modern, but the latter needs to be owned collectively. (Mehboob had rejected this as the subject for a good documentary, but was delighted to congratulate Chopra when it succeeded.)

Raj Kapoor, one of the greatest directors, producers and actors in Hindi films from the 1940s to the '80s, held a more romanticized view of the village. Although he had never lived in a village himself, he saw it as representative of a pure, unsullied India, exemplified by the village women whom he portrays in his films as innocent and pure. The city, on the other hand, is a place of corruption, lacking human values, although he also shows the glamour of the city, its sophisticated women and its opportunities to make money. These corrupting riches are later disavowed in the films, usually in a lengthy speech at the climax. Ashis Nandy analyses this popularly held view of the city, arguing that the village is usually regarded as the fantasy of a peasant or rural past as a lost paradise, contrasted with fears of the city and its amorality.[56]

The romantic films of the 1960s were usually about young urban people but they continued to show beautiful landscapes as locations for love, particularly the song sequences. The countryside is shown here as a version of the pastoral, somewhere to go on holiday, visiting parks and admiring mountainous scenery, whereas the city is always home. In Raj Kapoor's film *Bobby* (1973), the young couple visit libraries, cafés and swimming pools, but their romantic songs are shot in fields provided with beds of flowers, in the holiday destination of Kashmir or in a glamorized fishing village. In the famous song 'Hum tum ek kamre men band' ('You and me, shut in a room') the couple are locked in a log cabin and can indulge in the fantasy of being alone, while the scene moves from cosy domesticity to a jungle where lions prowl, marking this as beyond civilization and safety.

A gritty urban realism emerged in the 1970s with the introduction of the hugely successful 'angry young man' or 'industrial hero' seen in the films of Salim-Javed, such as *Deewaar* (*The Wall*, directed by Yash Chopra, 1975). The city of Bombay once again is split between glamour, represented by rooftop swimming pools and large suburban bungalows, and the crime-ridden docks and the street life of the urban migrant. Money, which is made from crime, is shown to be corrupting as the source of all glamour and comfort, while the impoverished teacher's son is obliged to steal to provide his parents with their daily food.

Bombay dominates the Hindi film's image of the city. One obvious reason is that the cinema industry is located there, but it is also India's economic capital and one of its most modern cities – at least until the last decade, when the high-tech cities of Bangalore, Hyderabad and, more recently, Madras have threatened its supremacy. Films show Bombay's money with its smart streets, houses, shops, hotels, night-clubs and public buildings, along with the industrial side of its docks and the public spaces used by most classes of society: its railway stations, beaches and parks.

One of the few films in the more popular idiom of Hindi films to show Bombay in a realistic manner in recent years is Ram Gopal Verma's *Satya* (1998). Set in a very Maharashtrian ambience, the film tells of a group of gangsters including Satya, a migrant who realises the way to advance in this city is through crime. The film depicts a lower-class gangster milieu through which the characters gain access to affluence, moving from working in bars to eating in restaurants and conducting their lives over the mobile phone. The dramatic cityscapes of Bombay are used in a manner rarely seen in a commercial film, as the city is shown in detail as a real space in which the protagonists live and work. *Satya* shows Bombay in detail: its beaches for romance (illus. 20), restaurants and for a public assassination, its rooftops providing privacy for meetings, its taxis and suburban railways (illus. 21) moving the actors across their networks, presenting realistic views of its streets, markets and shops. The city remains threatening, problematic and does not provide Utopian solutions, while it can be dehumanizing and lacking in human values.

This is in contrast to the depiction of the western suburbs of Bombay in the high budget films, where they appear associated with money, wealth and consumerism. These films have an altogether more posi-

20 Chowpatty Beach with Malabar Hill showing Bombay as a romantic location in *Satya*, 1998.

21 The Bombay suburban railway as a location for action in *Satya*, 1998.

tive view of the city as their concern is only with the rich. The privileged also visit overseas cities, which are shown in loving detail; London is a favourite, where major tourist attractions are shown, including Trafalgar Square, the Tower of London and the Houses of Parliament, as well as parks, shopping malls and pubs. The British Tourist Authority is keen to promote this use of British locations to encourage Indian tourism, and in 2001 produced a 'Bollywood map of Britain' so fans can visit the sights used in the films.

Romance: Capitalist and Consumerist Space

Hindi films offer further consumerist pleasures by showing designer, jewellery and sari shops, which many may recognize but few can afford to use. Expensive restaurants and bars also feature in films as places for romantic dinners or for young people to meet. The most important, and certainly the most expensive, locations are often in five-star hotels, which are used more widely as major public spaces by the wealthy, combining restaurants and coffee shops with other sites of consumerist pleasures, such as shopping arcades, beauty parlours and fitness centres and swimming pools. The style of furnishing typical of these hotels has spilt over into some domestic interiors and influenced office and commercial furnishing.

Indian monuments are used as spectacle or attraction rather than as having any connection with the story itself. Palaces (some of which are now heritage hotels) are used as houses, while palaces and forts appear as sets for dance sequences, as do gardens and the colonial hill stations. Sequences in Delhi may show the main roads around Edwin Lutyens's city but only as wide avenues and spectacle rather than bearing any historical meaning. Occasionally the use of historic locations may enhance the meaning of 'historical' films, such as the sets of Mohenjo-daro in Kamal Hasan's *Hey! Ram* (2000), where they suggest the unity of pre-partition India and the origins of Indian civilization, but in a contemporary 'social' film such meanings are rare.

Many films show the offices where the family's money is made. These are usually family businesses, which occupy a transitional position between feudalism and capitalism. The office arrangement is shown as a space constructed around the head of the family, with the offices of his sons adjacent, and complete with images of dead ancestors and loyal retainers, yet it is also furnished with icons of modern capitalism and the nation state.

Romance: Transgressive Space

One of the great attractions of the Hindi film is provided by showing spaces usually associated with transgressive (non-marital) sexual relations. The most celebrated of these is the courtesan's house, the sumptuous and elaborate furnishings of which suggest not only the glamour of prostitution but also the profitability of selling sexual pleasures. Its modern form, the nightclub, may suggest through its association with alcohol consumption and dancing girls, paid to perform in front of men, or it may be shown as an expensive venue for a sophisticated couple to visit.

Nightclub/cabaret

The nightclub features in too many sequences to mention. As a setting for songs it differs from the rest of the film in terms of style, even creating its own particular stars, notably Helen, who danced in these 'items' for around twenty years, and helping to promote some of the most successful dance directors, such as Saroj Khan. Sets for nightclubs have included some of the most fashionable and idiosyncratic in the Hindi film. From flashing disco floors to enormous record players, slides or giant eyes, as in *Teesri Manzil* (*Third Destination*, directed by Vijay Anand, 1966), the nightclub has been a designer's favourite. Dancers have worn fishtail dresses, for example Nadira in *Shri 420* (*Mr 420/The Fraudster*, directed by Raj Kapoor, 1955), miniskirts or cutaway dresses, usually associated with Zeenat Aman in such films as *Yaadon ki Baraat* (*Procession of Memories*, directed by Nasir Hussain, 1973). The space created is 'unreal', in that there are no such clubs in Bombay,[57] but it is an idealization of trends seen in music videos and Western musicals such as *Saturday Night Fever* (directed by John Badham, 1977). In films of the 1970s the setting often has a dance floor with tables and chairs, to which the dancer will come to sing a song full of meaning understood by the cinema audience, if not the audience in the nightclub. The dance floor will usually show a few bewildered Westerners trying to look as though this is the kind of place in which they feel comfortable. It is a space in which all of society's norms are transgressed: women wear sexy clothes, drink and dance for men's entertainment. The sequence allows the viewer to enjoy forbidden pleasures that are subsequently often disavowed by the film's narratives. During the 1990s nightclubs are shown as similar to the real nightclubs of Bombay and other cities, frequented by the young and wealthy for fun and dancing, as for example in the Valentine's Ball in *Dil to Pagal Hai* (1997), rather than being transgressive spaces.

22 Umrao Jaan (Rekha) dances in the sumptuously recreated historical *kotha* (house of courtesans) in *Umrao Jaan*, 1981.

The 'kotha' or courtesan's house

The 'courtesan' film is one of the most popular genres, in terms of their box office success rather than the number of films produced.[58] Films that have the courtesan in a minor role often portray her as Hindu, but where she is the heroine she is always a Muslim. Given that Lucknow and Delhi were two of the principal centres of courtly Muslim culture of their time, it is appropriate that the two great films in which the main heroine is a courtesan are set in nineteenth-century Avadhi Lucknow (*Umrao Jaan*, directed by Muzaffar Ali, 1981; illus. 22) and Delhi and the Punjabi princely state of Patiala in the early years of the twentieth century (*Pakeezah/The Pure One*, directed by Kamal Amrohi, 1971).

The courtesan has been a popular figure in film, where her attractions give rise to a variety of pleasures in the audience. She is portrayed as a victim of men's lust and as an object of the viewer's pity, but also delights the audience in being the object of the male gaze as she dances for his entertainment. The combination of a beautiful actress and the opportunity for incorporating poetry, music and dance into the narrative are important, but viewers also enjoy the spectacle of her body, together with the elaborate scenery and clothing, tied to a certain nostalgia arising from the decline and

23 Arun (Rajesh Khanna) and Vandana (Sharmila Tagore) in a log cabin in *Aradhana*, 1969, while the silhouetted couple sing a song suggesting sexual transgression. Vandana becomes pregnant as a result of this encounter.

disappearance of courtesan culture. These are certainly some of the most extravagant and beautiful sets and costumes in the history of the Hindi film.

The log cabin

As noted earlier, one of the most popular locations for romance is Kashmir, where the lovers may go on holiday or meet in song sequences. Within this trope, the log cabin features as a space offering further privacy, allowing the audience the pleasure of imagining complete solitude and remoteness. In *Junglee* (*The Savage*, directed by S. Mukherji, 1961) this makes the couple realize they are in love, whereas in *Dhool Ka Phool* (*Blossom of Dust, Lovechild*, directed by Yash Chopra, 1959) and *Aradhana* (directed by Shakti Samanta, 1969; illus. 23) the unmarried couples end up having sex (offscreen, of course), which results in the woman's disgrace. The scene in *Aradhana* in which the heroine changes out of a wet sari into a draped blanket provides in 'Roop tera mastana' ('Your beauty is intoxicating') one of the most powerful erotic song sequences in Indian cinema, while in *Bobby* (directed by Raj Kapoor, 1973) it is unclear what is actually happening in the room, although the couple sing a most innocently suggestive song, 'Hum tum ek kamre men band' ('You and I, shut in a room').

The Space of the Family – Domestic Interiors

The range of domestic housing in the Hindi film is huge, from that of the super-rich to the desperately poor. The houses are usually shown in a fairly realistic manner, although they are often glamorized. The houses of the wealthy include the following areas: staircase, library, bedrooms, hall, music room, garden and *pooja* (worship) room. The films of the 1950s showed a baronial or colonial style of interiors, while in recent films the lifestyle of the super-rich is increasingly 'modern' or 'Western'. Yash Chopra's lavish, modern interiors in *Waqt* (1965) set the model that others have followed. The theatre group in his *Dil to Pagal Hai* (1997) lives in a Manhattan-style loft apartment, complete with a Pepsi machine and a fireman's pole, showing a cityscape of skyscrapers beyond the windows. The setting allows the audience to enter into the lifestyle of the super-rich and enjoy vicariously the pleasures of conspicuous consumption.

In crowded and expensive cities like Bombay, only the well-to-do can afford to have bedrooms of their own. The very rich have their bedrooms arranged like mini-flats, each with an en suite bathroom, a desk and computer, and a television and seating area, as well as the more usual bed and cupboards. Many Hindi films depict lavishly appointed bedrooms for the unmarried hero and heroine. His is likely to be replete with consumer goods, weight-training equipment, television and telephone. The wall may be covered with pictures of him in various poses displaying his multi-faceted character, or it may have pictures of his beloved. Her room is likely to be filled with cuddly toys and very 'girly' goods, reminiscent of a 'Barbie' doll's room. There may be a modern bathroom shown as well. The bedroom is not only associated with luxury and wealth, but is an area for personal expression, where the boy can show his muscles and the girl her innocence. It is also, of course, an area associated with sexual activity, symbolized by the bed, although this is rarely referred to directly in the film.

The staircase

The staircase is one of the most striking and frequently seen motifs but it is by no means unique to Indian cinema. It is found in fairytales, including versions of Cinderella, where she leaves her glass slipper on the stairs on her flight from the ball at midnight. The stairway features frequently in opera[59] and also widely in Hollywood as a location for

24 The grand staircase marks out domestic space and privacy as well as showing great wealth in *Andaz*, 1949.

spectacle; hence it is seen most frequently in spectacular genres. In historical films it is the setting for swashbuckling fights, as when Errol Flynn or Douglas Fairbanks Jr fenced up and down the staircase, or it is used for the major dramatic scenes of domestic crisis – notably in *Gone with the Wind* (directed by Victor Fleming and others, 1939), when Scarlett falls down the stairs, resulting in a miscarriage, and for the final scene where Rhett Butler walks away, turning to say to Scarlett, 'Frankly my dear, I don't give a damn.' It has been used with high frequency from the earliest days of the great RKO and MGM musicals to today's television shows, in which celebrity hosts use stairways to make grand entrances. It is also used to give strong visual images of the steps themselves, as in the shots of the Odessa Steps in *Battleship Potemkin* (directed by Sergei Eisenstein, 1925). Why is there this fascination?

The staircase can be used for enormous visual impact as it allows figures to run down the steps showing youth and grace and allows for the display of spectacular costumes. It also introduces vertical movement into interior locations that would otherwise be on one plane (illus. 24) and creates opportunities for specific patterns in high-angle shots, giving a graphic effect. However, it is often its symbolic meaning that is most important, representing a liminal space and an arena for confusion. It also represents danger, since a fall down the stairs can be fatal, as witnessed in *Hum aapke hain koun...! (What am I to You?*, directed by Sooraj Barjatya, 1994).

The staircase is neither on earth nor above it. If this idea is extended to cover that of a stairway to heaven,[60] each step can show a different gradation and a shift of perspective as one approaches either end. It also marks the boundaries of public and private within the house since the upper space is forbidden to outsiders, replacing the courtyard of the traditional feudal palace and dividing the space vertically, and not just horizontally, into different quarters. At the top of the stairs there is often a galleried space for looking down or up to, which allows the look to cross from one area to another, even if the person cannot.

The size of the staircase is also an indication of class, as it wastes valuable space, rather than economizing by using the ladder found in lower-class housing: the grander the house, the bigger the staircase.

Sites of Authority

Among the regularly recurring sets in the Hindi film are sites of authority, whether centred around figures of pre-modern authority or around institutions of the modern state. These sites are often in competition with each other, as when the police arrive too late after natural justice has been done, or they are in direct conflict, as the young policeman may have to choose between his professional duty and his love for his law-breaking brother. Sometimes the feudal view is upheld, as in *Mother India* (1957), in which the mother kills her son for abducting their enemy's daughter. She is not brought to trial for murder, but rather is honoured by the new state, which asks her to formally open a dam, a symbol of the power of the modern.

The historical film shows an elaboration of a composite style of representations drawing on the (often Mughal) splendours of the popular imagination. They are set in royal courts in which the king, traditionally the giver of *darshan*, offers himself as a spectacle. Dressed in fine clothes and jewellery, and presented with grandiloquent speeches and recitations of his many names and dominions, he is positioned in splendid sets of mirrored, jewelled halls. His gaze may be contested, however, by even the lowest classes, such as the dancing girl in *Mughal-e Azam* (1960). This role, played by a great star, Madhubala, is also elaborately dressed and she adds the spectacle of beauty and talent in her song and dance 'Pyar kiya to darna kya?' ('If I've fallen in love, why should I be afraid?'; illus. 25). Her authority, however, is based on a greater power than that of the king, namely that of love, which allows her to question his judgement.

25 The servant Anarkali (Madhubala) defies the Mughal emperor Akbar, by singing of her love for his son in *Mughal-e Azam*, 1960.

The mythological film, India's oldest and unique genre, achieves Phalke's dream of showing India's gods and goddesses. Here the gods always maintain their *darshanic* gaze, often using the device of stasis to present an iconic image. A famous example of this is in the social film, *Kismet* (*Fate*, directed by Gyan Mukherjee, 1943), in which a staged show presents an image of Mother India against a map and icons of the country (illus. 26). The mythological also allows the display of special effects in the performing of miracles, which, like much of their setting, is drawn from the nexus of calendar art and urban theatre mentioned above.

The public space of the *ghats*, the steps to the river where women go for water and to wash, is one of the few public spaces traditionally permitted to women. Men rarely visit the *ghats*, but they are associated in legend with Krishna's teasing of the milkmaids. In Bimal Roy's version of *Devdas* (1955) the hero visits the *ghats* to meet Paro as a sign of his connection with Krishna and perhaps also of his 'feminine'[61] nature.

All of India's religious communities have traditions of pilgrimage, whether the Hindu *tirthas* or sites that map out the sacred land of Bharat (India), the Muslim *hajj* or pilgrimage to Mecca or the visits made to the *dargahs* or tombs of saints. Photographs or moving images

26 A tableau of nationalist images, including that of Mother India, in *Kismet*, 1943.

have some element of the power of these sites and can benefit their viewers.[62] These sites often have musical traditions associated with them, such as the devotional song or the Sufi *qawwali*. They may appear as the location for miracles, as does the shrine of Shirdi Sai Baba, revered by Hindus and Muslims alike as almost the patron saint of the Bombay film industry, in *Amar Akbar Anthony* (directed by Manmohan Desai, 1977). The blind Hindu mother approaches the saint as a devotee, while her son sings a song in his praise. Two flames move from the statue's eyes to the mother's, restoring her sight. Sufi *qawwalis* sung in *dargahs* may carry an inner meaning, such as at the tomb of Salim Chishti in *Pardes* (*Overseas*, directed by Subhash Ghai, 1997), where the *qawwals* sing of divine love, 'nahin hona tha lekin ho gaya pyaar, ho gaya mujhe pyaar' ('It wasn't meant to happen, but it did, I fell in love'), but their words may be interpreted as concerning the human love of the hero and heroine. Characters who are shown visiting religious sites are associated with such virtues as goodness, truthfulness and conformity. While several films in the 1970s show jokes being made in temples, where the hero may pretend to speak as a god, telling the girl to fall in love with him, as in *Sholay* (*Flames*, directed by Ramesh Sippy, 1975), this has not been seen of late, probably on the grounds that it would offend Hindu sentiments. Temples often appear as a scene for a 'love marriage', a device to excuse the heroine of any suggestions of sexual activity outside marriage, where the hero and heroine marry 'in the eyes of God' but the marriage is not recognized by society; this justification usually appears when the heroine is left pregnant after the hero's death, for example in *Aradhana* (directed by Shakti Samanta, 1969).

Domestic temples and religious objects also indicate a space in which such values are upheld. The girls in *Hum aapke hain koun ...!* (1994), for example, seem to live in a house that has a temple as part of its structure, while in the house where the boys live the gods are able to communicate their will via their images to a dog, who can carry the fateful letter to the hero just in time to prevent the wedding.

The authoritative spaces of the modern state also appear in the Hindi film, largely as markers of melodrama, of extreme positions. The courtroom is one of the most popular of these, and courtroom drama is required so frequently that this is one of the few standing sets available at Film City (see chapter One). This genre sometimes seeks to uphold wider principles: B. R. Chopra's *Kanoon* (*Justice*, 1960), for example, a family melodrama about a father-in-law and son-in-law, made without songs and mixing film noir and courtroom drama, is a plea against capital punishment. Yash Chopra's *Waqt* (*Time*, 1965), a drama that can easily be read as an allegory of Partition, telling the story of three brothers separated from their parents, and unknown to each other, has many encounters with the law. The father is imprisoned for murdering an orphanage official who had mistreated one of his sons. When the eldest son, a professional thief, is framed by his boss, he is defended by his brother, a lawyer, and his youngest brother is a witness (illus. 27). The family is reunited in the courtroom itself, showing the all-embracing reach of the law of the state in restoring the law of the family.

Other sights of modernity are frequently found in films, where the ordinary citizen is rendered powerless by forces beyond his/her control and often has to be guided by a professional. The best example is of hospitals, usually private rather than state, which feature in many films as places where extreme emotions are experienced. The most crucial, of course, occur when someone is taken 'serious' (critically ill), and trivial concerns and emotions are put aside for rawer and deeper emotions in both the characters and the audience. In such scenes the patient will be draped in blood-stained bandages and surrounded by as much hospital equipment as possible. The death in hospital of Pallavi (Sri Devi) in *Lamhe* (*Moments*, directed by Yash Chopra, 1992) was drawn out to evoke pity in the audience for both her and the people she was leaving behind. In other scenes the hospital can form a plot device, as where the three brothers separated as children in *Amar Akbar*

27 Ravi (Shashi Kapoor) takes his oath in the courtroom drama which leads to the denouement of *Waqt*, 1965.

Anthony give blood to their seriously ill mother without any of them knowing of the relationship. This shows a clear link of blood, as they give blood directly rather than through a blood bank, and also makes them into an 'artificial' family until the true connections are uncovered. In *Dil to Pagal Hai* (1997) the second heroine's hospital visit precipitates the search for a new female dancer and also allows a backdrop for a staged performance to cheer her up.

The armed forces are shown frequently in films. The rare genre of the war film portrays the army and air force at close quarters, acting heroically and upholding the values of the nation. The films of J. P. Dutta, especially *Border* (1997) and *Refugee* (2000), have dramatic desert settings in which the forces are depicted starkly, struggling to control the enemy in the face of their more private desires. Many films feature a member of the armed forces, often to give the character a moral or heroic stature, such as that accorded to the fathers of illegitimate children, who die serving their country, an event that occurs in *Aradhana* (directed by Shakti Samanta, 1969) and in Yash Chopra's *Kabhi Kabhie* (*Sometimes*, 1975) and *Silsila* (*The Affair*, 1992). In recent years the integrity of politicians and lawyers has been questioned in some films, but the army has never been held up to ridicule or portrayed in anything less than a heroic light.

Specific Sets

Of all the sets that have appeared in Hindi films there are two that are outstanding in terms of attraction and the way they illustrate several points made above. Among the close contenders would be those for any of the courtesan films, but it is hard to choose one at the expense of another, and in these films the sets are so closely connected with the costumes and other features that they cannot stand alone. One of the most famous art directors is the artist M. R. Acharekar, who won three Filmfare Awards[63] and whose sets for *Aan* (*Savage Princess*, directed by Mehboob Khan, 1952) are among the most stylish in Hindi film history (Mehboob, a great fan of Cecil B. De Mille, made films on a truly epic scale). My choice, however, is for the sets that Achrekar built for the dream sequence in *Awāra* (*The Vagabond*, directed by Raj Kapoor, 1951).[64] Among contemporary designers, the work of Nitin Desai is outstanding but it was Sharmishta Roy's sets for *Dil to Pagal Hai* (*The Heart is Crazy*, directed by Yash Chopra, 1997) that changed the look of Hindi films.[65]

Awāra's basic storyline rehearses the nature versus nurture debate in an Oedipal manner that almost compels a psychoanalytic reading, not least as the real-life father (Prithviraj Kapoor) and son (Raj Kapoor) play two of the lead roles. In a striking parallel with the exile of Sita by Rama, Raj's father, Judge Raghunath, throws his wife out of the house after she has been abducted by the bandit Jagga, believing that she is no longer 'pure'. Raj becomes a criminal in order to survive, trained by Jagga. He befriends and then falls in love with Rita, the ward of Judge Raghunath. Raj kills Jagga and almost murders Raghunath. A courtroom drama ensues in which Rita raises key questions as to Raj's responsibility for his actions, given his upbringing. He goes to prison for three years, promising he will train as a lawyer, while Rita promises to wait for him.

The dream – or nightmare – sequence in *Awāra* is the big 'item' of the film, nine feet of footage, which is said to have taken three months (and considerable amounts of money) to shoot and was added to the film at the last minute as a major attraction (illus. 28).[66] The first shots set the scene, showing a spiral staircase surrounded by clouds, presumably heaven. Dancers appear among carvings of loops and swirls, singing and sliding down chutes. Rita (Nargis) stands at the top of a flight of stairs, topped by a barley-twist column, dressed in fine fabric, sequins and shiny hair ornaments, dusted with glitter and singing a love song, 'Tere bin aag yeh chaandni' ('Without you this moonlight is like fire'). Raj, dressed in a black T-shirt and trousers, then appears in hell, where he sings of his desires for love and spring, 'yeh nahin, yeh

78

28 Raj (Raj Kapoor) and Rita (Nargis) climbing the spiral to heaven in
Awāra, 1951.

nahin zindagi' ('This is not, this is not life'), as he is surrounded by
flames, dancing skeletons and other monsters. In the last sequence he
emerges through clouds to the sound of 'Om namah Shivaya' ('Homage
to Lord Shiva') at the bottom of a flight of stairs leading to a Trimurti
(composite image of Brahma-Shiva-Vishnu), when Nargis bends down
to take him by the hand and lead him to heaven. Dressed in an embroidered bodice and skirt, she sings 'Ghar aaya mera pardesi' ('My traveller has come home') in front of a statue (of the goddess Devi?) with
flashing lights in the background. She begins to climb the spiral and
Raj follows her. They then climb more stairs towards a Nataraja (dancing Shiva) as Nargis appears in dancing clothes. They begin to walk
along a twisting road when a giant Jagga appears, holding a shining
knife. Raj falls down, yelling 'Rita', as she reaches over him but cannot
save him. A montage of images, including one of Raj yelling as Rita
appears superimposed, dissolves as Raj wakes up, shouting 'Maa,
mujhe bachao' ('Mother, save me!').

Heaven is dry ice, statues of deities and dancers in pale, bright light,
while the dark torments of hell have dancers who look very like the
evil spirits conjured up by special effects in a film by Phalke, although
no effects are used here. There seems to be no direct connection

between heaven and hell, but heaven has many a spiral staircase, chutes and slides, as well as other stairs, suggesting further possible ascents. The sequence is shot in black and white, using contrasting textures, reflections and lighting to great effect.

The scene is not only stunning visually and aurally, but it condenses into a dream many fears and anxieties relating to the film's key themes of love, religion, women, motherhood, punishment and crime, which it then projects onto the sets themselves.[67]

Sharmishta Roy trained as an assistant to her father, Sudhendu Roy, who worked for Yash Chopra from the 1970s until *Lamhe* (*Moments*, 1992). Among his most celebrated sets was the *basti* or slum he built for *Mashaal* (*The Torch*, 1984), although this was not one of the films for which he won his three Filmfare Awards. Sharmishta inherited his team of workmen when she made her debut as an art director. Although she designed the sets for Aditya Chopra's *Dilwale Dulhania Le Jayenge* (*The Brave Heart Will Take the Bride*, 1995), it was her work on *Dil to Pagal hai* (1997) that really made her mark as an art director, winning several awards, including the coveted Filmfare Award for best art director.

Yash Chopra asked Roy to produce a new look for a young, hip theatre crowd. This meant a move away from a traditional living space, divided into rooms, to a kind of Manhattan loft-space, with futons, galleries and exercise machines, and such unlikely props as roll-down screens of landscapes, a fireman's pole, a Pepsi machine and a VW Beetle covered in graffitti (illus. 29). The main heroine lives with her aunt in a traditional house, although her bathroom seems to be located in her bedroom rather than separate from it. The sets seem to lack continuity – the heroine's bedroom has a balcony for one song only, while the props in the theatre troupe's apartment come and go, and it is never clear who lives there or if there is a coffee bar inside it.

The film also used some real indoor locations in Bombay, notably Shopper's Stop, one of the first department stores in Bombay, and the Bombay Stores. Many of the audience outside Bombay assumed these were sets as they fitted so seamlessly into the look Roy created, suggesting once again the close connections between sets and other design.

These set designers, who now charge considerable fees, are important and influential figures in the creative work of a film and are part of the marketing package. The overall attention to detail brought to the sets is quite different from the less professional approach followed until quite recently. Sharmishta is also one of several women working in male-dominated parts of the industry on an equal footing with their

29 A Bombay flat as a Manhattan loft in *Dil to Pagal Hai*, 1997.

male counterparts. She admits that her entrance to the industry was made easier by her father's position but she now stands on her own merits, acting as an important role model to other women considering working in the film industry.

Clothing

As in Hollywood, Indian cinema has had a close relationship with the fashion industry, both as a source of inspiration and of marketing. In the early days the wardrobe department consisted mostly of tailors, who made designs chosen by the stars and the producers. The stars began to use their own dressers and advisers, but it was only recently that specialist dress designers became important. Their budgets are now considerable and they have become celebrities as the fashion and model industries boomed in the 1990s. The first celebrity designer was Bhanu Athaiya, who won an 'Oscar' for her costumes for *Gandhi* (directed by Richard Attenborough, 1982); in the 1990s Manish Malhotra developed an instantly recognizable look that has been much copied outside the film industry as well as within.

As with sets, few producers have kept their costumes at all or in careful conditions. The major exception is R.K. Studios, where they have preserved the entire wardrobe from all their films. This has been possible because the family has retained control of the studios, but perhaps their theatrical background has made them realize the value of their collection. The collection is dry-cleaned regularly and is in excellent condition. Costumes, such as that of the vagabond in *Awāra* are kept in their totality – hat, suit and shoes – and can be located swiftly by the keepers.

In the nineteenth century many of the urban élites began to wear British clothing, at least for formal wear. However, largely following Gandhi's adoption of Indian clothing on his return to India in 1915, many of the dominant Congress party adopted a new uniform of *khadi* ('homespun cloth'), although in the more generous covering afforded by the *kurta-pyjama* (long, loose shirt and trousers). Fifty years after independence, *khadi* remains the Congress uniform for men, although it has come to be mocked in Indian cinema, where the *khadi*-clad politician is usually associated with civic corruption.

The early genres, the mythological, the devotional and the historical, drew on the modern visuality, notably that of photography, chromolithography, religious processions and performances, folk and urban theatre, and foreign cinema.[68] 'Social' genres, however, set in contemporary India, drew on a hybrid of contemporary Hollywood films, in particular their style of glamour, make-up, hairstyles and some of the men's clothing, although dress, especially for women, was largely local (illus. 30). In Bombay, for example, most of the studios during the silent period were Gujarati, and a Gujarati *mise-en-scène* is the norm during this time, while in Calcutta a Bengali style emerged. The evolution of an Oriental style in Hollywood, typified by the films of Valentino, Douglas Fairbanks Sr and Cecil B. De Mille's biblical epics, introduced a way of depicting the East that was often incorporated into Indian films.[69] The 'Punjabification' of the film industry in the 1940s (see chapter One) affected the industry at all levels from producers, directors and writers of dialogues and lyrics, to the male stars. During the last fifty years, nearly all the major male stars of Hindi cinema, who represent an idealised form of masculinity, have been Punjabi.

The post-independence period saw Western clothes becoming the norm again for the urban, upper-caste male, with 'Indian' clothes reserved for wearing in the home (the vest or *kurta* worn with a *lungi* or sarong) or for strictly formal occasions – the *bandgala* (lounge suit with 'Nehru' collar) or the *sherwani-pyjama*. This trend was mirrored in the films, with male stars becoming famous for their style, whether 'Debonaire' Dev Anand's quiff or Shammi Kapoor, 'India's Elvis'. The greatest superstar of the Hindi movie, Amitabh Bachchan, very tall, thin and not conventionally handsome, set the trend that has contin-

30 Pratap (Ashok Kumar), the Brahmin boy and Kasturi (Devika Rani) as a Dalit ('untouchable') in *Achhut Kanya*, 1936.

ued to the present for 'cool', outrageously stylish high fashion for men, often eclipsing his female co-stars. Bachchan's representation was fetishistic, his first appearance usually being of his feet, shod in black leather, as the camera slowly panned up his long body. His legs, which were used in the movie as weapons of destruction, were clad in the widest flares or bell-bottoms, often impossibly white. Bachchan regularly appeared in a vest, but his body was for action, not offered for display, while his fashionable clothing became his trademark. His roles tended to be masochistic and he often died at the end of the film, in the arms of his buddy or his mother.

The action films of the 1980s saw the macho action-hero dominate the screen, but this figure was replaced in the 1990s by the short, muscular hero with a pretty face. Salman Khan, one of the most popular, takes his shirt off several times in each movie to show his pumped body, frequently wearing gym-gear and American sportswear. The suburban look of Tommy Hilfiger and Nike trainers is the informal uniform, while the men wear double-breasted suits for formal occasions, showing that men's clothes as ever are designed for careers and leisure, although they are supplemented by a number of fancy outfits for the song and dance numbers.

One striking feature of the male stars is that, unlike most men under forty in India, they are clean-shaven. Most young men wear moustaches, a sign of masculinity that has become proverbial – 'mooch nahin: kooch nahin' ('No moustache: no nothing') – although older men often shave. Only élite and middle-class men and *jankhas* ('effeminate men') shave, a rule followed by the movie star even when playing a street guy.[70] This fashion is not followed by many movie fans, although they do follow the fashion for haircuts seen in the movies. Just as the quiff and the crew cut were fashionable in the 1960s and sideburns in the '70s, during the 1980s the short front and long back cut was very popular. In *Viraasat* (*Inheritance*, directed by Priyadarshan, 1997) the hero, Anil Kapoor, returns from the USA with long hair, but cuts his hair and grows a moustache after his father dies and he takes up his role as village landlord. Hairweaves and wigs are popular among the balding stars; beards are for intellectuals, baddies, Muslims and Sikhs.

The male at the end of the twentieth century is groomed, maintained, exercised and dressed in the clothes of consumer society, an object of his own narcissistic gaze while inviting the gaze of the audience on his often fragmented body in a way traditionally associated with women.

Unlike the men, the female stars who play north Indian, upper-caste women are often from other regions of India, some of the top stars being Bengali, Maharashtrian and south Indian, most of whom are upper-caste (usually Brahmins) and said to be lighter-skinned than the lower castes. The body shape of the stars has changed radically over the years. The early stars had big breasts and hips, were often large and rarely athletic. Although some were always slim, the 1990s has seen the star becoming increasingly thin, some even having a worked-out/gym look. Within films a different look is required for different types of heroine: former models are used for modern, Westernized women, while more curvaceous women play the traditional roles.

In a patriarchal society women's bodies do not belong to themselves, but to the patriarchal male. At the most extreme, couples do not meet before marriage, the family deciding on the choice of partner, with beauty less important than the moral qualities of the bride and her family. In such families, the older members decide which clothes are important for the young woman, any attempts by her to exercise her own choice being a source of family conflict.[71] These rules have been relaxed considerably in recent years, although the romance followed by family negotiation, as seen in most films, glosses over many important issues in the ownership of women's bodies. This appropriation of the woman's body is further complicated in the cinema, where the woman is the object of gaze.[72] This is reinforced in Indian cinema by the operation of the star system, which creates an image of glamour rather than a realistic depiction of women and may be further complicated by the structures of Indian spectation.

The relationship between women's clothes in movies and in real life is not one of reflection, but the codes of cinema require clothing to fill particular semiotic functions, which I attempt to trace below.

The sari is seen as the national dress of Indian women, but this is only a recent fashion. A taboo on wearing stitched clothing has meant that a variety of methods of draping different lengths of cloth have been practised in India for at least two millennia. Today there are two main lengths, the nine-yard sari, worn only by married women, although now rarely by the upper classes and mostly restricted to the lower castes and classes. Instead the norm is for the six-yard sari, now found worn in two major styles, the so-called Gujarati style, where the *pallu* (the patterned end) is worn draped over the front, or the more commonly worn style with the *pallu* hanging loose over the left shoulder. The saris themselves are very different, being made in an enormous variety of weaves, prints, borders and textiles, many regionally marked. A widely understood grammar of wearing the sari exists, with specific occasions requiring different saris according to season, time of day and degree of formality. For example, a wedding in north India requires, if at all possible, a costly Banarsi sari (heavy silk, with *zari*, gold thread), while for any religious occasion a silk sari is necessary (some orthodox women still wear a silk sari for eating everyday). The choice of colour is also important: red, green and yellow are the choice for festive occasions; widows traditionally wear white or pale colours, while black is not a popular colour, being worn largely as a Western fashion.

The sari is often seen as an eternal and unchanging dress, but not only is its widespread popularity and standardization of drape recent, but it is as subject to changes in fashion as any other clothing. One year may see a trend for heavy weaves, followed by cottons with hand-painted designs, followed by chamois-silks (illus. 31 and 32).

The *choli* ('blouse') became popular in the nineteenth century and has now become almost mandatory, with many styles of sari including a blouse-piece in their fabric. Otherwise blouses are usually made in a fabric that matches the sari, but fashion sometimes demands a contrasting colour. Blouse styles change radically from season to season as regards degree of tightness, length of sleeves, shape of neckline and so on. Versions drawing on ethnic backless bodices, traditionally worn with skirts and veils, have remained popular among the more daring for several years while other ethnic styles, such as the

31 Paro (Suchitra Sen) and Devdas (Dilip Kumar) meet on the *ghats*. Their clothes are 'traditional', in particular the Bengali drape of her sari. *Devdas*, 1955.

32 The wife, Shobha (Jaya Bachchan), meets the mistress, Chandni (Rekha), in a sari shop with her husband Amit (Amitabh Bachchan). Chandni's plain silk sari and blouse are high fashion items. *Silsila*, 1981.

jacket-style, have been popular as a heavily embroidered or beaded item, worn with a plain sari.

The sari is the orthodox form of Hindu dress, some temples refusing admission to women not wearing them. Other communities also wear saris, the Parsis preferring small borders and sleeveless blouses, although many wear Western clothes; while women in some Goan Christian communities wear saris, they can be distinguished from others who only wear Western-style dresses. Some Muslims also wear saris, but it is increasingly thought an inappropriate form of dress for Muslims in terms of its association with Hindus and because it shows the body and the arms; it is becoming largely confined to weddings, although the *sherara* (a long culotte-type skirt) is usually preferred for the bride. Despite its frequent showing of the midriff and cleavage, it is widely regarded as a particularly chaste dress[73] and as the appropriate dress for women at home and at work.

Saris are important social markers as regards age, marital status and class beyond the mere fact of cost and maintenance of the garment. They are rarely worn by young, middle-class and elite women except for formal occasions. These groups prefer Western-style clothes or the *salwar-khamees*. However, after marriage (see below), and especially after having children, the sari becomes increasingly popular, especially for middle-class girls who live with their in-laws.

The sari is heavily laden with cultural meanings of nostalgia, tradition, womanhood, nationalism and social status, the full range of which are developed in the Hindi movie. Mothers or mother-figures always wear traditional, sober saris. In older movies that contrasted the heroine with the vamp, the heroine almost invariably wore a sari as an emblem of her chastity and goodness. In recent years the unmarried heroine, who is usually a teenager, wears Western clothes before marriage but changes into *salwar-khamees*, but more often the sari, after marriage. In one of the big hit films of 1999, *Biwi no 1* (*Wife Number 1*, directed by David Dhawan), the wife and mother of two always wears a sari, although her rival wears Western-style fashion. When the wife decides to produce a portfolio of modelling shots, her unfaithful husband is outraged at her wearing the same clothes as his mistress, reminding her of her status as married and a mother. The two young heroines in the top film of 1998, *Kuch kuch hota hai* (*Something Happens*, directed by Karan Johar), both wear Western clothes. The hero fails to realise he is in love with one, since she is his best friend and dresses as a tomboy, and marries the other. When they meet again after he has been widowed, the heroine has begun to wear a sari and the hero soon realizes that he is in love with her after all. A heroine who is not a mother, however, often wears a type of sari and sari blouse that would not be acceptable for a mother, most often a transparent chiffon sari. Thus the sari becomes a meeting-point for the maternal and the erotic in the movies, a conjunction supported at many other points in the movie.

The *salwar-khamees* or Punjabi suit, originally a Muslim dress that became popular in north-west India, has also become a national and even international dress through the influence of Jemima Khan and Diana, Princess of Wales. The suit comprises trousers (loose *salwars* or tight *churidars*), a long shirt and a scarf. The materials and colours may be the same, contrasting or mixed. The stylistic variations are endless, the scarf alone carrying a range of meanings according to whether it is used to cover the head, the breasts or worn like a Western scarf.

This outfit is a popular option for younger women, being easy to maintain, comfortable and modest in covering the limbs and even the head. Although Punjabi women and Muslim women of all ages and statuses wear this outfit, it has recently become the standard dress of many college girls, unmarried women and working women. Regarded by many as a frumpy outfit, it has been glamorized largely within films. During the 1950s it is shown as a typically modest outfit, but the 1960s saw the introduction of the tight-fitting top, with more glamour added by Sadhana's introduction of the *churidar* trousers in *Waqt* (1965). One of the most striking uses of the *salwar-khamees* in recent films has been Manish Malhotra's outfits for *Dil to Pagal hai* (1997), where they were worn by the 'traditional' heroine in contrast to the other heroine, the DKNY, sportswear-clad best friend of the hero. Once again, the hero falls in love with the girl in Indian clothes, who only wears a sari for dream sequences, her Western clothes being for holidays in Europe, nightwear and stage performances. In this film the outfits have much transparent material, are cleavage-revealing and the scarf is used more for pictures of billowing material than for modesty.

While ethnic chic is a fashion associated with activists and intellectuals, although very popular at the beginning of the 1990s, the Hindi film has invented its own version of the village belle, the *gaon ki chori*, who usually appears in a skimpy version of a regional costume, with knee-length skirts and backless shirts. While some village women may show their backs, they do not show their legs and they usually cover their heads, if not their faces. Madhuri Dixit wore such an outfit in *Khalnayak* (*The Villain*, directed by Subhash Ghai, 1993) for her infamous song 'Choli ke peeche kya hai?' ('What's under my blouse?'). The heroine has her head covered for the opening of the song, but the camera's close-ups on her heaving breasts and naked back dispel any suggestion of modesty, despite her protest that her heart is in her blouse.

While many Hindu women veil themselves in the presence of older men by covering their heads and sometimes their faces, the veil is largely associated with Islam. This is true in the films also, and it plays important roles in some genres, such as the Muslim social and the courtesan films. In the Muslim social, the hero catches a glimpse of the heroine, but her veil (the full *burqa*) often leads to a tragedy of mistaken identity. The heroine in the courtesan film may wear a veil, but her honour is not that of wider society. In her famous song 'Inhe logon ko' ('Ask these people') the heroine of *Pakeezah* (*The Pure One*, directed by Kamal Amrohi, 1971) clings on to her honour (hence the name her beloved gives her, Pakeezah), accusing men of trying to rob her of it by removing her veil. The veil is erotically charged by the idea of concealing and revealing, and numerous songs in Hindi films are about veils, even though the heroine no longer wears one herself.

Women in India took longer than men to adopt Western clothes, which have remained restricted to certain groups. They are worn as uniforms by, for example, schoolchildren, nurses and police. Certain communities, some Christian and some Parsis in particular, wear Western clothes, although the form varies from an old-fashioned 'frock' to the latest designers. They are also popular with modern, urban women, although mostly before marriage and children. Western clothes are seen as more sexy and more 'fun' by young urbanites, but it is felt that one has to have a good figure (i.e. be slim) in order to wear them. Western designer clothes, in particular sports clothes, cannot be purchased in India, adding a further element of glamour to their acquisition. In film, the sports clothes wear their labels proudly, *Kuch kuch hota hai* being emblazoned with the Tommy Hilfiger and DKNY labels (illus. 33)

Perhaps more important than outerwear in India has been the impact of two parts of the Western wardrobe, underwear and nightwear. The bra, the strangely erotic and chaste garment of the twentieth century, has been widely adopted in India at all levels and, although not shown directly in films, the recent fashion for the truss-like Wonderbra has been all too obvious. In India one traditionally slept in one's day clothes, but now kaftans have become popular, along with a rise in Western-style nightdress/pyjamas or a T-shirt with a gown. Nightdresses are often featured in movies to provide a certain eroticism, in particular as preludes to songs of the 'dream sequence' type.

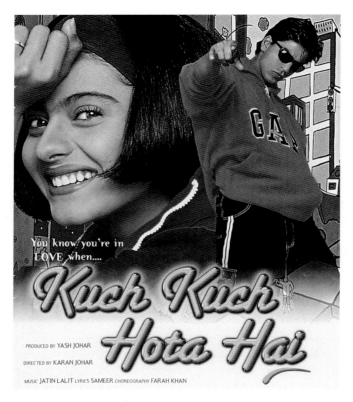

33 Designer-labelled leisurewear in *Kuch kuch hota hai*, 1998.

Although one rarely sees a naked body in a Hindi film, there have been debates around this, sparked largely by a scene in Shekhar Kapur's *Bandit Queen* (1992), in which the heroine is stripped by her attackers. This proved a major attraction for some viewers, although the Hindi cinema's elaborate codes of eroticism are far more sensual than the presentation of a humiliated woman. The Hindi cinema's most controversial outfit is the swimsuit, popular in the films of Raj Kapoor, whether his *Awāra* (1951) or *Bobby* (1973; illus. 34), but deemed unsuitable for a round in the Miss World contest held in India in 1996. This is, however, far less erotic than Raj Kapoor's other device, the wet sari, which not only reveals the heroine's body to the point of nudity but is also associated with the erotic mood of the rainy season and of sweat (illus. 35). It also allows a display of those parts of the body that are seen as most erotic in India – the trunk (breasts, waist, hips and back); the limbs, although they must be covered, are not seen as particularly erotic but can be vulgar when displayed.[74]

LOVE THAT DEFIED
ALL BARRIERS

34 Bobby (Dimple) wears a bikini while Raj (Rishi Kapoor) wears '70s sunglasses in *Bobby*, 1973.

35 Viday (Urmila Matondkar) enjoys a soaking in the Bombay rain in a 'wet sari' sequence. *Satya*, 1998.

36 The former Miss World, Aishwarya Rai, in *Taal*, 1998.

The film heroine's body must look good in all these outfits, for she is likely to be required to wear the whole range in a film (illus. 36). This totality of costume is similar to the fashion show, in which the Indian designer is required to present all types of clothes, from Western to a whole range of Indian (especially the wedding outfits), although she/he may specialize in one. These designers came to world notice when their clothes were worn by several Oscar nominees in 1999 and after Abu (Jani) and Sandeep (Khosla) designed outfits for Sophie Marceau in the James Bond film *The World is not Enough* (1999). Many of these designers provide costumes for films, sometimes being consultants for particular stars and dressing them in their off-screen appearances.

Heroines wear a huge number of outfits in the films, not just for the occasions required by the script but for song sequences, which may be fantasies allowing them to wear otherwise incongruous outfits, and nearly all of which often involve many changes of clothes. These changes of clothes have many functions, partly as the modern idea of romance is based around consumption, whether dress, travel or going out, but also to show the heroine's adaptability – both physical (in looking good in a variety of styles) and in her ability to put on and put off clothes as masquerade.

Jewellery is not just a means of displaying wealth in India. Traditionally, a woman's only legal possession is the jewellery she is given on marriage; it never belongs to her husband and is a mark of a woman's own wealth (illus. 37). It conveys religious meanings ranging from the mark of a married woman (see below) to astrological functions, notably in the use of stones as protection against malign planetary activity. A woman will almost always have her ears pierced in childhood; nose piercing is common among certain groups. Hair also has complex significance,[75] ranging from the erotic (long, loose hair) to the ordered (long, groomed, and tied back for women), and hair is covered for specific occasions. Widely varying haircuts are also seen, often shown by using wigs in films, from sleek bobs to big, fluffy

37 Umrao Jaan (Rekha) wears the full range of a courtesan's jewellery in *Umrao Jaan*, 1981.

hairstyles, but hair-colour is usually a natural black, although streaks have become increasingly popular. Women never show any body hair in India, and for middle-class and elite women the beauty parlour is an important monthly visit, where the hair is trimmed, the face is tweezed, threaded, waxed and bleached, while exposed limbs and underarms are waxed. Pubic hair is not shown in films, and is often removed for religious as much as cosmetic reasons. Manicures and pedicures are fairly commonplace, the latter being popular since the foot is regularly exposed in the standard footwear of the open sandal, from the flat to the platform. The foot is further decorated by anklets, married women of many communities wear toe-rings on their second toe, and feet are decorated with henna at the time of family weddings. Given the ritual impurity of feet and footwear, and their consequent importance as a sign of submission, it is not surprising that many films exhibit foot fetishism to varying degrees.[76]

While Hindu men undergo various ritual initiations, a woman's only initiation is the rite of marriage. The importance of marriage in Indian society is hard to underestimate, whether in terms of religion, economics or society. This important event requires a particular form of dress for all participants, with the most costly clothes required. The spectacle of the wedding, as much as its romantic associations, has meant that most films incorporate a ceremony requiring the most sumptuous clothes and jewellery. Traditionally, the woman changes the way she dresses after marriage, to appear as the auspicious married woman (*saubhagyavati*), a form of dress in which she will be cremated if she dies before her husband, or will have to abandon on his death. The colour and form of outfit worn by the bride varies between communities and regions. Given the Punjabi atmosphere of the Hindi movies, the dominant representation is of the Punjabi wedding, with many people referring to a 'Yash Chopra wedding', after the creator of the look in some of India's most popular romantic films (illus. 38). The film will show the bride in full red for her wedding dress, the groom with his face covered with flowers, wearing a turban.

After marriage the bride may or may not wear the complete outfit of the *saubhagyavati*, but will often begin wearing colourful saris, more jewellery, and always a *bindi* ('auspicious mark on the forehead'). The jewellery is an essential part of dress, marking wealth, religion and region. The absolute minimum worn will be earrings, a necklace (often the black beads of the *mangalsutra*, 'the wedding necklace'), bangles (red glass is traditional in north India as a minimum, but gold is worn when it can be afforded) and a ring (seemingly incorporated from the Christian tradition, but worn on any finger). The absence of jewellery

38 On their wedding night, Vijay (Shashi Kapoor) removes his bride's (Raakhee) wedding jewellery during a song sequence in *Kabhi Kabhie*, 1976.

is always a statement, usually of widowhood, but has also been adopted by feminists and other activists, although some may wear some oxidized silver 'folk' jewellery rather than more costly gold.

A popular comic feature of Hindi movies is to have a hero appearing dressed as a woman. This is usually at some point in the story when the hero needs to pass himself off as a woman, or it can be purely for comic effect. One of the most popular songs of the 1990s, 'Didi tera dewar deewana' ('Sister, your husband's brother is crazy') from *Hum aapke hain kaun ...!* (1994), involved men and women cross-dressing. The women of the house hold a six-month pregnancy ritual to ensure the birth of a son. This is intended only for women, so the men of the house try to enter in disguise. The younger son dresses as a pregnant woman, while a female friend dresses as the younger son. This is seen as being purely fun and part of the happiness of the celebration, perhaps because the transgression of gender boundaries brings a further intimacy.

The purple dress worn by the heroine in this song (illus. 39) is indicative of the wider influence of the Hindi films on fashion, becoming one of the most copied items of recent years, with girls asking their tailors to make this outfit for family functions. This is part of a trend that has been widespread since the earlier days of movies[77] and has been observed in many other societies, for instance among the female fans

39 Prem (Salman Khan) and Nisha (Madhuri Dixit) in the famous purple outfit, which was much copied. *Hum aapke hain kaun...!*, 1994.

of Hollywood stars in the West, who copy clothes, hairstyles and make-up, along with gestures and ways of speaking.[78] Madhuri Dixit was the undisputed top box-office star when this outfit became widely copied, her popularity augmented by the phenomenal success of the film and in turn this particular song. She is one of several stars who have always been at the forefront of setting trends. In the 1960s Sadhana cut a fringe in her hair to conceal her broad forehead and this became a style copied by girls all over India. For *Waqt* (1965) Sadhana wore *churidars*, which had previously been considered 'Muslim' dress, and created a fashion that has endured for decades. Rekha, the star who transformed and monitored her appearance more than any other, set a whole range of fashion styles from the clothes she herself selected for her film roles, such as the 'Rekha blouse' and her styles of make-up.

Film has also been an important way of introducing Western dress styles to an Indian audience. In the 1990s the heroine can wear Western clothes, which no longer carry any negative implications, but now represent a facet of her character, namely her ability to be at home anywhere in the world. Western clothes now mark her as modern and cosmopolitan but will usually form only a part of her wardrobe and, as in earlier films, all married women wear some form of Indian clothes and usually have long hair (illus. 40). The clothes worn in films are often from labels favoured by the new generation of stars and directors, who wear these clothes in their everyday lives as a variety of fashion

Some love stories... live forever

Yash Chopra's

Mohabbatein

an aditya chopra film

40 The characters of the young couples in *Mohabbatein*, 2000, are marked by their clothing. Kiran (Preeti Jhangani) on the right, is a widow, so wears more traditional, though not staid, clothes in light colours.

statements: casually informal, yet markers of foreign travel and wealth; or sporty as part of their new healthy lifestyle. American sports clothes, rather than European formal or eccentric clothes, mark the norms of the so-called transnational or global fashion.

The fashion of films has interacted with the growing consumer culture of 1990s' India, which has also seen an explosion of new media, including cable and satellite television, the magazine industry, advertising and 'sex 'n' shopping' novels. Television in particular has drawn heavily on film for its programmes, circulating images from the film to ever-wider audiences. The best-selling magazines are film-based and show images of the film stars in screen costumes and other outfits. Youth programmes and Western television have increased awareness of Western designers, although their clothes, perfumes and accessories still have to be purchased overseas, often on shopping trips to Dubai or holidays in the US, UK or Australia. Many of the Indian middle classes and élites have family settled abroad, creating a circulation of goods through visits to India and overseas, allowing new forms of style to emerge.

Beauty pageants, regarded in the West at best as kitsch survivors of the pre-feminist 1950s and '60s, have become hugely popular in India, due in part to their achieving major success in both Miss World and Miss Universe. The Femina Miss India competition is watched avidly by television viewers and the beauty queens are household names, like supermodels in the West. The next move for a beauty queen is into the world of films: Sushmita Sen has had moderate success, while Aishwarya Rai has established herself as the top female box-office star.

Fashion flows move in multiple directions as the Western clothes in film and the clothes worn by the film personnel interact with 'street fashion', often originating in African–American communities and subsequently being adopted and adapted by many British Asians. India has continued to remain a source for mainstream Western fashion 'hippy chic' (and not so chic) as well as for luxury items, such as pashmina shawls, silks and jewellery. The mixture of Indian and Western clothes remains eclectic: Indian jewellery may be mixed with Western clothes, the *bindi* or vermilion mark has mutated into stick-on motifs embellished with eye and lip pencil designs; the shawl can be worn with formal Western clothing; sari-borders are found on jeans; toe-rings and nose-rings are associated with Western 'grungy' styles.[79]

The Hindi movie has eschewed these hybrid trends, the stars wearing completely different styles in separate scenes and even displaying several changes of style within a song sequence. These outfits remain as distinct as the rounds of the Miss World contest dedicated to evening wear and swimsuits. The cinema continues its fondness for songs about clothes, even though it has changed the tone of its lyrics from 'My red muslin scarf flew up in the breeze' in *Barsaat* (*Rain*, directed by Raj Kapoor, 1949) to 'Even my shirt is sexy, even my trousers are sexy', as sung in *Khuddar* (*Self-respect*, directed by Iqbal Durrani, 1994).

This chapter has made some steps towards an analysis of two aspects of film style in the Hindi film. These are important within the films themselves as part of its overall style or look, but they reach out beyond the film to wider society. Changes in the films have been contextualized within a changing society, such as the rise of a consumerist society in recent years in a small, but disproportionately powerful, section of Indian society or to the transnational status of the

Hindi film. It has shown how settings and clothing may be linked to some of the major attractions of the Hindi film, particularly the songs, where the most exotic sets and locations are used and for which several costume changes are often required. It has also noticed that these areas of design are now being given greater importance by producers, who are well aware of their market and the viewing practices of their audiences.

While constant comparison to Hollywood becomes tedious, there is a striking difference between the use of settings and clothing in Hindi films and that in Hollywood. This is again to do with the issue of realism. The settings shown in Hindi films are not necessarily presented in a realistic way, in particular in the songs, when there may be cuts to locations thousands of miles away. Many of the sets in Hindi films are not realistic either, in that they do not exist in India, nor probably anywhere else. The audience is not so naïve that it fails to notice these facts (although the stars may be so remote that some people may imagine they do have houses like those of the characters they are playing). The films' appearance arises from the function of melodrama, which makes settings show inner feelings and emotions and which places characters socially and hierarchically. The clothing shown in Hindi films may be worn by a very small minority of people, and even then perhaps it is not quite as revealing as it appears on screen, but this is to present an extreme form of modernity, glamour and fashion. The public might not copy the outfits directly, but they may take elements to incorporate into their own dress designs made for them by their local tailor.

3 The Art of Advertising

'The marvel of the century / the wonder of the world / Living Photographic Pictures / In Life sized Reproductions ...' – so proclaimed the first advertisement for the first film to be shown in India. It was presented in the form of a simple typeset message in a box and printed in the *Times of India* on 7 July 1896. The arrival of the Lumière brothers' *cinématographie* marked a period of technological advancement and rapid development that saw India become an independent nation state, together with its industrialization and urbanization. Film and film advertising were a product of this dynamic environment and as such were regarded as indicators of modernity. The subsequent technological, economic, social and political developments that defined the progress of modernity were reflected in the changing face of advertising. Each distinct phase in development marked a distinct aesthetic change in advertising. Thus, in addition to promoting film, advertising employed the aesthetic vocabulary of the period to reflect the ideas, beliefs, attitudes and values of their cultural environment. Film advertising reflected the *Zeitgeist*.

From Text to Image

The practice of placing advertisements in newspapers for the promotion of products and services had been in force since the first printed newspapers appeared in India in the eighteenth century. Modelled on examples from England, advertisements would be categorized under headings and printed on the back pages.[1] The Lumières' notice was placed under the 'new advertisements' section next to those publicizing shippers and cargo carriers. The *Times of India*, however, only advertised foreign films and therefore publicity for early Indian films was confined to a few important dailies.[2] The release of one of the first Indian feature films, *Raja Harishchandra* (directed by D. G. Phalke, 1913), was advertised in the *Bombay Chronicle* as 'a powerfully instructive subject from the Indian mythology. First film of Indian manufacture. Specially prepared at enormous cost. Original scenes from the city of Benares. Sure to appeal to our Hindu patrons.'[3] When the film was taken to a provincial town it failed to raise much interest. Phalke then readvertised it with greater success as 'a performance with 57,000 photographs, a picture two miles long!'[4] The emphasis on length appealed to an audience used to seeing stage plays that lasted over six hours. Furthermore, Phalke's reference to photography echoed Louis Lumière's slogan of 'Living photographic pictures ...'. These statements not only captured the essential nature of the product – the natural extension of photography into film – but also transferred the values associated with one to the other. Thus, as photography was valued for its ability to capture reality with a truthfulness and objectivity previously unobtainable, film was valued for its ability to bring those 'real' but static images to life.

Newspaper advertisements were supported by other forms of street publicity. The imminent arrival of a film would be heralded with great fanfare. Decorated bullock carts were paraded around villages and towns, accompanied by musicians blowing horns and banging drums (see illus. 79). D. G. Pradhan, publicity designer for Wadia Movietone, recalls that when he entered the film industry in the late 1920s, working for Maneka Pictures, he was taught how to make plaster-cast models of the stars and to paint banners, cut-outs and posters, which were then used to decorate these bullock carts.[5] Following the example of early theatre publicity, handbills, single sheets of paper outlining the details of the film, were distributed from the carts. As with early newspaper advertisements, handbills were initially entirely text-based (illus. 41). As printing technology advanced there was a gradual progression from simple printing to the use of ornate, decorative fonts and the inclusion of line drawings and woodcut images.[6]

In the 1920s a new form of advertising emerged in the shape of film booklets. These appear to be unique to Indian cinema and contained images and a synopsis of the film. One of the earliest surviving examples is for the silent film *Prem Sanyas* (*Light of Asia*, directed by Franz Osten and Himansu Rai, 1926), the first jointly produced Indo-German film which told the story of the life of Gautama and the founding of Buddhism. Two different booklets were produced to accompany the German and Indian releases of the film. The lavishly produced Indian version was printed after a special showing of the film at Windsor Castle and contained glowing reviews taken from all the major newspapers of India. A substantial section of the booklet was filled with a detailed account of the narrative and it was generously illustrated with black-and-white stills from the film. The production of the souvenir booklet suggests that it was made for distributors and exhibitors (theatre owners) to encourage them to show the film, rather than for the audience. With the arrival of sound in the 1930s music and song quickly became a key component of Indian film. The booklets incorporated song lyrics written in both Hindi and Urdu. They were produced and distributed prior to the release of the film as forms of pre-publicity,

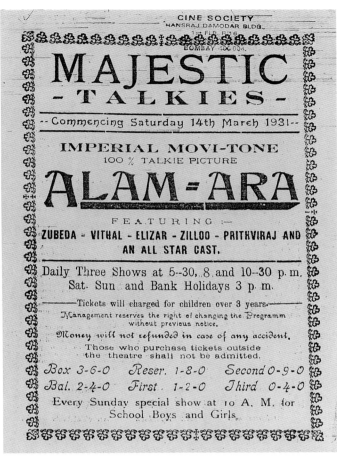

41 Alam Ara, 1931, printed handbill. Cine Society, Bombay.

and small-town exhibitors often reproduced the song lyrics for their audiences. Some booklets were sold directly to the public and had the price of four annas printed on them. Fondly remembered as 'song booklets', they were considered to be an important part of the cinema-going experience, as they brought the music to the audience at a time when sound recordings were not available.[7]

The importance of the booklets, however, lies not only in the text but in their pictorial content. The images used on the covers and inside offered distributors, exhibitors and the public an immediate indication of the film's theme, style and visual appeal. Thus, for *Light of Asia*, the covers for the German and English versions differ, as they catered for different audiences. The Indian version (illus. 42) conveys the theme of

42 *Light of Asia*, 1926, booklet cover, Indian version.

the film through its simplicity of design. Orange in colour, it has an outline of the map of Asia with rays of light emanating from a point marking Kapilavastu, the birthplace of the Buddha. At the centre of this is an image of a seated Buddha. In contrast, the German cover (illus. 49) was rendered in a more modern European style. Stylized rays of light derived from the Art Deco movement (see below) are combined with bold coloured designs taken from Indian sculptural forms and set against a vivid red background. Together, they conveyed the exotic nature of the film to a German audience, who may have been unfamiliar with the story and image of the Buddha. Images on booklets were supported by those on posters and hoardings.

Film from its inception was seen by film makers as a medium for creating a 'work of art', thus appropriating the status usually associated with the fine arts. This status was never fully extended to the images created for advertising, even though the artists responsible for them have adhered to styles and techniques appropriated and derived from the fine arts. These artists introduced a dynamic new visual force to India's already rich culture. They ushered in a new age dominated by the cinematic image that extended beyond the movie theatres and into the wider landscape. The starting point for this new ocular era was the imagery created by Phalke in his films produced between 1913 and

1937, projecting a strong visual aesthetic that was to have a lasting influence on Indian cinema and was itself subject to many influences, the most significant of which was the painter Ravi Varma.

The 'Ravi Varma Aesthetic'

Ravi Varma is credited with creating a dynamic new aesthetic style that had a huge impact on Indian visual culture and contributed to the birth of the nationalist movement. He was the first Indian artist to appropriate successfully the materials and techniques of Western academic art and apply them to Indian subject matter. This fusion meant that his paintings were regarded as important signifiers of both modernity and nationality.[8] Varma illustrated episodes from the Hindu mythological epics and, through the use of the Western techniques of chiaroscuro and perspective, he rendered them with a realism that effectively brought them to life. Influenced by the traditional art of Tanjore, as well as the majestic settings and romantic themes of nineteenth-century European neo-classical history paintings, his work was similarly characterized by grand locations and properly proportioned figures, draped in robes with animated gestures and emotional expressions.

Realism as a pictorial convention was imported into a country that had no similar aesthetic tradition. Consequently the phenomenal success of Varma's paintings resulted from his presentation of a familiar subject matter, the Hindu gods, in a manner that had never been seen before, simultaneously highlighting their physicality and glorifying their divinity. This reconstruction and glorification of the past captured the imagination of the educated élite, and his paintings were seen to project a new art with a particularly 'Indian' sensibility, and as such appealed to nationalist aspirations.[9] To meet the public demand for his paintings Varma set up a printing press outside Bombay in 1892 to enable him to reproduce his paintings as oleographs. These mythological prints were hugely successful and went into mass circulation alongside similar prints produced by other presses, such as the Poona Chitrasala Press[10] and the Calcutta Art Studio.[11] With the proliferation of these prints it was appropriate that early mythological films adopt the same styles for their posters. This was particularly evident in the poster for *Sati Savitri* (directed by Baburao Painter, 1927; illus. 50). The style was more rigid and clumsy than Varma's fluid forms but was typical of the majority of cheaply produced prints in circulation at that time. The artistic and patriotic sentiments projected by Varma in his prints were also echoed by Phalke. He too wished to bring the gods to life, and his mythological films borrowed much from the aesthetic style that Varma and the other print studios had defined. Phalke acquired an intimate knowledge of these paintings while working at Varma's printing press in 1905, and his proficiency with printing technology led him to establish his own highly successful art printing and engraving press before becoming a film maker.[12]

In 1932 Phalke released *Setu-Bandhan* (*Bridging the Ocean*) and evidence of Varma's influence can be seen in the accompanying film booklet (illus. 43). It was lavishly produced to stress the importance of the film, and included thirteen pages with photographic stills of the courtly scenes and dramatic episodes. The neo-classical sets, actors' costumes and make-up were typical of Varma's stylistic impact. In addition, there was a long passage explaining the section of the *Ramayana* on which the film was based, together with an even longer description of the making, cost and significance of the film. Phalke's primary concern, however, and one that he repeated continuously, was that the film be viewed as a work of art:

The author has every hope of being rewarded with the deserving appreciation of his humble adventurer in the domain of art where after a ceaseless service and faithful devotion at the feet of the goddess of Art over a quarter of a century he still remains an obsessive devotee and a helpless explorer.[13]

This sentiment was reflected on the front cover of the booklet, where Varma's aesthetic style is most apparent. Like his mythological paintings, this illustration captures and dramatizes a moment of history. The god Rama is depicted standing on the top of a cliff with the sea below, waves crashing against the rocks, and the great expanse of the sky before him. Rama is posed with his bow and arrow ready to fire, thus suggesting the next thrilling point of action, and his distant figure against the soaring cliff serves to emphasize the grand scale of the task ahead. The image is very similar to one of Varma's oil paintings entitled *Rama Humbling the Seas*.[14] Before Varma's application of Western techniques to the representations of Indian gods, Rama had been depicted in the flat two-dimensional format of the traditional Rajasthan or Pahari miniature paintings. Here Rama is shown as a young man and his body is given a sense of reality, thereby bringing him from the past into the present.[15]

It was through the depiction of the female form, however, that Varma made his greatest impact on film and specifically poster design. His paintings are characterized by voluptuous long-haired women draped in saris, posed against stone columns, surrounded by neo-classical architecture or luscious green scenery (illus. 44). The realist mode of representation enabled him to give a greater fullness and sensuality to their bodies. In 1892 he exhibited a series of paintings of women from across India. Representing regional types, they were depicted in their local costume surrounded by objects associated with the more affluent sections of their communities. Like Varma's mythological paintings, these also conformed to orientalist and nationalist ideology, whereby the status of a woman was considered to be a signifier of the nature and condition of society and thus central to the construction of a national identity.[16] Though Varma's paintings depict regional types,

THE HINDUSTAN FILM Co.

PRESENTS

SETU-BANDHAN

A BEAUTIFUL EPISODE FROM RAMAYAN

(100 % TALKIE)

WRITTEN, DIRECTED AND PRODUCED

BY

Mr. D. G. PHALKE

43 *Setu-Bandhan*, 1932, booklet cover.

44 Ravi Varma, *Portrait of a Woman*, c.1895, oil on canvas. Victoria & Albert Museum, London.

the aesthetic style in which they are represented serves paradoxically to negate regional variations as identified by dress and environment, and instead creates a homogenized all-India figure of a woman. Thus, the overriding image that persists is of a full-figured woman adorned in Indian attire with a rounded pale face and a graceful and dignified stature, and this came to represent the ideal figure of Indian woman-hood.[17] It was this image, disseminated to the wider public through oleographs, that was later translated into film imagery, film posters, popular prints and other forms of advertising and packaging.

Two examples of work influenced by Varma can be seen in the poster for the film *Diler Jigar* (*Gallant Heart*, directed by S. S. Agarwal, 1931; illus. 45) and the booklet for *Devi Devyani* (directed by Chandulal Shah, 1931; illus. 46). Although rendered in different media, Varma's realist aesthetic was replicated in an almost formulaic way. Thus, both images depict women reclining on a chaise-longue, draped in ornate saris and adorned with strings of pearls and gold bracelets. Both women are in similar environments that place them in a wealthy social class, and are surrounded by almost identical objects, such as an ornate pedestal with a vase containing flowers. The poster for *Diler Jigar* was painted on canvas with oil paints and signed by G. B. Walh. Its large scale (145 x 94 cm) suggests that it was probably

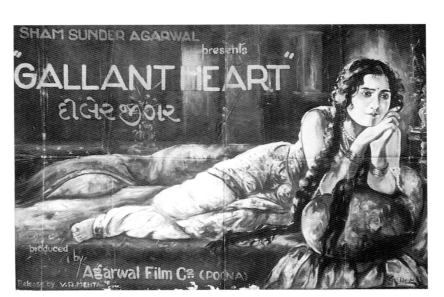

45 G. B. Walh, *Gallant Heart*, 1931, poster.

46 *Devi Devyani*,
1931, booklet
cover.

made to hang over the cinema entrance. The booklet cover for *Devi Devyani* uses a reproduction of a black-and-white photograph, beautifully hand-tinted in subtle colours, with the details of the costume finely picked out with gold embellishment.

The transference of Varma's imagery to film was the beginning of a constant exchange between mythological prints and film images. The production and popularity of mythological prints increased over the years, and today these are known as popular prints, bazaar prints or calendar art. A characteristic of these images (which Varma initiated) is the 'elision of the sacred and secular', whereby 'goddesses were seen as luscious women, and luscious women as goddesses'.[18] The work of the artist S. M. Pandit is a prime example. During the 1940s and '50s his studio was responsible for the design of many film booklets, posters and other forms of film ephemera, such as matchboxes and incense-stick packets. The many films he produced artwork for included *Dr Kotnis ki Amar Kahani* (*The Immortal Story of Dr Kotnis*, directed by V. Shantaram, 1946; illus. 77), *Andaz* (*A Matter of Style*, directed by Mehboob Khan, 1949) and *Barsaat* (*Rain*, directed by Raj Kapoor, 1949). As can be seen in his depictions of *Draupadi* (directed by Baburao Patel, 1940; illus. 53) and of the actress Nargis on the booklet cover for *Barsaat* (illus. 54), his work was characterized by a delicacy and refinement that transferred a sense of unearthly divinity to film stars and an earthly physicality to mythological subjects. Pandit went on to become a painter of mythological subjects producing popular prints that emphasized (even more so than Varma's depictions) the physicality of the female form.

The Bombay School of Art

The poster for *Kalyan Khajina* (*The Treasures of Kalyan*, 1924; illus. 47) was illustrated in a style that differs greatly from the Ravi Varma aesthetic. The film tells of the adventurous exploits of the Maratha emperor Shivaji, the most dramatic moment being when, on inspecting some crates full of treasure, he is confronted not by a box full of coins but by a woman.[19] The film was awarded a medal at the British Empire Exhibition in Wembley, London.[20] The poster, possibly the earliest known to survive today, depicts Shivaji bowing before a woman. The two figures are dressed in Mughal period costume and rendered in a realist manner. Unlike Varma's imagery, however, there is no sense of sensuality or voluptuousness in the depiction of the woman, and the overall feel is a little stiffer and more delicate and restrained.

The poster was designed by the director of the film, Baburao

47 Baburao Painter,
Kalyan Khajina, 1924,
poster.

Krishnarao Mistry, who, as a self-taught painter and sculptor, appropriated the name Baburao Painter.[21] Although he was not formally
trained, stylistically his work aimed to imitate that of the Sir Jamsetji
Jeejibhoy School of Art (Bombay School of Art), one of four schools set
up by the British government during the 1850s in Calcutta, Madras,
Bombay and Lahore with the intention of disseminating a uniform art
education policy across India. Students of the fine arts were instructed
in European academic art and taught to draw and paint from life studies, the desired goal being the growth and perpetuation of a class of
Indians with a taste for Western art. During the early part of the twentieth century the economic and political movement of Swadeshi,
which aimed to replace European goods with Indian products, had
been gaining momentum. The schools in Calcutta and Bombay
became involved in this discourse, and within the ideological frame-
work of cultural nationalism they sought to identify an 'authentic'
Indian art, one that would project a national identity for India. While
Varma's work was once regarded as patriotic, under the Swadeshi

ideology of art it was rejected. His paintings were deemed to be crude and vulgar and academic realism was seen as Western and foreign and therefore incompatible with Indian subject matter.[22]

While the Calcutta school received greater attention through its development of the Neo-Bengal style, the Bombay school offered a strong alternative. Although their aesthetic styles were vastly different, both advocated policies of 'Indianization' and looked to the art of India's past for inspiration. They turned to the wall paintings of the Ajanta caves, which were painted between about 200 BC and AD 600 and were considered to be the pinnacle of India's artistic heritage. In the 1870s the students of the Bombay school under John Griffiths, their teacher for decorative painting, made an extensive survey of the mural paintings, producing copies and studying them for their realist rendering of the human form and their subtle use of light and shade. Under the leadership of Gladstone Solomon in the 1920s, the school established a course for the revival of mural painting, believing that 'the true work of the modern Indian artist was to revive the ancient and national methods of artistic expression and to revitalize and restore them'.[23] Any revival of past styles had also to be underpinned by a close study of nature and of the human figure, hence emphasis was placed on accurate representation through the ideals of Western realism and projected through a variety of styles, all of which were deemed as being equally Indian. This course became the school's strongest claim to the creation of a national art.

It was this sympathetic combination of realism and reference to the past that was used to illustrate the poster for *Kalyan Khajina*, the tasteful style gaining the admiration of Gladstone Solomon.[24] The delicate realism used in the depiction of the human face and form was characteristic of the school, and two notable artists working with this style were Bide Viswanathan and L. L. Meghanee. A particularly fine example of Viswanathan's work can be seen in the booklet for *Atmatarang* (directed by Sohrab Modi, 1937; illus. 48), while Meghanee was responsible for *Kangan* (directed by Franz Osten, 1939) and *Azad* (directed by N. R. Acharya, 1940), among others. The art-school style was appropriated by film directors and by studios that had a particular sensibility and knowledge of the fine arts and wished to use it to highlight the alternative or special nature of their films. Thus, Baburao Painter's appreciation of it was not only evident in the poster for *Kalyan Khajina* but was more accurately rendered on the booklet cover for his film *Pratibha* (1937; illus. 51). Here the graceful depiction of a woman holding a *lota* (water pot) was typical of the figure studies executed at life-drawing classes in the art schools, where emphasis was placed on the realism of the female form. Similar aesthetic sensibilities were reflected in the advertising for the films *Amar Jyoti* (*The Eternal Flame*, 1936) and *Duniya na Mane* (*The Unexpected*, 1937), both of which were directed by V. Shantaram. His studio, Prabhat, became known for its sympathetic approach to difficult subject matter, and his art department, headed by Sheikh Fattelal, who was responsible for creating spectacular stage sets, was considered to be the best in the country.

Despite the general tendency for many studios to produce cheap posters with little regard for aesthetic quality, the influence of the Bombay School of Art on film advertising was evident in the ensuing years. It is likely that many of the school's students would have become involved with the booming film industry at some point in their careers. Furthermore, untrained artists working within the industry were highly aware of the status associated with those who had art school tuition, and would try and emulate it. D. G. Pradhan, publicity designer for Wadia Movietone, recalls how he entered the film industry

48 Bide Viswanathan, *Atmatarang*, 1937, booklet cover.

49 *Light of Asia*, 1926, booklet cover, German version.

50 *Sati Savitri*, 1927, poster.

51 *Pratibha*, 1937, booklet cover.

without any formal training and learnt on the job, as was typical of the way early studios functioned. He started off painting lettering for hoardings and posters and was then taught a variety of other skills. He was, however, always conscious of the training being given to art school students. Unable to afford the fees, he took evening classes from M. R. Acharekar, a student of the Bombay School of Art who went on to become deputy director of the school. The result of Pradhan's training can be seen on the booklet cover for *Krishnabhakta Bodana* (directed by J.B.H. Wadia, 1944; illus. 52), where he rendered the female figure with a delicacy typical of the art school students. Pradhan introduced Acharekar into the film industry, where he was able to supplement his income by designing posters for the Wadia studios. Acharekar went on to work for R.K. Studios in the 1950s and become a highly successful art director, producing spectacular sets for such films as *Awāra* (*The Vagabond*, directed by Raj Kapoor, 1951). He also continued to paint, and a solo exhibition of his works, including an oil painting of Nargis, was held at the Jehangir Art Gallery in Bombay in 1955.[25]

52 D. G. Pradhan, *Krishnabhakta Bodana*, booklet cover, 1944.

It was Pradhan's awareness of the distinct qualities of the art school style that led him to employ Acharekar specifically to do the artwork for *Raj Nartaki* (*Court Dancer*, directed by Modhu Bose, 1941). The poster[26] and booklet cover both used the key image of a court dancer combined with a montage of smaller illustrations. The poster was more elegantly rendered than the booklet, and both were signed by Acharekar and Mirajkar, one of his students. The booklet made for the Western market used only one single but strong image. The artists illustrated the influence of the Ajanta paintings through the elegant rendering of the dancer, in the delicacy of her fingers and their expressive dance gestures and in her detailed costume. The influence of classical painting and sculpture on Acharekar's work was seen in a book he published in 1949 entitled *Rupadarsini*. This provided a valuable guide to students and connoisseurs on how to approach the human form in Indian art (illus. 55). That this style was chosen to advertise *Raj Nartaki* was highly appropriate. Its references to classical Indian art and nationalist ideals paralleled the message that was being projected in the booklet made for Western audiences. The booklet publicized the

53 S. M. Pandit, *Draupadi*, 1940, booklet cover.

film as the first to be made in English, and proceeded to proclaim the glory of India: 'Our India – Ancient India, the fountain head of all civilisation and culture of the world is today an almost forgotten country. Few people outside this country know of its glorious tradition in art, culture and science ...'.[27] This was reinforced with extracts from the writings of Max Müller and others. Released in 1941, during World War II, these references to India's past clearly aimed to project a national identity for India.

This style appears to have been used for the promotional campaigns of only two of the many films that Wadia Movietone released, *Raj Nartaki* and *Asia Sitara* (*Star of Asia*, 1937; illus. 56), thus demonstrating how this and subsequent styles or movements in the fine arts were referred to whenever there was a need to communicate more than the basic information about a film. In these instances, the mode of representation was often used to reflect or reinforce underlying messages about current cultural and political issues.

Images of Modernity: The Art Deco Style

In the 1930s great changes began to take place in the film industry. The silent screen gave way to sound. *Alam Ara* (directed by Ardeshir Irani,

54 S. M. Pandit, *Barsaat*, 1949, booklet cover.

55 Advertisement for M. R. Acharekar's book *Rupadarsini*, 1949–50 from *MARG*, vol. III/ii.

56 M. R. Acharekar and Mirajkar, *Asia Sitara*, 1937, booklet cover.

1931) was the first Indian film with sound, and it fully utilized the new opportunities available to it through the incorporation of music, song and dance. This fuelled an expansion of the film industry, with greater numbers of skilled specialists in the form of sound engineers, camera operators and lighting technicians required to feed the demand for films. Increased mechanization within the industry was paralleled

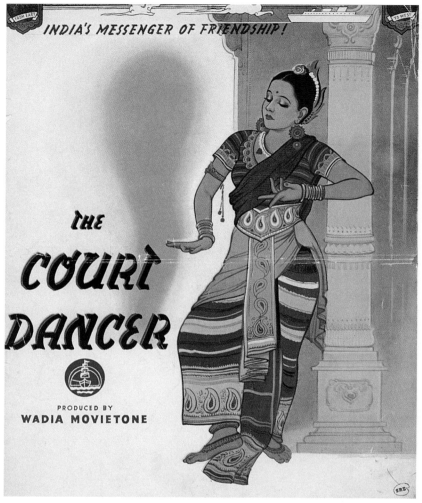

INDIA'S MESSENGER OF FRIENDSHIP!

THE
COURT
DANCER

PRODUCED BY
WADIA MOVIETONE

57 M. R. Acharekar and Mirajkar, *Raj Nartaki*, 1941, booklet cover.

by technological advances and industrial progression in other industries across India, and was an indicator of the rising tide of modernity. This was a period of economic growth and business opportunities for Indian capitalists, and many Indian manufacturers, textile mill owners in particular, had profited from the wartime interruption of imports.[28] The rise of these mills and factories and of the industrial working classes was represented in films like *Mazdoor* (*The Mill*, directed by M. Bhavani, 1934), and this expansion in Bombay's workforce provided a large proportion of the new cinema audience. Jithubhai Mehta, a

58 H. Parekh, *Madam Fashion*, 1936, booklet cover.

publicity agent at the time, recalls how he targeted this audience by
changing the distribution of handbills from the mornings to the after-
noons to catch the workers as they returned after their lunch. He also
tailored the bills to suit the location in which they were distributed.
Thus for Bhuleshwar, an area defined by its temple, a few lines from
the Puranas or mythological texts made the publicity more effective.

In the wealthy Napean Sea Road area he used illustrations of beautiful women.[29]

During this period a new aesthetic style began to emerge in film advertising. Art Deco established itself after the Exposition Internationale des Arts Décoratifs held in Paris in 1925 and became the primary aesthetic movement of the inter-war years. Having started in Europe it quickly spread across the globe. Art Deco came to be recognized as a universal symbol of modernity that encompassed the processes of mechanization and industrialization. The style was a decorative response to these changes and influenced everything from architecture, furniture, fashion and jewellery to packaging and the graphic arts. It was characterized by the simplification of forms and the use of straight lines, smooth curves, stylized representation, cubic patterning and repetitive motifs.[30]

The global spread of the style was facilitated through the tools of mass communication, such as film, graphic arts and advertising. In India cinema was the vehicle through which Art Deco established itself. Completed in 1933, the Regal in Bombay was the first theatre to be built exclusively for showing films. It was designed by the British-trained architect Charles F. Stevens and was equipped with a café, soda fountain and balcony. The interior was opulently decorated by the Czech artist Karl Schara. Two other Art Deco cinemas were built in Bombay in 1938, the Eros and the Metro, both of which were elegantly designed with lavishly decorated foyers.[31] The Regal and the Metro showed largely Hollywood films, thereby exposing Indian audiences to the values and aesthetics of the period. Booklet covers for *Madam Fashion* (directed by Jaddanbai, 1936; illus. 58), *Jung-e-Jawani* (*Modern Youth*, 1937; illus. 60) and *Fashionable India* (directed by Mohan Sinha, 1935; illus. 59), a big-budget musical spectacular about living in the modern age, reflected the ethos of the time and the lifestyle that the new urban élite of Bombay aspired to. They were a rising class in the 1930s and, like the factory workers, they formed another growing portion of the cinema-going audience. The sleek, athletic figure on the cover of *Modern Youth* was stylized like an Art Deco figure, and the accompanying illustration of a cinema served to highlight the fact that film, along with fashionable clothes and fast cars, was part of the glamorous and luxurious lifestyle that defined modernity. In India, as elsewhere, Art Deco was seen to be synonymous with these associations.

The appropriation of Art Deco by Indian artists was most evident in film graphics, where pictorial realism was replaced by stylized imagery and geometric symbolism. Here the influence of Cubism was apparent. Defined by Pablo Picasso and Georges Braque, Cubism depicted objects

59 'Fashionable India', 1935, booklet cover.

from multiple viewpoints rather than one, and so presented them as fractured and multi-planed objects. The Calcutta-based artist Gaganendranath Tagore experimented with Cubism as an alternative to the Neo-Bengal style, believing that for India to progress artistically it had to look beyond national boundaries and explore modern international art movements. It was this internationalism that was reflected in many film booklets of that period. They showed a move away from previous aesthetic styles towards forms of representation that were distinctly modern in feel. The cover for *Ayodhya ka Raaja* (*The King of Ayodhya*, directed by V. Shantaram, 1932) was depicted in a style similar to British travel posters of the period (illus. 61). Here the juxtaposi-

60 G. Sanjeev, *Modern Youth*, 1937, booklet cover.

tion of contrasting blocks of colour to form the shapes and shadows of the boat, along with the smooth curved edges and stylized waves and clouds, give an elegant feel to the image. The bold, uppercase typeface used for the title completed the modern look. That same year *Maya Machhindra* (*Illusion*, directed by V. Shantaram, 1932) was released. Two posters were produced, one in Hindi (illus. 62), which has

61 *The King of Ayodhya*, 1932, booklet cover.

62 *Maya Machhindra*, 1932, poster. National Film Archive of India, Pune.

'Varmaesque' depictions of the actors' portraits, and the other in English. The latter version (illus. 63) has a single stylized portrait set against large stripes of colour. The design has all the sharp, clear boldness of an Art Deco image. Both films were made by Prabhat Studios and, as with its use of the Bombay School of Art style (as well as its logo, which was in an Art Nouveau style), these posters provided more evidence of the studio's aesthetic sensibilities, and its realization that the style of a poster was able to convey messages about the film as well as the *Zeitgeist*.

Art Deco was used as a means of communicating the idea of progress, and it is effectively employed in the booklet cover for the film *Dr Madhurika* (directed by Sarvottam Badami, 1935). The actress Sabita Devi plays a 'modern' wife who neglects her home and husband for her career. On the cover (illus. 64) she is shown looking into a microscope set against a background of laboratory equipment. The rendering of the laboratory through the use of repeated geometric shapes and the smooth and rounded forms of the conical flasks and test tubes reflects the theme of modernity. The style also spread across India, as illustrated by the booklet cover for the Calcutta-based film *The President* (directed by Nitin Bose, 1937). The film tells the story of the expansion of the cotton mills, and the arrival of the industrial age is dramatically depicted in the repeated grey and black geometric forms of the buildings, smoking chimneys and machine cogs (illus. 65). The invasion of the machine was further emphasized by the absence of human forms in the design. However, so as not to alienate the cinema audience, another booklet for the same film reflected the more human side of the story by using an image of the star actress on the cover.[32]

The progress of modernity also focused attention on other social issues. This was a period when the nationalist movement was gathering momentum and Mahatma Gandhi was leading his non-violent demonstrations against the British. Among the issues that Gandhi spoke out against was the plight of 'the untouchables', a theme addressed by the film *Achhut Kanya* (*Untouchable Girl*, directed by Franz Osten, 1936), which deals with the love affair between two people from different castes, an untouchable girl and a Brahmin boy. Once again Art Deco was used to communicate the idea of modernity. The booklet cover (illus. 69) illustrates the main characters in a realist manner but the typography was in an Art Deco style, which aptly conveys the fact that this film was addressing a traditional social issue within today's modern environment. The choice of typeface was particularly relevant, as it is almost identical to a font designed by the graphic artist Cassandre (Adolphe Mouron) in 1929. The font, named Bifur, used thin lines juxtaposed with dark blocks to suggest a sense of modernity and grandeur.[33] This was characteristic of the work of Cassandre, whose powerful images were meant to symbolize the union between art and industry and which defined the French Art Deco graphic style.[34] During this period typography became an integral part of the booklet cover design, and there was an inventiveness and experimentation about them unsurpassed in any subsequent period.

Handbills too were no longer simple text-based leaflets; they had achieved a level of sophistication whereby a greater degree of imagination was used in their production. A handbill for *Daku ki Ladki* (directed by Moti B. Gidwani, 1933) was particularly striking, a single folded sheet offering a montage of images in full colour. The text was minimal and gave the title, film company and star names, and concisely stated that this was 'A gripping story with emotions, thrills and suspense'. Similarly the handbill for *Jailor* (directed by Sohrab Modi, 1938) cleverly integrates the concept of a jailor into the typographic

63 *Illusion* (*Maya Machhindra*), 1932, poster.

design by using the links of a chain to form the title (illus. 66), and this extends to the inside of the handbill, where the enlarged links of the chain are cleverly used to display a selection of images from the film.

Many of the booklets and posters of the time were unsigned. However, a group of them can be attributed to the artist J. Mistry, who not only signed his name but also began to develop a logo for himself, the changing form of which can be seen on the covers of *Mahageet* (*Eternal Music*, directed by Hiren Bose, 1937; illus. 67) and *Ver Ni Vasulat* (*Vengeance is Mine*, 1935; illus. 68). These are just two of the covers showing how Mistry incorporated aspects from the stylistic movements of the time, such as the Art Deco details in *Mahageet*, as

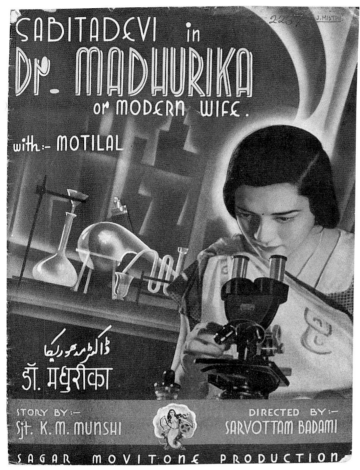

SABITADEVI in
Dr. MADHURIKA
or MODERN WIFE.
with:- MOTILAL

STORY BY:—
Sjt. K. M. MUNSHI

DIRECTED BY:—
SARVOTTAM BADAMI

SAGAR MOVITONE PRODUCTION

64 J. Mistry, *Dr Madhurika*, 1935, booklet cover.

well as imagery from Hollywood, for example in *Vengeance is Mine*, where he placed a profile of Sabita Devi's face horizontally across the bottom edge of the booklet against a stark black background, thus creating a very strong dramatic effect (the artist designed a series of booklets for films featuring this actress). Again, the choice of typography was integral to the design. Today this could be mistaken for a 1930s Hollywood image: the artist was obviously influenced by American films and advertising, which had been prevalent in India since the mid-1920s.[35] Hollywood actresses were also featured in advertisements for such products as the Lux 'Beauty Soap of the Stars' campaign. In 1941 Lux 'Indianized' its advertising by signing the

65 *The President*, 1937,
booklet cover.

66 *Jailor*, 1938, handbill.

67 J. Mistry, *Eternal Music*, 1937, booklet cover.

actress Leela Chitnis as its first Indian model.[36] This type of promotion was highly sought after, as there were very few other means of exposure for actresses at the time. *Mauj Majah* and *Kiren* were the first Indian-language film journals, in circulation from 1924 and 1932 respectively, and both printed Indian and foreign film advertisements.

The use of Art Deco in India did not survive beyond the end of the 1940s, perhaps because it was viewed as another foreign style. In Europe it had been used as a symbol of Western modernity and helped in the articulation of autonomous national identities.[37] In India the nationalist movement wanted modernity but wanted it on Indian terms, and Art Deco was seen as a form of Western cultural imperialism.[38] Paradoxically the style was evident in other forms of advertising during the late 1940s and the 1950s, where it was used to convey a nationalist message. Two notable examples were the magazine advertisements for Tata Industries (illus. 70) and Raymond Woollen Mills (illus. 71). Tata used an iconic image of a stylized muscular man with angular features in a series of pictures that depicted him as a monumental figure providing power and running numerous industries. Similarly, Raymond Mills used multiple images of spinning wheels to advertise its factories. These advertisements transferred all the aspirations to modernity and

68 J. Mistry, *Vengeance is Mine*, 1935, booklet cover.

69 *Achhut Kanya*, 1936, booklet cover.

70 Magazine advertisement for Tata Industries, 1953–4.
MARG, vol.vii/iii.

industrialization that were inherent to the Art Deco style of the 1930s
to the newly independent nation state of India.[39]

Towards Independence: Images of Nationalism

Ever since the arrival of cinema India had been searching for an identity that would define the 'Indian' nation, and each ensuing decade had
seen this search become more acute. In the 1930s the progress of
modernity had been accompanied by a fear of the erosion of tradition
against the onslaught of Westernization. In the 1940s, with World War

The ceaseless click-clack of looms! Patterns unfold themselves, resolve into crisp designs of chequered loveliness, and the fabric is there, soft and warm and elegant for YOU. An exclusive Indian product JAYKAY fabrics compare favourably with the best that the world can produce. For strength, beauty, compactness of weave, and dependability JAYKAY fabrics are unexcelled.

71 Magazine advertisement for Raymond Mills, 1949-50, *MARG*, vol. 111/i.

II raging, it was the call for independence that grew ever stronger. Many of the films of the period addressed this dilemma through a wide range of subject matter, from stories of war heroes to grand historical spectaculars, from romances to the realities of Indian life. Linked through their patriotic themes the films were emotionally charged to arouse feelings of anger, compassion, nostalgia, admiration and pride. One of the primary graphic means of evoking these emotions and conveying the nationalist theme was through the depiction of the map of India, as seen on the booklet covers for *India Today* (1933; illus. 73), *Janma Bhoomi* (1936) and *Mother India* (directed by Gunjal, 1938; illus. 72). With the rise of the Independence movement, popular prints in particular were quick to use the map as a symbol with which to stir patriotic fervour. In these images the map was merged with images of freedom fighters, nationalist leaders and Hindu gods and goddesses, thereby creating visual metaphors that personified India and presented each of these individuals as a symbol of the nation.[40]

One of the most important films of this period was *Dharti ke lal* (*Children of the Earth*, directed by K. A. Abbas, 1946). It told the story of the Bengal famine of 1943 in which millions died as a result of the diversion of food supplies away from the people of Bengal to British

72 *Mother India*, 1938, booklet cover.

and American forces on the Burmese front. Made in Calcutta as a contribution to the war effort, the film aimed to inform the entire nation of this tragedy and was part of a 'growing "nation-building" ideology'.[41] Unusually, it was advertised in the Bombay-based art journal *Marg*, which was founded that same year by Mulk Raj Anand. That the advertisement was placed here served to present the film as a work of art and to highlight its alternative nature (it was the first to be made in the 'realist' mode), thus placing it above the average commercial film being produced at the time. The black-and-white image (illus. 74) was a clever reduction of the key elements of the film into a stark and striking design, which aptly conveyed the dramatic and serious nature of the film. The roughly drawn line of human silhouettes represented a key point in the film when hundreds of starving villagers marched to the city in search of food. This was juxtaposed with the delicate art

73 *India Today*, 1933, booklet cover.

74 Magazine advertisement for *Dharti ke Lal*, 1946, *MARG*, vol. 1/i.

school style representation of a female portrait. Echoed in this advertisement was the work of two artists: Somnath Hore's sketched skele-
tal figures[42] and Chitraprasad's dramatic black on white woodcuts.[43]
Both artists had been witnesses to, and affected by, the famine and
both chose to depict its harsh realities, creating images that today
stand as important documents of the time.

A series of patriotic films was released during this period, including
Shaheed (*Martyr*, directed by Ramesh Saigal, 1948), *Shabnam* (directed
by B. Mitra, 1949), *Samadhi* (*Monument of Remembrance*, directed by
Ramesh Saigal, 1950), *Azad* (*Freedom*, directed by S.M.S. Naidu, 1955)

and *Dr Kotnis ki Amar Kahani* (directed by V. Shantaram, 1946). Their posters reflected nationalist ideals in varying degrees. Most were quickly produced with little thought to design, as the title was the primary means of conveying the film theme. In *Shaheed* (illus. 75) the wearing of the Gandhi cap was an additional indicator. Portraits were the main components of these posters and most were barely recognizable. In contrast, the poster for *Samadhi* (illus. 76) consists of an amalgamation of images ranging from a female figure holding a gun to the depiction of the nationalist hero Subhash Chandra Bose. The design relies on the cumulative effect of multiple images to convey the film's theme, though like *Shaheed* the actual images were clumsily rendered.

The most effective advertising was for *Dr Kotnis ki Amar Kahani*. A synopsis of the film was given in the inside cover of the booklet, but it was preceded by a statement that proclaimed its overtly nationalist status: 'In this picture we have purposely avoided the use of "popular wrong" nomenclature Indian and India and have used instead the "nationally correct" words Hindostani and Hindostan'. Dr Kotnis was part of a medical team sent to fight alongside the Chinese during the Japanese invasion. The synopsis itself left no doubt about the moral message: 'This story is stronger than fiction of a gallant young patriot. Dr Kotnis was the youngest and luckiest of all as he was the one who never came back home. He died serving the sick and the wounded on the battlefield in China. Young Kotnis lived for the cause of world freedom and loved his life at the altar of liberty'. His heroism was captured on the booklet cover (illus. 77), which shows him carrying a body out of the debris of a collapsed building. The figure of a Buddha standing serenely in the background over Dr Kotnis and his Chinese wife not only conveys the idea of peace over war but was used as an image of unification symbolizing the 'solidarity of their nationalist struggles'.[44]

Towards Independence: Images of India's Past

The search for a national identity extended to other genres, such as the historical, which focused on significant events and figures from the past and were a combination of fact, myth, legend, and folklore.[45] As a reflection of the way India envisioned itself, films constructed a self-image for the nation by borrowing from different indigenous sources, and often this was based on a glorification of the past. Consequently, historical films functioned as tools for reinforcing patriotic sentiment. *Humayun* (directed by Mehboob Khan, 1945) was one of the most important of this genre and was set in the court of this sixteenth-century Mughal emperor. It was made at a time of political crisis when negotiations between the Hindu Congress party and the Muslim

75 *Shaheed*, 1948, poster.

76 *Samadhi*, 1950, poster.

डॉ.कोटनीस की
प्रमर कहानी

Rajkamal Kala Mandir Picture
Dr KOTNIS KI
AMAR KAHANI

77 S. M. Pandit, *Dr Kotnis ki Amar Kahani*, 1946, booklet cover.

league over the governing of India were at deadlock. In a country with a Hindu majority, film makers were reluctant to handle Hindu–Muslim subjects for fear of censorship.[46] However, projecting contemporary problems into the past through historical films was one way of addressing those issues. The Mughal period lent itself to the exploration and portrayal of Muslim sensibilities, and its representation as the golden age of racial and religious harmony projected a national synthesis that was a key aspiration of nationalist ideology.

The advertising for historical films projected this nationalist ideology through images that reflected the glory of India's past. These films relied on the aesthetic reproduction of sets and costumes for their impact. Visually spectacular scenes were created through the use of grand architecture, opulent settings, sumptuous costumes, ornate jewellery and a cast of hundreds, all of which evoked the 'essence' of the Mughal period. Thus the booklet cover for *Humayun* (illus. 78) aimed to reflect that vision and achieves it by using as one its design features a portrait of the emperor adorned with a jewelled turban. The film's historical period was also projected through the incorporation of domed buildings in the background and enhanced by the style in which the image was rendered. The use of profiled portraits echoed the Mughal school of painting, a device also used for the poster of *Shah Jehan* (1946),[47] and the diagonal layering of the portraits was a convenient way of accentuating the stars. A poster produced for the re-release of the film in the 1980s used the same image but with the incorporation of a further 'essence' or signifier of the Mughal age, the addition of fighting figures on horseback in the foreground, which conveys the idea of a grand epic with battle scenes involving hundreds of extras.

Unlike *Humayun*, the film *Chandralekha* (directed by S. S. Vasan, 1948) was not a story based on historical fact but it was a period film employing the same theatrical characteristics of magnificent stage sets and costumes. Produced after the war in both Tamil and Hindi, the film was meant to provide entertainment for the masses or, as the director said, 'pageantry for our peasants'.[48] It featured a spectacular drum dance (see illus. 19) and the longest sword fight in Indian cinematic history, projecting a magnificent Indian past through sets that recreated a 'Hollywood-style orientalism ... which became a landmark in the codification of an Indian mass entertainment ideology after Independence.'[49] This was the first film by a Tamil studio that attempted an all-India distribution, and no expense was spared for the publicity campaign. A. K. Shekhar designed both the sets and the campaign, which included posters, booklets and full-page newspaper advertisements.[50] Following the example of Hollywood, Gemini Studios also produced a publicity brochure for distribution to exhibitors and the press. In America, showbooks or pressbooks had become a well-established means of publicizing a film by the 1930s, with studios employing special editorial staff and artists for this purpose. These contained advice for theatre owners, movie reviews, ready-made newspaper advertisements, feature articles, details on how to stage publicity stunts and images of the range of posters available. Some pressbooks also offered star portraits that could be cut out for use by the theatres.[51] The production of these pressbooks does not seem to have caught on in the same way in India and the *Chandralekha* brochure appears to be the first of its kind.[52] It contained a synopsis of the film along with a step by step pictorial account of the key points of the narrative. It reproduced glowing reviews from the film premières held in various Indian states and provided pre-prepared text for use by local theatres. The booklet also had 'layouts for women's pages' with a pictorial account of suggested marketing activities such as 'How to drape an Indian sari: Theatre demonstrations have a big draw ', along with information on the film costumes, which were 'hand-woven garments of silk and gold', and one particular gold embroidered riding jacket, which 'cost a fortune and is perhaps the most expensive single piece of outfitting ever used in a motion-picture'. Despite the obvious benefit of pressbooks, the expense involved in their production meant that Indian film publicity continued its less systemized approach whereby local theatres across India were free to produce their own forms of publicity, including their own poster designs.[53]

The visual imagery of the sets and the advertising aimed to deflect attention away from the realities of the aftermath of war and the partition of India, and to present this as a form of escapist entertainment. Accordingly, photographs included in the pressbook not only capture the huge crowds gathered outside the theatres but also show the impressively decorated South Indian cinemas with their large hoardings and figurative cut-outs (illus. 79). The climactic scene from the film provides the main graphic motif used throughout the book: female dancers on drums. Small line drawings illustrate the use of poster-adorned carts and musicians for street advertising, and these also suggest that the original posters for the film used the drum dance motif along with an image taken from the cover of the film booklet (not the pressbook). It is surprising that this image was used on either the booklet or the poster, as its subtle depiction of a woman leaning against a tree failed to convey the excitement of the film (illus. 80). There were, however, two further posters of differing sizes produced either for the Hindi version of the film or for a later re-release. In this instance both aimed to reflect the film's spectacular nature. Thus, the designs are structured around powerful images that symbolize the film's defining moments. In one the sword fight is represented by two men in the classic duel position with swords crossed, and the dance by a dramatic and expressive dance pose (illus. 82). Its impact relies on the image of the dancer being taken from a low viewpoint and reproduced on a larger scale than the other images, thus projecting a sense of monumentality – a grand figure towering above and dominating the scene. The bold typography and use of bright orange, purple and yellow add to this sense of monumentality and gave a modern look to the design.

The representation of splendour and spectacle, therefore, was the most effective way of advertising historical films and conveying both their nationalist and escapist aspirations. *Sahib Bibi aur Gulam* (*Master, Mistress and Slave*, directed by Abrar Alvi, 1962) is a historical set in Calcutta at the turn of the twentieth century and, rather than glorifying the past, it focuses on the decline of the *zamindars* (land-owning classes) and the trials of one family within that process. Here the advertising was more subtle, the booklet cover (illus. 81) using two forms of line drawing superimposed upon each other to depict the key signifiers of the film theme. Thus, grand architecture, a horse and

78 *Humayun*, 1945, booklet cover.

79 Photographs from the press booklet for *Chandralekha* showing street
and theatre advertising, 1948.

80 *Chandralekha*,
1948, booklet cover.

carriage, a dancer and a *huqqa* pipe are some of the elements that place the film in a historical setting. In contrast, the poster design (illus. 83) emphasizes the male-female relationships that govern the narrative. This poster may have been produced for a later re-release of the film and therefore the images represent scenes that acquired an importance for the public after the original release. The only indication of the historical nature of the film is the inclusion of a Persian-style wine bottle, which also serves as a means of indicating that alcohol is one of the narrative themes.

The Studio System: Image and Memory

One of the defining features of the film industry during the inter-war years was the growth and decline of the studio system, and the eventual rise of the star system. After World War I, the industry saw the expansion of the studios, each of which had a team of directors, cameramen and art directors, who defined the distinctive style of the films that were produced there. Actors and actresses were employees of the studios and their status was below that of the studio as a whole, a system that gave poster designers greater scope since they did not have to include the stars on their designs. Thus, when deciding which film to see, the public looked to studio identity as represented by its logo. Logos helped the public to associate a particular type of film to a particular studio; they helped to trigger people's memories, simultaneously reminding them of what the studio stood for as well as the other films made by them. Two of the most famous early logos represented the Prabhat and Gemini studios. Both incorporated the idea of the bugler or trumpeter into their symbols, with Prabhat's 'Tutari girl' (see illus. 63) and the Gemini twins (see illus. 82) looking as if they were announcing or heralding the arrival of sound into the cinema.

Wadia Movietone, a studio established in 1933 by the brothers J. B. Wadia and Homi Wadia, used as its logo an image of a galleon sailing into the distance. The Wadia family (*wadia* means shipbuilder), originally served as master shipbuilders to the East India Company and later to the Government of India,[54] and the logo not only stood for the family's illustrious past but also alluded perhaps to the notion of exploration and venturing forth into a new enterprises. The studio was responsible for one of the more unusual genres – the stunt film – and became known for a series of films featuring 'Fearless Nadia'. She represented courage, strength and idealism, and these fantasies of power and action fed the nationalist movement. The stunt film also built upon the fascination with modern technology, as demonstrated by the booklet covers for *Miss Frontier Mail* (directed by Homi Wadia,

guru dutt films private limited presents
Sahib Bibi aur Ghulam
साहिब बीबी और गुलाम صاحب بی بی اور غلام

81 *Sahib Bibi aur Gulam*, 1962, booklet cover.

1936; illus. 84) and *Deccan Queen* (directed by Mehboob Khan, 1936; illus. 85). Many of Nadia's stunts were performed on top of trains.[55]

After the war the need for entertainment that appealed to the masses placed the emphasis on fast production and greater financial returns. Film makers were under pressure to incorporate key elements that were known to attract large audiences. This gave rise to the 'formula film' whereby song and dance, archetypal characters, romance and rebellion began to appear as components combined in one film, and the stars became the single most important factor. Thus, the rise of the stars saw the decline of the studios, although two continued to operate into the post-war years. They were Mehboob Productions, founded in 1942 by Mehboob Khan, and R.K. Films, set up in 1948 by Raj Kapoor. Between them they were responsible for some of the most memorable and successful Indian films ever produced. Both had a studio identity based on the quality of their films: Mehboob produced grand melodramas while R.K. Studios dealt with socio-realist subject matter. Their reputations persisted through the years due to the constant showings and re-releases of some of their most successful films.

Advertising also played its part in the perpetuation of studio identity. To coincide with the re-release of some of its classic films in the 1980s, Mehboob studios redesigned its posters for *Najma* (1943), *Humayun*

82 *Chandralekha*, c.1948–70s, poster.

83 *Sahib Bibi aur Gulam*, c.1962–1970s, poster.

(1945), *Anmol Ghadi* (*Precious Time*, 1946), *Anokhi Ada* (1948), *Andaz* (*A Matter of Style*, 1949), *Aan* (*Savage Princess*, 1952), *Amar* (1954), *Mother India* (1957) and *Son of India* (1962). The activation of memory was a key factor in the redesign. As the public was already familiar with these films, the primary function of the new publicity was to create an image that would most effectively trigger people's memories. Contemporary design interpretations therefore highlighted scenes, images and stars that over time had become key signifiers of the films, and consequently became key elements within the new posters. All were designed by Raj Tilak of Seth Studios and to retain their studio identity they were stamped with the Mehboob logo. There was a stylistic similarity in some of the new designs but all were characterized by a certain uniformity in their quality of production and the use of simple, bold and effective imagery, thus helping to perpetuate a dynamic studio identity.

The posters for *Najma* (illus. 86), *Humayun* and *Andaz* (illus. 87) place particular emphasis on the star portraits, thus capitalizing on the status they had appropriated over time and making them the key to activating memory. The posters recreate a particularly striking device originally used on the booklet cover for *Humayun* (see illus. 78), which saw the rendering of the human face in profile and the layering of profile over profile. Sharp light and dark contrasts and the use of warm shades of red, brown and yellow heighten the dramatic effect. These designs were also effectively enlarged for reproduction on large-scale 'six-sheeter' posters used for display above cinema entrances and on billboards.[56] With *Anokhi Ada*, the most memorable aspect of the film was the 'love triangle' theme, hence the new design reduces the original more complex one to its basic components of the three central characters in order to convey that theme in an instant. In the case of *Aan*, the key image on the new poster (illus. 89) is that of a sword fight replicating the pose used in the *Chandralekha* poster. As a trigger it works on two levels, both as a reminder of the scene in the film while simultaneously alluding to the most famous sword fight in India's cinematic history. The advertising potential of this one particularly striking image was demonstrated by the fact that the original poster (which was reproduced as a hoarding-size six-sheet poster at the same time as the redesign), did not include an image of the sword fight. The original designs for many of Mehboob's films were made by Bide Viswanathan. His earlier small-scale work was of the Bombay School of Art style (see illus. 48) and the original poster for *Anokhi Ada* still bears evidence of this. With this, as with *Aan*, Viswanathan incorporated multiple images to convey the theme, and for *Aan* elements of

84 *Miss Frontier Mail*, 1936, booklet cover.

the original design, such as the typography and descending staircase, were included in the new poster. The new designs therefore refined the originals by either adding or subtracting images according to their perceived contemporary impact or relevance.

R.K. Films built its studio identity on the socio-realist subject matter of its films as well as on the stars who acted in them. The studio logo was inspired by the poster for *Barsaat* (1949; illus. 88), which depicts Kapoor, who plays a musician, holding a violin in one hand and a fainting girl, Nargis, in the other. This image represents the great love between the two characters and was reduced to its basic stylized form to produce the logo. It symbolized the first success story of the studio and was incorporated into subsequent reprints of the *Barsaat* poster.

Images of an Independent India

The attainment of independence did not resolve the search for a national identity, rather it served to highlight the complexities

85 *Deccan Queen*, 1936, booklet cover.

involved. Post-independence India was caught between the need to modernize and continue its technological advances, against the fear of cultural decline. The city was at the centre of the many social and economic changes taking place at the time, perceived as the source of employment and wealth, and cities like Bombay and Calcutta attracted thousands of rural workers in search of a better life. For many, however, the hardships of village life were replaced by the hardships of sordid city slums with their culture of crime and exploitation, as aptly illustrated on the booklet cover for *Dekhi teri Bombai* (*I Have Seen Your Bombay*, 1961; illus. 90). For them the city epitomized the erosion of social structures and the loss of moral values. Film makers explored the social and moral dilemmas arising from this expanding urban landscape, thereby attracting the new urban audiences that would identify directly with these issues.

Set up in 1948, a year after Indian independence, R.K. Films explored the changing environment and made the city its focal point in films such as *Awāra* (*The Vagabond*, 1951), *Boot Polish* (1954) and *Shri 420* (*Mr 420/The Fraudster*, 1955). *Boot Polish* has been described as an 'allegorical representation of the newly independent "infant" Indian

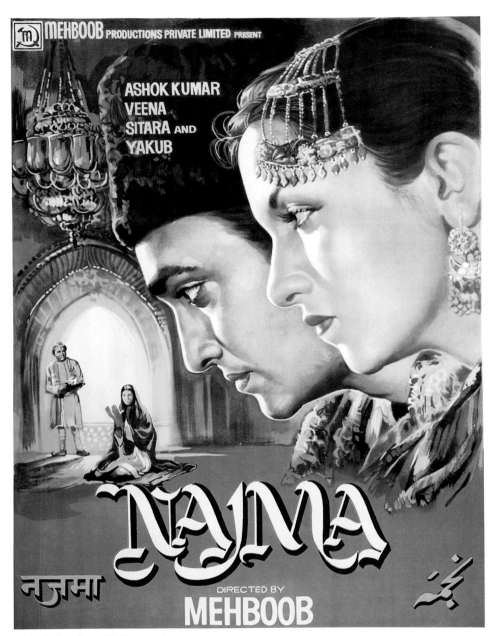

86 Seth Studios, *Najma*, 1980s, poster.

87 Seth Studios, *Andaz*, 1980s, poster.

nation',[57] telling the story of two orphans forced to become beggars in Bombay and their struggle to make an honest living by shining shoes. The original poster showed the children looking hopefully into the horizon and projected a sense of optimism for the new India (illus. 91). However, a poster produced for a re-release of the film reproduced a direct visual translation of the title, so the use of a black-and-white

88 *Barsaat*, reprint of original 1949 poster design.

photograph of a boy polishing a shoe left no doubt as to the film theme and served as a means of triggering memory for those who were already familiar with the film. In *Awāra* Kapoor modelled himself on Charlie Chaplin and took on the persona of a rebellious law-breaking vagabond, who also had a vulnerable side and was perceived by audiences as the archetypal loveable rogue. This character was revived in

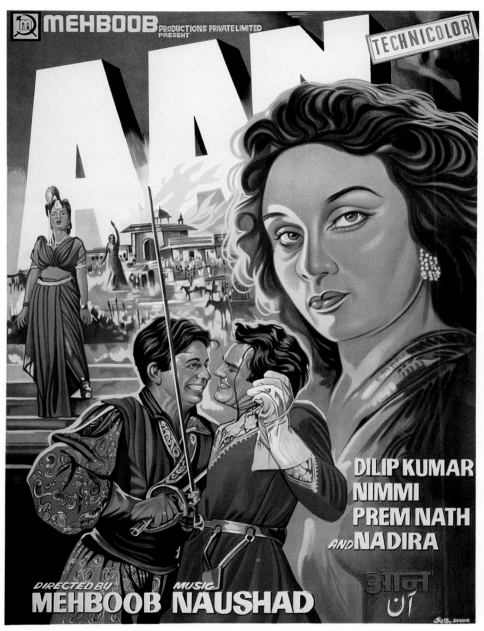

89 Seth Studios, *Aan*, 1980s, poster.

Shri 420 and both films revolved around the love affair between the characters of Kapoor and Nargis, with the city environment presented as a cause of the narrative dilemma.

After the success of *Barsaat*, the pairing of Kapoor and Nargis captured the public's imagination and the advertising for *Awāra* and *Shri 420* built upon that love affair. The knowledge of the real-life affair between the two added further power to the images.[58] The *Awāra* poster (illus. 92) uses as its key graphic image a classic moment from the film when Kapoor is shown kissing Nargis's bare shoulder after having put a stolen necklace around her neck. The image is particularly evocative and would have seized the public's attention, but it would not have conveyed the other themes of the film. The poster for *Shri 420* (illus. 93) built upon Kapoor's character, the revival of which was represented by an image of his now-famous tramp costume, while the inclusion of Nargis's portrait drew attention to the love affair. Furthermore, the depiction of a row of buildings in the middle ground separating the two figures served to indicate the narrative dilemma of the film, both the more general themes of city life and modernity and the more specific theme of urban housing.

90 *Dekhi teri Bombai*, 1961, booklet cover.

This image of Kapoor has since become one of the most famous in Indian cinema history and refers to one of the most famous film songs of all time, 'Mera joota hai japani ...'. The nationalist sentiments of the song state that, while he was dressed in an odd assortment of clothes from around the world, his heart and soul were Hindustani. To the public, Kapoor's 'Hindustani' soul encapsulated the very essence of the Utopian society that the films of the 1950s aimed to create. This was a Utopia situated in the modern world but one in which the traditional and basic values of hard work and honesty were seen to triumph over greed and corruption. Kapoor's character was hugely popular in India, the USSR and the Middle East because he stood for these universal values. However, the true exposition of these value systems and the social structures that underpinned them were not to be found in the cities but in the

91 *Boot Polish*, reprint of original 1954 poster design.

villages of India where they were firmly rooted. In opposition to the depictions of the city underworld, films idealized village life and made it the basis of their projection of a national identity for India.

Released in 1957, *Mother India* explored this Utopian society. Set in rural India, the film tells the story of Radha (played by Nargis) and her progression from a young bride to the revered 'Mother' of the village. An endless series of gruelling trials against both man and nature become the vehicle through which she displays her courage, strength and moral resolve. She is an embodiment of the values and codes of behaviour derived from 'mythology, cult worship, social traditions and customs',[59] the very basis of traditional Indian society. Living within these defined social structures allows her to gain a symbolic position of power with which to lead the transition to a new mechanized India. Radha thus came to personify a national identity for the new Independent India, and it was this powerful and iconic image that the souvenir booklet aimed to project (there was also another much simpler booklet produced at the same time). The souvenir booklet was lavishly produced and gives a twenty-two-page step by step synopsis of the film and its making. Unlike other booklets it excludes the song lyrics, usually one of the major components, and is entirely in English. Each page is illustrated with a richly painted image. On the front page (illus. 94) there is a dramatic side profile of Radha rising out of the flames, with much smaller roughly drawn figures below her, and the only text is the title in bold capital letters. The effectiveness of the image is due to the technique used in rendering it. Using photographic stills from the film the portrait of Nargis was painted over with oil paints. Unlike Ravi Varma's use of oil paints, however, which gave his depictions of women a sense of depth and reality, here the paints give texture and volume to the realism imparted by the photograph below.

The artist responsible for the paintings was L. L. Meghanee,[60] who had previously worked for Bombay Talkies and R.K. Studios before Nargis brought him over to Mehboob. His earlier painting style was that of the Bombay School of Art and this work represented experimentation with a new style. The exaggerated and rough brush strokes give an effect similar to that of Western Expressionist painting. Expressionism was concerned not with the realistic portrayal of a subject but with the expression of inner emotion. Aesthetically, the transmission of emotion was achieved through scale, intensity of colour, brush stroke and texture. This was a time when artists who later came to define the Indian contemporary fine arts movement were experimenting with international styles and techniques, and groups such as the Progressive Artists (1947–53) had embraced

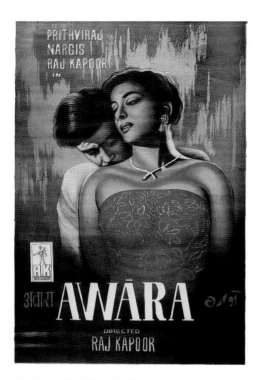

92 *Awāra*, reprint of original 1951 poster design.

93 *Shri 420*, reprint of original 1955 poster design.

94 L. L. Meghanee, Souvenir booklet cover, *Mother India*, 1957.

Expressionism and Cubism.[61] Meghanee's appropriation of a new style may therefore have been a response to these developments, as well as a need to produce something significantly different to match the unique and epic nature of the film. For the cover of *Mother India*, the brush strokes and use of colour enhance Radha's facial expression, intensify the reds and oranges of the flames, which are reflected in the title itself, and emphasize the dramatic nature of the entire image. The other images were not all executed in the same manner; rather, key photographs illustrating the most dramatic points in the narrative were selected and painted around so that the background had an Expressionist feel. The entire booklet is charged with an emotional and passionate intensity that aimed to glorify India and its traditional ways. Thus, the opening text quoted the Indologist Max Müller:

If I were to look over the whole world to find out the country most richly endowed with all the wealth, power, and beauty that nature can bestow – I should point to India.

If I were asked under what sky the human mind has most fully developed some of its choicest gifts, has most deeply pondered on the greatest problems of life … I should point to India.

And if I were to ask myself from what literature, we in Europe … may draw that corrective which is most wanted to make our inner life more perfect … more truly human … again I should point to India.

The booklet contains elaborate explanations on the moral dilemmas of the narrative, integrating these with information on village life and thereby propounding a deeper understanding of the Indian nation and the value systems that formed it. Rural life is projected as the essence of India, whereby 700,000 villages are inhabited by 'an ancient peace-loving people' who lead a 'harmonious community life' and whose entire existence and 'eternal character' are based on 'honest, hard toil'. Tradition and destiny are the two key elements that are continually mentioned and articulated through Radha. She is described as a 'jewel of Indian womanhood', with continual references to mythology and comparisons to Sita and Savitri. Thus throughout the booklet Indian womanhood continues to be projected as a symbol of the nation as it had been from the very beginning of the nationalist period: 'From India … this epic drama of an Indian mother, the nucleus round which revolves the tradition and culture of ages in this ancient land'.[62]

An image of a mother cradling a baby in her arms symbolized that statement and was used on the original poster design (illus. 95). When Mehboob Studios redesigned the poster in the 1980s, however, it aimed to convey a sense of the monumentality of the film and to reflect the status it had achieved as a national epic and one of the greatest Indian films ever made. The new design (illus. 96) refined and reused an image from the booklet that shows Radha with her arm stretched out, pulling a plough, and is captioned: 'The grain of rice on your table does not tell the grim tale of the toil which grew it'.[63] Thus Radha's heroic struggles were immortalised in one inspirational iconic image that stands for endurance, power and the Indian sense of morality. A sense of monumentality is achieved through the depiction of her body from a low viewpoint so that the viewer looks up at her. The viewer's eye is drawn from Radha's tightly clasped hand, down her outstretched arm, which forms a diagonal across the poster, and comes to rest on her face. The expressive nature of the painting impresses upon the viewer the feeling of anguish and pain seen in her face and her straining neck, along with the ache of the taut muscles in her fingers. Behind her the great expanse of land and cattle is matched by an equally large expanse of sky and glorious sunset, all in rich shades of orange, red, yellow and brown. The

three-dimensional lettering adds to the sense of scale.

The power of the *Mother India* imagery was such that both the style and format of the booklet were directly copied for *Resham ki Dori* (*Rope of Silk*, directed by Atma Ram, 1974). The emotional intensity of the imagery was also captured by another series of posters featuring Guru Dutt: *Sahib Bibi aur Gulam* (1962; see illus. 83), *Pyaasa* (*Thirst*, 1957) and *Kagaz ke Phool* (*Paper Flowers*, 1959; illus. 97). These posters used simple, bold imagery to convey intense passion. Guru Dutt's films were not all successful at the time of their release, but since his death in 1964 they have been recognized as classics of the cinema. *Pyaasa* and *Kagaz ke Phool* look at the place of the artist within the new structures of the modern independent state, the creative individual against a hostile environment and a society motivated by material wealth. Both are highly poignant narratives involving passionate relationships between the characters played by Dutt and Waheeda Rehman, and in both cases the posters focus on this element at the exclusion of all else. Thus for *Pyaasa* the sole image is of Guru Dutt gently kissing Waheeda Rehman's forehead. The strong use of

96 Seth Studios, *Mother India*, 1980s, poster.

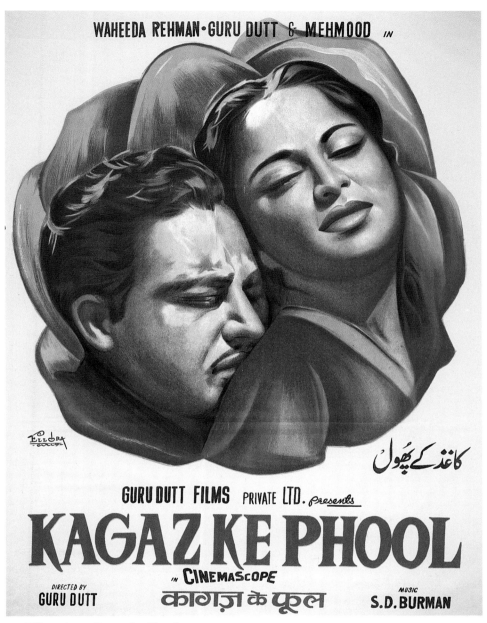

97 Ellora Arts, *Kagaz ke Phool*, 1959, poster.

chiaroscuro conveys the tenderness and passion of the moment. For *Kagaz ke Phool*, the title of the film, which alludes to the artificial world created by the film industry, became an integral part of the design. Thus, the booklet uses a simple image of a red rose juxtaposed with some film-making equipment. The poster, however, is much simpler and more striking. The key image is a depiction of a large rose and encompassed within it is an image of Dutt shown kissing the back of Waheeda Rehman's shoulder and she resting her head on his. Coloured entirely in red, this image fills the poster and conveys the passion, anguish and sorrow of the narrative.

Internationalism and Images of Youth

While the post-war period had been a time of inward reflection for India, a time spent searching for a definition of 'Indianness', the 1960s saw a move towards a more international outlook. Within the film industry one of the signifiers of this new mood was the use of Western locations. *Sangam* (*Union*, directed by Raj Kapoor, 1964) was the first Indian colour film to be partly shot in Paris, Rome, London, Venice and Switzerland. The film was described as an 'earnest and ambitious effort to synthesize the modern European culture with that of ancient India through an immortal story of love and friendship'. An image of the iconic Eiffel Tower was used on the front cover to symbolize both the love story and the international theme. Within the booklet (see illus.11) the statement 'Ageless as Asia, Exciting as Europe' projects the ethos of the whole film. Its use of bright colours, modern typographic style and colour photographs of the five cities presents the West as an exciting, exotic and modern place where romantic fantasies can be played out,[64] while the image of the East conforms to orientalist ideals and is portrayed as 'ancient' and 'ageless', thereby confining India to the past.

The 1960s was a period of economic growth in the West and this was accompanied by the spread of a new liberal culture. In Britain this manifested itself through the rise of consumerism, new music, increased sexual freedom, new fashions and hairstyle trends, all of which were fuelled by an overriding sense of experimentation and excitement. In India this world was seen as glamorous and cosmopolitan and was made visible through fashion and youth culture. Fashion was determined by films like *Jewel Thief* (directed by Vijay Anand, 1967),[65] which replicates the black eye make-up and bouffant hairstyles characteristic of London's pop generation. One of the best examples of this look can be seen on the publicity for the film *Ankhen* (*The Eyes*, 1968). The natural focus in the design of both the poster and the

98 *Ankhen*, 1968, booklet cover.

booklet cover (illus. 98) is the eyes as they refer to the title of the film, but the 1960s appearance was enhanced through the clever use of typography and the juxtaposition of image and colour. These images however, presented a lifestyle that in India was only ever appropriated by the few who could afford it.

The film that epitomized youth culture and 1960s fashions was the teenage love story, *Bobby* (directed by Raj Kapoor, 1973; see illus. 34). The poster (illus. 99) is rendered in the style of American psychedelic posters of the 1960s and is characterized by swirling bands of bright colours set against a black background, rounded 'bubble' lettering and fluid floral forms. In the West psychedelic posters were a symbol of youth culture and represented a new liberalism that manifested itself through the growth of folk-protest music, radical student activism, civil rights and anti-Vietnam movements, hippy fashions and the drug LSD. The use of LSD was synonymous with this era, and the effects of the drug, which heighten the senses and result in glowing colours and resonating sounds, gave rise to the term psychedelic, meaning literally 'mind-manifesting'.[66] By using the psychedelic style, the *Bobby* poster was not implying that this culture existed in India, rather it alluded to a period associated with youth culture, fun, romance and rebellion.

99 *Bobby,* 1973, poster.

Crisis in India: Images of Violence

The 1970s was a period of internal crisis in India, one in which there was great political, economic and social upheaval. The war in 1971 leading to the formation of Bangladesh, and the state of emergency imposed by the government, were coupled with rising inflation, increasing numbers of urban poor and rising levels of Mafia and drug-associated crime. The emergence of a new genre of film was seen as a response to the state of the nation and reflected the emotion, anger and aggression of the period. Centred on the theme of revenge, the films were characterized by action-packed scenes of unprecedented violence.[67] They also gave birth to a different type of hero, the anti-hero. In the past he had been the weak and ineffectual victim but in his new guise he was a powerful man who brought about revenge or 'justice' through the ubiquitous force of violence. He was usually an outsider to society and inhabited the criminal underworld, he exhibited great physical strength and martial skills, but often had a tragic and introspective side to his character.

This new genre was paralleled by a new graphic style whereby film poster art of the 1970s was defined by the technique used in rendering the images. Oil paint applied in bold and distinct brush strokes became the characteristic feature. The process involved using photographic stills from the film to form the basis of the poster design, which were then painted over with gouache or oil paints (illus. 100). The rough brush strokes of the paint had the effect of adding texture, emphasizing facial expressions and enhancing the overall emotional impact of the poster. Although overpainting had been used before in the advertising for *Mother India*, where its expressive nature suited the emotional content of the film, the technique became much more widely used in the 1970s. The artist responsible for this particular phase in poster design (and for many of the important posters of the time) was Diwakar Karkare. He was trained at the Bombay School of Art where he was taught to use oil paints and he developed the technique of over-painting with the aim of bringing his art school education to the film industry. The style was regarded as new, dynamic and expressive, and suited the highly emotional intensity and melodramatic characteristics of this new genre. It was also instrumental in the promotion and perpetuation of the characteristics that defined the new role of the anti-hero (see chapter Four). The impact of the style was such that it not only became synonymous with films of the period but is today the style most frequently associated with Indian film poster art as a whole.

The film that epitomized this decade was *Sholay* (*Flames*, directed by Ramesh Sippy, 1975), and the phrase 'Flames of violence blazed across the horizon ...', which was used in the booklet, captured the essence of both the film and the advertising. The film has been described as an 'Indianized Western' that tells the story of a man who hires two ex-convicts to seek revenge for the murder of his family and the mutilation of his own body. Evil and violence are shown as the ever-present forces of society and are presented without restraint in a manner that had never been seen before. The film's visualization of violence had the effect of glamorizing it, and the advertising played its part in this. The advertising aimed to project the monumentality of the film, and the simplicity of the poster and booklet designs, all designed by C. Mohan, were extremely effective in doing this (illus. 101). The striking typography became the main feature of the advertising. The lettering is formed from rocks and stones that represent the boulders and desert setting of the film. Its three-dimensional quality give it a monumentality echoed in the wording at the top: 'The greatest star cast ever assembled – The greatest story ever told'. Posters possibly produced for the UK release of the film also contain all the elements of a successful design, a bold image, bright colours and a minimum of lettering (illus. 102). Here, the sense of monumentality is evoked through that distinctive typography as well as the star portraits and the manner in which they are rendered with an inferno of flames surrounding them. Two posters were printed, both using star portraits in the centre of the design and representing the two screen relationships: one with Dharmendra and Hema Malini, and the other with Amitabh Bachchan and Jaya Bhaduri. The original advertising campaign in India, however, had been focused solely on Dharmendra as the lead actor to capitalize on his star status at that time.[68] The technique of overpainting was used to depict the male faces and serves to emphasize their defiant and stern expressions. Painted in shades of yellow and orange, they appear to be rising from within the flames, in effect merging with them, and the brush strokes enhance the blazing flames. In contrast the female portraits, while depicted in the same shades of colour, are smaller and have a smooth photographic appearance that highlights the difference between them, the male being from outside the law and directly involved with the 'flames of violence'. Below them, also in orange and yellow, is the title in bold three-dimensional lettering on a scale that fills one third of the poster.

Unlike these other forms of advertising, the lobby cards were the exception in that chosen images highlight not the violent nature of the film but its diversity, the scenes depicting a range of emotions that, when displayed together in a cinema foyer, would project the film as an all-inclusive epic, with something of interest for everyone. *Sholay* became one of the most popular films ever made; the poster design also made an impact and was crudely and heavily borrowed from in the poster for *Qurbani* (directed by Feroz Khan, 1980), which copied both the title and the blazing background.

The 1970s and '80s saw the 'formula' film become a well-recognized and structurally definitive format. Even though all the elements of the formula, such as the song, dance, romance and action, had been integral to Indian cinema since the 1940s, they became more exaggerated during this period. The posters of the period contributed to this: rather than focus on one or two elements within the film, the poster incorporated all or most elements. Thus for films like *Kabhi Kabhie* (directed by Yash Chopra, 1976; illus. 104), *Amar Akbar Anthony* (1977), *Naseeb* (*Destiny*, directed by Manmohan Desai, 1981) (illus.103) and *Alaap* (directed by Hrishikesh Mukherjee, 1977), we have a montage of many images depicting the central themes, the main characters and some of the key scenes from the films. The main characters are given prominence in that their portraits are larger than the other images and provide a focus for the design and the viewer. Overpainting would either be used across the entire poster to give some sense of cohesion to the myriad of images or would be applied to specific parts such as the portraits to enhance and emphasize them.

New Technology and the Cinematic Image

From the beginning of the 1990s film advertising began to change. With increasing sums of money being spent on campaigns a greater degree of sophistication was brought into the entire process. The development of technology fuelled changes that saw the characteristic overpainted montage poster of the previous two decades replaced by images that were defined by simplicity and elegance. Image creation was now driven by the opportunities offered by computer-aided design. Photographic stills fed into the computer could be manipulated on screen, allowing for the smooth superimposition, juxtaposition, reduction, enlargement and colour contrasting of images and text with relative ease.

One of the first films to use this new technology was *Dilwale Dulhania Le Jayenge* (*The Brave Heart Will Take the Bride*, directed by Aditya Chopra, 1995). Three different posters were produced, all of which focus on the romantic theme of the film but which inform the audience of the different strands and locations of the romance; thus one depicts the couple dancing in Western clothes while another shows them in traditional Indian clothes. By focusing on the two main characters, the images maintain a simplicity that has become a charac-

100 Close up showing Diwakar Karkare's technique of overpainting.

101 C. Mohan, *Sholay*, 1975, booklet cover.

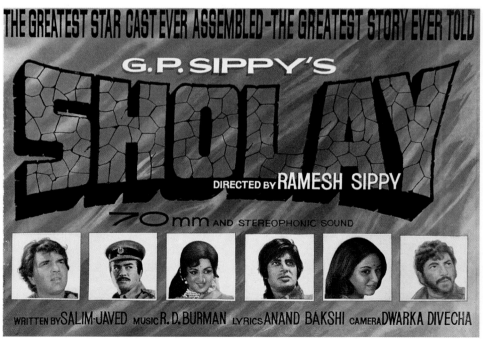

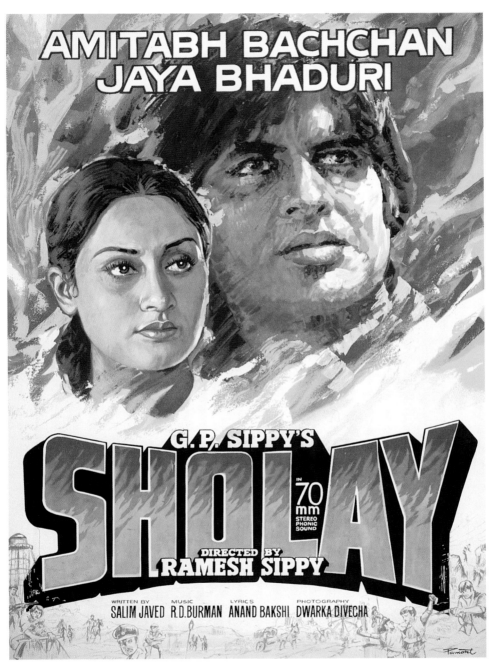

102 C. Mohan, *Sholay*, 1975, poster.

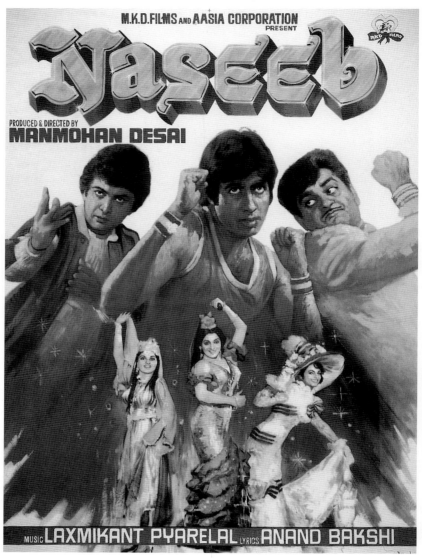

103 Diwakar Karkare, *Naseeb*, 1981, poster.

teristic of the posters of this period. For *Pardes* (*Overseas*, directed by Subhash Ghai, 1997; see illus. 18), the poster format returned to the earlier designs and used an amalgamation of images to convey the film theme. The male and the female portrait indicate the romantic theme, while diagonally opposing images of an American cityscape and the Taj Mahal serve to highlight the East–West narrative dilemma. However, the computer-aided technique that allowed for the diffusion of images and the subtle transition of image to image differentiates this poster from the clumsy montage effect of the 1970s and '80s. These slick, glossy posters match those produced in the West and as such they have become indicators of modernity. They also reflect an important shift in film theme, from a decade defined by the *masala* film (see chapter Four) and its depiction of violence to films defined by themes of family, love and romance.[69] The films illustrate modern, affluent lifestyles and the new poster technology projects that image of India, thereby pushing representations of India into the twenty-first century.

With technology providing the primary creative tool for the production of these posters, the role of the traditional artist has been displaced by the computer specialist. H.R. Enterprises, for example, is one of the pioneering design companies responsible for these changes,[70] and is run by two publicity 'designers' who are not trained artists but have an extensive knowledge of computers.[71] The relative ease of production has led to an influx of computer-generated posters and as a direct result the established art-school trained artist Diwakar closed his studio, believing that posters no longer require any artistic input. More recently Yash Raj Films set up Design Cell, its own in-house design company, and the 'designer' Fayyaz Badruddin is also a computer specialist. The decision to set up the studio was taken in 1998 after it was felt that the vision of the director could be easily transferred to posters through the use of computer technology. Thus, although Yash Chopra, Diwakar's one-time patron, cites a preference for painted posters since there is an element of 'art' in them and a greater emphasis on emotion, he sees the new posters as having a more modern appeal.[72] To the new breed of publicity designers, hand-painted posters appear old-fashioned in comparison to these glossy, slick designs, which are considered essential to attract audiences who are more sophisticated, internationally aware and image conscious. Advertising is therefore not about 'art' but about selling an image. For the film *Gupt* (directed by Rajiv Rai, 1997), the designer Rahul Nanda created an image for the poster that was totally unconnected with the original film – the actors dressed in black leather jackets projected a modern trendy image that reflected the ethos of the film. The strength of the image, however, was such that the script was rewritten to include a scene with those outfits.[73]

Just as the poster artist has been displaced by the arrival of new technology, so too has the hoarding artist. Rajesh Vaidya, who runs one of Bombay's leading firms, Balkrishna Arts, believes that they are one of only four studios surviving today.[74] The company, situated in a gully

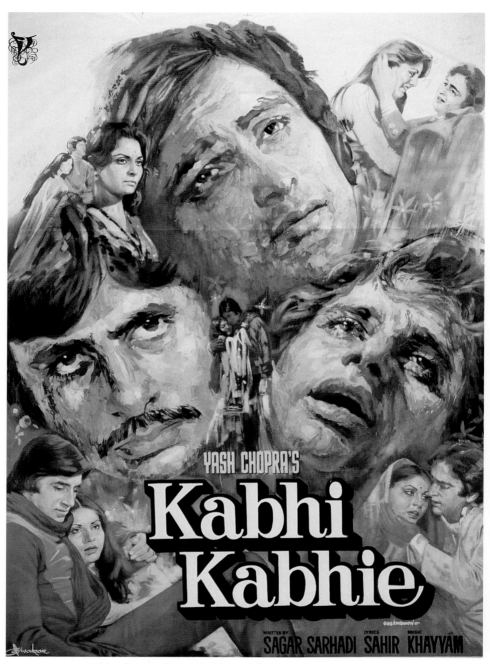

104 Diwakar Karkare, *Kabhi Kabhie*, 1976, poster.

off a main road in the West Dadar district of Bombay, produces every year some four or five hundred hoardings, which are usually commissioned by the local film distributors. It is a small family-run business, whose working processes and painting techniques have been handed down from father to son.[75] That they consider their work to be 'art' is evident from their pride in talking about their profession and in the fact that they have kept and continue to keep photographic evidence of some of it. The firm's history (covering more than fifty years) is chronicled through these snapshot photographs and through a stock of old stills and film booklets that bear the markings of the hoarding painters: pencil lines drawn horizontally, vertically and diagonally marking a scale to allow for the transfer and enlargement of the image onto the hoarding canvas. As one of the few remaining firms Balkrishna Arts appears to be surviving well, particularly as the increased interest in Indian popular culture has led to several international commissions in the last few years, the latest being for an exhibition at Tate Modern in London.[76] This has served to further their own sense of worth as artists. However, while hoardings have been typified by roughly drawn, rapidly executed, highly exaggerated and emotive images, ironically some painters are now mimicking the computer-generated posters thus displacing their own characteristic expressive interpretations. An example is the hoarding for *Mohabbatein* (illus. 105), which is just like its printed version, suggesting that these artists are showing their ability to compete with technology while at the same time signalling a loss of artistic freedom.

Today for each new film release a publicity campaign consists of three primary areas, printed material, television commercials and newspaper advertisements. *Mohabbatein* (*Loves*, directed by Aditya Chopra, 2000), produced by Yash Raj Films, is a very recent release and provides a good example of the advertising process. Publicity for the film starts from the first day of filming with photographic stills being taken all through the shooting. Work on the posters begins twelve weeks prior to the release of the film and the design has to be with the printers eight weeks before release. For *Mohabbatein* twelve different posters were produced in total, eight one-sheet designs with a print run of 250,000, one four-sheet design with a print run of 15,000 and three six-sheet designs with a print run of 30,000. Four weeks before release the distributors are supplied with lobby cards, booklets and the one-sheet posters free of charge, but distributors have to pay for the larger poster designs used on bill boards and above cinemas. Local distributors therefore decide whether they wish to purchase these or commission hoarding painters. Yash Raj Films has sixteen all-India distributors who are responsible for the advertising within their own regions, including street publicity, local displays and cinema decoration. Two weeks before release the art work has to be displayed in the cinemas. Alongside paper publicity goes television advertising. 'Soft' publicity starts twelve weeks prior to release, and with *Mohabbatein* this took the form of short trailers shown ten times in one day but spread across different channels. Two weeks later the music for the film was released to allow time for the music companies to capitalize on their income and for the audience to become familiar with the songs. The easy availability of cassette recordings means that most film booklets no longer reproduce song lyrics. Aggressive television advertising started two weeks before the release; this meant that trailers were shown up to six a day on one channel at peak viewing time. While the film is running the publicity continues in the form of newspaper advertisements that reproduce the poster designs with details of local showings.[77]

The advertising aims to sell an image for Yash Raj Films, a studio or brand identity that emphasizes romance and youth. *Mohabbatein* was the first poster campaign designed in-house by Design Cell. The film follows the romance of three different couples and the opposing attitudes of a teacher and the head to these romances. The large-scale posters use images of all of the eight central characters or the three couples (see illus. 40), while the smaller posters focus on different elements of the film. Three of these concentrate on the two teachers played by the two lead actors, Amitabh Bachchan and Shahrukh Khan, their antagonism towards each other being emphasized through their facial expressions, posture and clothing. Thus Amitabh is always shown wearing black, standing perfectly straight and with a stern expression, whereas Shahrukh is shown wearing pale colours, in a relaxed pose and playing his violin to show his sensitive nature. A key motif running through the posters is an orange maple leaf that has been taken from a scene in the film and has been projected as a symbol for the film.

Mohabbatein's campaign included one other form of advertising, the Yash Raj website. The company was one of the first to take advantage of this new technology and to realize its potential as a medium for global exposure. An interesting feature of the site, which also indicates its importance, is a diary supposedly written by a crew member working on the film set. The entry for June 2000 (about twelve weeks prior to the release of the film) reads:

The countdown begins! The shooting is over ... The publicity material has begun to take shape and we have decided to use the internet to give the

105 Hand-painted hoarding for *Mohabbatein*, Balkrishna Arts, 2000.

first glimpses into *Mohabbatein* at the Yash Raj Film website. So we are gearing up for an extensive web-peek into the film – everything from the making of the film, behind the scenes, previews of the music to the first introduction to the characters and stars who play them and a chance to chat on-line!

The site does in fact do justice to this statement. It is extensive, offering interviews with the director, cast and crew credits, listings of theatres showing the film, poster releases, movie trailers, screensavers, e-cards, music, photosets, contests, fan sites and a diary of the making of the film. However, the most dynamic feature is the opening film sequence. This starts with a gust of wind blowing orange leaves across the screen and is followed by the statement 'There was a man who believed in love ...' with an image of Shahrukh's character. With each new gust of wind we are given another statement and introduced to another character: thus Amitabh is 'a man who did not believe in love' and then 'there were the love stories...', followed by images of the other six characters (see also illus. 40). The film closes with the sentence 'Some love stories are meant to last forever' and within fifty seconds the viewer has been given a concise and entertaining synopsis of the film. The site, which also offers archival information on Yash Chopra and his previous films, was the recipient of an 'International Web Page Award' for the best film website in 2000. Thus, as a form of global advertising, the potential for creative freedom and audience accessibility is infinite. Films are advertised not only through their company sites but through magazine sites such as *Filmfare* and *Screen*, as well as through those dedicated to Indian film and the more general entertainment and arts Web pages.

Computer technology has therefore ushered in a new era that has seen the displacement of traditional forms of artistic production, and has seen the marketing of a film become an all-encompassing process that plays as important a role as the product itself. Now, more than any other period in Indian film history, the cinematic image dominates India's visual landscape and through the medium of the World Wide Web will become ever more pervasive.

4 Advertising and the Communication of Meaning

The primary aim of a film poster is to advertise a specific film. It may also, however, often convey other messages and is multi-layered in terms of the meanings that can be read from it. Posters, through their depiction of key components from the film, are able to communicate both simple messages about the films they are advertising as well as more complex cultural meanings by 'triggering a hierarchy of responses'.[1] This hierarchy means that certain elements within a poster are immediately and universally understood while other elements require a specific cultural knowledge to be understood.[2]

The Star Image

It is evident that the majority of film posters (both Indian and Western) use portraits of the star actors and actresses as their key component. These portraits are the most natural and obvious starting-point for a successful advertisement since they activate this 'hierarchy of responses' by capturing the viewers' attention and prompting them to look further at the poster. The success of a portrait in alerting our attention is dependent on two factors. Firstly, an image of a human face is instantly engaging because it is familiar to us all. If we look at any mix of images it is the representation of the face, over any other image, that is most likely to draw our glance. The dynamic nature of portraiture is such because the structuring of human relationships from the earliest stages of life (from when a child gazes at its mother) are based upon physical appearance and facial recognition.[3] The face is also the 'primary field of expressive action'[4] where all forms of emotion can be made visible, and is therefore able to hold the viewer's attention at a far deeper level than other visual images. As a result, on one level the image of a face is instantly and universally engaging, and we do not need to recognize the person to be drawn to it. Secondly, a portrait on a poster attracts greater attention because it is immediately recognizable as a representation of a cinematic star. It is, however, only recognizable within a specific cultural environment: an Indian film star will be unknown to the wider Western audience where his or her films are not so popular and the poster will not evoke the same response.

Within its own cultural context, the portrait of a star on a poster not only sparks recognition but also arouses expectations (see chapter One). It projects a persona or identity associated with the star that has been constructed over a period of time. This identity is usually extensive in that it covers all aspects of their character and is both a multi-media and inter-textual creation, in that the various forms of media and promotional activities that surround the star inform and constantly build upon each other.[5] This process begins with actors or actresses forming their own star identity or 'symbolic biography'[6] through the films they appear in and the characters they play, and through the documentation of their public and private lives in the media. This is enhanced by the photographers and artists who produce the images that are seen on the plethora of promotional material accompanying a film release. At the same time members of the public who watch the films and see these images develop their own perceptions of the star. They too are able to affect the way a star is represented by the choices they make, which are manifested through their attendance at the box office as well as through other media, such as fan magazines and clubs. The star identity is therefore cumulatively constructed by the star, the artist and the public, which implies that within the star's portrait there is a 'concurrence of self representation, artistic interpretation, and viewer expectation' appropriate for the portrayal of such a star.[7] Consequently when it is used on a poster it not only projects that identity, it also reinforces it, and in so doing it simultaneously arouses the public's attention to the film and raises expectations about it.

An example of this process, and the way in which the visual medium in its many forms constructs and defines the stars' identity and the extent of their authority, can be seen in the formation of Amitabh Bachchan's star persona and his elevation to a national icon (see chapter One). Regarded as the most successful Indian actor of all time, Bachchan developed his persona of the 'angry young man-hero' in the 1970s. *Zanjeer* (directed by Prakash Mehra, 1973) was the first film in which he took on this role, and the character traits developed here were built on in subsequent roles and transferred from one film to the next. Consequently over a period of time he was presented as a strong independent figure, ready to fight for justice, physically powerful but also introverted and in some cases ultimately tragic. The public's perception of Bachchan in terms of his personal characteristics, physical appearance and mannerisms developed and were transferred from one film to the next. Film magazines provided a 'barrage of information on Bachchan, his relations to other stars (male and female), his relations to 'starlets', his achievements in stunts that are used to confirm his masculinity, his ambitions and desires, and speculation about his personal likes'.[8] Other promotional material projected the 'material phenomenon' of Bachchan, his 'physical body, physiognomy, gestural repertoire, physical agility, and costume'.[9] Booklets and lobby cards presented him in a myriad of aggressive fighting poses, brandishing guns and riding motorbikes (illus. 106), while the posters tended to focus on his face. The poster for *Muqaddar ka Sikandar* (*Man of Destiny*, directed by Prakash Mehra, 1978; illus. 107) is a particularly good example and shows Bachchan on a motorbike set against a background of four large portraits; he is depicted as though riding out of the centre of the poster and is further differentiated from the others through the use of contrasting colours.

A comparable cumulative construction in terms of promotional art is the persona of James Bond. From the first film produced in 1961 to the most current releases the posters have carried the distinct 007 logo of a gun barrel extending from the top of the figure 7, and have been characterized by: 'Red-hot colours ... phallic guns pointing north ... the suave man in evening clothes, sporting the "stud-can't-help-it"

106 *Deewaar*, 1975, lobbycard.

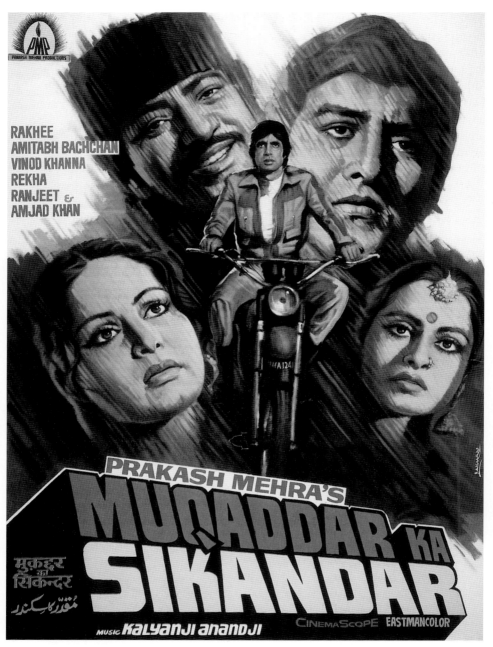

107 *Muqaddar ka Sikandar*, 1978, poster.

grin ... half-clad pneumatic lovelies melting over him ... underwater slugfests, jetpacks, and marauding choppers ... slyly suggestive copy lines ... (such as) ... "James Bond does it everywhere" ... "No body does it better"...'.[10] The campaigns, for which the best illustrators were hired and paid large salaries, aimed to convey in 'a stylish and classy way' the girls, the action and the gadgets, the key idea being that 'Bond is cool'. With Bachchan, although he did not play the same character in every film, he often played the same character type of the 'angry young man', and it was this that was projected in the advertising.

Visually, however, it was Bachchan's facial distinction, as depicted on posters in particular, that added considerably to the construction of his star identity. During the 1970s and '80s several artists from different studios worked on various film posters, but many of the notable examples were the work of one artist, Diwakar Karkare. Within these posters the artist sought to create a resemblance to the subject as well as to convey the actor's star identity, a knowledge of which he would have accumulated over time from Bachchan's on- and off-screen characterization. A survey of the posters shows how certain facial characteristics came to be identified as his defining features, with a particular emphasis being placed on them, thereby making them the key to affect recognition. With Bachchan it was his heavy-hooded eyes. Usually depicted looking directly at the viewer or into the distance, they projected a disturbing piercing quality to his gaze. Within the films the eyes were used to display a range of emotions, with many close-ups demonstrating the changes in temperament from calmness to anger and rage.[11] Similarly, his full lips were enhanced to impart a quiet brooding air of discontent to his expression. Depicted thus by the artist, these properties assumed the form of a mask projecting the constructed star identity or 'social role' that the actor had appropriated.[12] For the public the properties of the mask acted as symbols with which to identify the subject, and were the trigger for sparking recognition and bringing forth all the associations attached to the star's persona.

Furthermore, these depictions of Bachchan were not merely representations, they were iconic images, an iconic image being a static image in which 'many symbolic meanings converge'[13] but which is not necessarily of a religious or mythological nature. Here the artist created an iconic image by using three specific devices: placing the portrait at the centre of the poster, often on a larger scale than the other portraits; directing the gaze of the star to meet that of the viewer; and, thirdly, using the aesthetic process of overpainting when rendering the portrait. This process of applying oil paints over a photographic portrait was most commonly adopted during the 1970s, the period when Bachchan's persona was created, and therefore the process became associated with images of him. The paint, often applied with a knife in thick textured strokes, provided a means for artists to place their own interpretation over the photographic image, primarily allowing them to express and emphasize emotion. The technique itself was an amalgamation of European academic portrait painting and portrait photography, both of which enjoyed widespread popularity in nineteenth-century India. The images of Bachchan therefore acquired greater meaning through the transference of this technique to twentieth-century poster art.

European portraiture became a highly valued art form in India from the end of the eighteenth century, when artists such as Tilly Kettle, John Zoffany and Thomas Hickey first began painting portraits of British residents. They created a taste for portraiture in the Indian nobility which associated these paintings with the status and power of the British ruling classes. In Europe, portraiture had been associated since the sixteenth century with figures of authority, and magnificent full-length paintings of monarchs and grand images of heroic leaders, depicted within their powerful historical contexts, came to define the élitist function of the genre. These images represented sitters as 'worthy of love, honour, respect and authority', and painted their virtues into a 'permanent reality'.[14] Portraiture came to perform a dual function: it not only portrayed persons of authority but, through the historical development of the genre, the act of portraiture also came to bestow authority on the portrayed. Thus, authority with all the associations of status, power and wealth became both the object and effect of portrayal.[15] Hence, in an effort to appropriate these values, the Indian nobility commissioned their own portraits, initially from British artists and then by Indian artists trained in the European manner. Although Ravi Varma was the first Indian artist successfully to employ oil paints and the conventions of realist portraiture, by the late nineteenth century many Indian artists had been trained in this manner in the government art schools and were helping to cultivate a 'Westernization of visual taste' in the Indian public.[16] By its very nature this genre emphasized the centrality of the figure; this was not, however, an exclusively Western convention. Indian art had a tradition of isolating figures or placing an iconic figure at the centre of a narrative scene. This is evident in early sculptural forms and in miniature painting of the Mughal period through to the mid-nineteenth-century Pahari and Sikh schools.[17] These were, however, imagined and idealized portraits and they lacked the realism of European painting, which posed the figures in a way that brought the subject into direct eye contact with the viewer, thus closing the psychological gap between them.[18]

With the arrival of photography in the 1840s, this full 'frontal encounter' between the subject and the viewer became an established convention within the Indian visual vocabulary. Photography had a huge impact on portraiture. Valued for its ability to capture reality, it immediately acquired the status and authority attributed to the painted image and was initially a privilege of the nobility. However, the relative ease of photographic reproduction and the introduction of *cartes-de-visite* soon made photographic portraiture accessible to a wider public.[19] It was the union of photography and painting that resulted in an exciting new aesthetic, creating images that projected an enhanced or heightened reality. While paint had always been used to embellish black-and-white prints, in India this became a whole new art form.[20] Studios established systems whereby up to six artists were involved in the process of painting a photograph. Black-and-white images were richly decorated in bright colours until there was little or no evidence remaining of the photograph underneath. The face and costume were immaculately detailed and often completely new features were added, such as extra ornamentation and elaborate backdrops. The face and form were occasionally highlighted to meet the Indian canons of beauty, thus displaying a particularly Indian sensibility.[21] The final picture was a lavish, brightly coloured image and the care and attention taken to produce it was evidence of the significance attached to the process.

While photographs captured reality, overpainting can be seen as a means of embellishing and enhancing that reality. The most common painted photographic images were those of Indian princes and wealthy noblemen. Placed in the centre of the image, with appropriate backdrops, props, costume and overpainting, they were presented as regal, majestic figures. Isolated and elevated in this manner these images projected the wealth and status of the subject, but they also conveyed onto the subject the wealth and status associated with the production of the image itself – associations which, as described above, were transferred from oil painting to photography. Today, with the prevalence of colour photography, the practice is only still employed for the creation of memorial photographs. Here, existing black-and-white images of the deceased are coloured and embellished according to the wishes of their relatives, often with the addition of new elements. These painted images display a sense of 'hyper-reality, a solidification of certain features and an intensification of the gaze through the sharp reworking of the eyes'.[22] Overpainting, therefore, continues to be a means of heightening reality.

Diwakar Karkare, who was responsible for many of the posters that use the overpainting technique, aimed to convey this 'enhancing of reality' in his work. From 'Studio Diwakar', which he set up in 1965, he worked for all the best-known producers and directors, including B. R. Chopra, Yash Chopra, Raj Kapoor, Manmohan Desai and N. N. Sippy, and produced posters for such films as *Deewaar* (*The Wall*, directed by Yash Chopra, 1975), *Amar Akbar Anthony* (directed by Manmohan Desai, 1977) and *Silsila* (directed by Yash Chopra, 1981). A student of the Bombay School of Art, he sought to apply his knowledge of academic painting to poster art and developed a new style that changed the conventional concept of poster design. It was first employed in the poster for *Daag* (*The Stain*, directed by Yash Chopra, 1973). For Diwakar,[23] this experimentation with a new technique allowed him to bring something 'new and different' to the photographic image, enabling him to show emotions and enhance facial expressions. He believes that he was able to do this owing to his understanding of oil painting and his knowledge of the use of light, shade and depth in portraiture. Portraiture was for him the most important element of his work: while at school in the 1940s he had been inspired by the freedom movement to paint portraits of the nationalist leaders. His subsequent training and the influence of his teacher, also an academic portrait painter, meant that in his application of this training to poster art he aimed to elevate the status of this popular art form. This belief in his work as a form of art resulted in the closure of 'Studio Diwakar' in 1988, as he felt strongly that the increased use of computer technology within film advertising was displacing the artist, and that the new poster designs required no real artistic input. Diwakar returned to painting portraits and continues to do so today.

While conventional portraiture through the nineteenth century was concerned with the artist's ability and desire to convey the true identity of the person portrayed, to convey more than a mere likeness of the subject,[24] the aim of the poster artist is to project the 'mask' or the star's constructed identity. The photographic stills used by the artist also play their part in the process. Even more so than the poster artist, the stills photographer is always credited in the film booklet, thereby acknowledging the importance of this role. The 'look' of the star is created by the stills photographer through the images isolated during the making of the film. It is their images that capture the star's identity in relation to the defining moments of the film; these are often idealized images created through lighting and editing, and it is these that form the basis of the poster design. Thus, in the depictions of Bachchan on the posters of the 1970s and '80s we see a convergence of all of these

108 Diwakar Karkare, *Deewaar*, 1975, poster.

many processes and it is they that created and conferred many symbolic meanings on to this one iconic image. The techniques of oil painting, photography and overpainting were amalgamated to produce a richly textured image that highlighted the facial characteristics and emotional expressions constituting his 'mask' or star identity. The conventions of realism, centrality and 'frontal encounter', as mentioned above, 'closed the psychological gap between the subject and the viewer' and brought the gaze of the two together in what might be considered a form of *darshan*. This term is applied to a culturally rooted practice that describes the exchange of the mutual gaze between a worshipper and a deity (see also chapter One). While much could be made of this 'ocular interaction with the divine', particularly with the type of attention and reverence shown to Bachchan today, when expressed in relation to poster design it must be termed a 'secular *darshan*'.[25] This mixture of European and Indian techniques and conventions has together imparted status and authority on to the poster images, thereby presenting Bachchan as a majestic iconic figure - a prime example of which can be seen in the poster for *Deewaar* (illus. 108).

These images, however, relate to a specific period in Bachchan's career (the 1970s and '80s), and as he continues to act so contemporary representations further augment his persona, contributing to this ongoing process. Throughout much of the 1990s the technique of overpainting, with its historical associations, was gradually almost replaced by computer-generated imagery, by which photographic stills are manipulated on the screen to produce an ultra-modern, polished, clean, sharp image. This new technology brings its own associations of modernity and confers a new status to film imagery. This is conveyed on to Bachchan's image and so his persona is regenerated through these new modes of representation. That his image continues to be given a central position in a poster design is a reflection of his status, which is due to the longevity of his career and his continuing success within the industry. In comparison, the positioning of the star on a Hollywood poster is determined by contracts drawn up between the star's agents and lawyers and the film company well before filming starts. Financial agreements therefore determine which star has the primary position and how large their portrait will be in relation to the others.[26]

A star's portrait on a poster, therefore, is full of meaning. It not only serves to alert our attention to the poster but is also able to trigger a deeper level of recognition and understanding in those who have the appropriate cultural knowledge.

The Cultural Construction of Meaning

The star's portrait is often only one element of a poster design and is usually surrounded by a montage of images. Montage, first used in the Surrealist art movement, is a way of creating meaning through the juxtaposition and placing of images. It is possible to bring together into one frame isolated images that occupy separate spaces and separate times within the film. Placed on a plain background without any contextual scenery, the aim is not to present them as a unified image, as for example in a photographic still, but rather to build into the image the very concept of multiplicity – that these images were from many different spaces and many different times.[27] It was this that gave, and continues to give, the poster its dynamic nature.

The tool of montage is used by most film poster artists across the world, although there are cultural differences between India and the West in the way posters are constructed. In early Hollywood poster designs the characters were placed within the narrative of the film at a point of narrative enigma. Rather than presenting the beginning or end of the narrative they present a moment of narrative friction, which is supported substantially by the use of text.[28] Contemporary Western posters present a dramatic enigma that requires the public to see the film in order to discover the conclusion. The enigma is conveyed through the use of provocative images and text providing incomplete or paradoxical information about the film, thus teasing and enticing the public to go and see it.[29] Today, text in the form of quotations from media reviews of the film is commonly used to convey the 'media seal of approval' for a film. These have become a key feature of any public-ity campaign, serving not only to publicize the film but also to boost the status of the reviewer whose name appears on the poster.[30] More text, through the inclusion of the names of the film studio, producer and director, also reflects the status of the film. In contrast, Indian posters rarely use text. With the scale of national and international distribution enjoyed by the Indian film industry, text is seen as a cultural barrier. On early posters the title and the names of the stars would appear prominently in English, with the Hindi and Urdu titles in smaller lettering nearby. From the 1980s onwards it has been more common for only the title of the film and the names of the producer, director and music director to be included, and printed solely in English. To the public, these three figures are a marker of the style, content and quality of the film, and stress the importance of music to its success. Occasionally the names of the actors are included, but the more well known the actor, the less need to print the name.

The minimal use of text highlights how these posters communicate primarily through the recognition of visual images. Therefore, unlike Western posters' use of image and text to present an enigma, Indian posters convey the familiarity of the form and content of the Indian film. The imagery used reflects the culturally determined conventions of film, such as the circular narrative, the incorporation of a range of emotions, the blending of the song and dance spectacle along with fight sequences into the narrative and the different 'types' or archetypes of character. All of these are key components of what has come to be termed the 'formula' or *masala* film, a genre that started to develop in the post-war period and today defines Indian cinema. Posters depict either a few different elements from this *masala*, thereby reflecting the main theme of the film, or they incorporate all of them into one image reflecting its all-inclusiveness. A key device for a poster to indicate that the film does include all these various elements is through the depiction of emotions. Thus, images of kissing couples, men fighting or sorrowful faces are easily and universally understood and aptly convey such themes as romance and action.[31] While this was the dominant trend in film posters up to the 1990s, however, more recent poster designs focus on one element of the narrative, such as the romance, and choose to project that as the main theme. This implies that these posters are more universally understood than those of the past, but a consequence of this universality is that they convey less information about the culture in which they are produced.

Character Types

Other key components of the Indian film include character 'types'; these, however, are not universally recognized and when depicted on posters are only fully understood by those with a knowledge of that culture.

Indian film is understood through the familiarity of its narrative and the familiarity of its characters. Characters are depicted as social types who are defined by their differences to each other. Thus good characters will be set against bad, rich against poor, weak against strong and traditional against modern. These oppositional structures form the basis of characterization, resulting in typical roles such as the long-suffering mother, the wife, the vamp, the good brother, the bad brother and the villain.[32] Their character traits are easily recognizable and often transfer from one film to the next. Part of the process is to cast the same actor in the same role type and in doing so they trigger the public's recognition, as was seen above through the analysis of Bachchan's character. The symbiotic relationship between the actor and the character means that the public is equally familiar with both and transfers meanings and associations from one to the other. Thus, when a viewer sees the image of a star on a poster, they immediately recognize both the star and the character, as well as all the social and moral associations that go with that role. Consequently film posters use the viewer's familiarity with character types as a code with which to convey a greater sense of the theme of the film.

The operation of these cultural codes can be seen in another poster for *Deewaar* (illus. 109). The familiarity of narrative and recognition of stars enables the poster to convey a complex message. In the first instance, the viewer's attention is drawn to the poster through the use of bright colours and through inclusion of Bachchan's portrait. His hooded eyes and full lips make his 'angry young man' persona immediately recognizable. Furthermore, placing him at the top of this pyramidal structure reinforces his star status. The older woman would be recognized as a typical long-suffering mother, a character type that projects her as an idealized image of a woman whose purpose in life is to care for her son. She is willing to sacrifice herself for the good of her family name, and becomes a symbol of suffering. Her desire is to be saved from her suffering by her son, and for him in turn to maintain or gain her approval, and thus to be saved by her.[33] The mother assumes the role of moral judge. Accordingly the inclusion of the mother figure in the poster almost automatically implies a filial or similar type of relationship between the two male portraits. A classic theme of Indian cinema is the lost-and-found theme (particularly during the 1970s).[34] Usually this involves the early separation of two brothers who grow up in totally different environments, from which they develop into people with opposing characteristics, thus falling into the oppositional structures of good/bad, strong/weak, traditional/modern, rich/poor. The final scene brings them into confrontation in some way, leading to their reconciliation and a resolution to the narrative. The poster is able to convey this filial relationship owing to the viewer's familiarity with the oppositional structure of archetypal characters within Indian film. This, along with the viewer's recognition of Bachchan in his 'angry young man' role set against the softer, more tender expression of the other portrait, serves to reinforce this filial relationship. Similarly, the two female figures become associated with the two men as wives or girlfriends because of their associated character types as well as their positioning in the poster.

The good/bad brother relationship has furthermore been seen as a means of addressing the good/bad characteristics of one person that within the Indian film medium may manifest themselves through two characters – a device known as 'splitting' or 'doubling'. In the case of *Deewaar*, Bachchan's face has been split in two by colouring one half

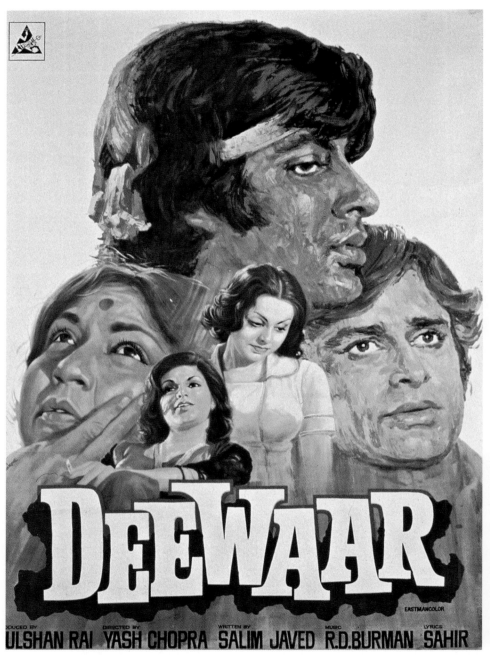

109 Diwakar Karkare, *Deewaar*, 1975, poster.

110 Diwakar Karkare, *Deewaar*, 1975, poster.

in reds and pinks and the other in shades of blue (illus. 110). While the artist, Diwakar Karkare, may not be aware of the 'splitting' device as used in the film, he has suggested that the light tones can be said to represent goodness and the dark shades represent vicious or bad qualities.[35] He used the same device in an earlier poster for *Sagina* (directed by J. K. Kapoor, 1974). Colour is therefore a means of communicating information and is one of the most flexible ways of achieving a variety of effects, such as attracting attention to the poster or creating a sense of scale and distance. There is systematic use of colour to indicate mood, in very general terms, including red for passion and green or other dark hues for evil. Colour is not, however, a means of applying symbolic meaning to images.[36]

Female Character Types

Female character types also commonly feature on (usually pre-1990) film posters. Their visual representations are split into a dual structure whereby the qualities of the 'traditional' Indian woman are opposed to those of the 'modern' Westernized woman. This oppositional structure was a product of both nineteenth-century orientalist thought and the Independence movement.[37] At a time when criticism levelled by Christian and Utilitarian thinkers at the degenerate state of Indian society focused on the treatment and status of its women, the orientalists constructed an identity for the Hindu woman based on textual sources of the past, such as the Vedas, Puranas and the epics. This highlighted a golden age for India in which women were seen to possess an equal status to men. They were valued for their intellect and as religious companions to their husbands, they were pious, devoted to their family, refined and cultured.[38] For the Nationalists, this glorification of Indian womanhood located in the ancient past fitted with their search for an 'authentic Indian' identity; and as a nationalist construct this identity existed in opposition to Western culture and therefore modernity, which was seen to be inherent to it. Hence the 'traditional' was set against the 'modern' and it was this oppositional structure that was translated into film.

On posters this opposition manifests itself through the clothes and accessories worn by the women. This clearly defines their character types and function as a code or language with which to identify them.[39] Women depicted in saris or rural/tribal costume with their hair tied back neatly are seen to play their traditional roles as virgin, wife and mother and are expected to possess all the moral values associated with the ideal Indian woman. An example of this can be seen in the poster for *Devdas* (directed by Bimal Roy, 1955) on which there are two female characters, one of whom is a prostitute (illus. 111). Both are wearing saris, but one is depicted with her hair neatly tied back while the other has loose hair falling over her shoulder, thus projecting the difference in their character types. The majority of the images of women on posters are shown in saris, which indicates the typical nature of the heroine to be found in Indian films. Depictions of the female portrait also feature significantly, and here the influence of the

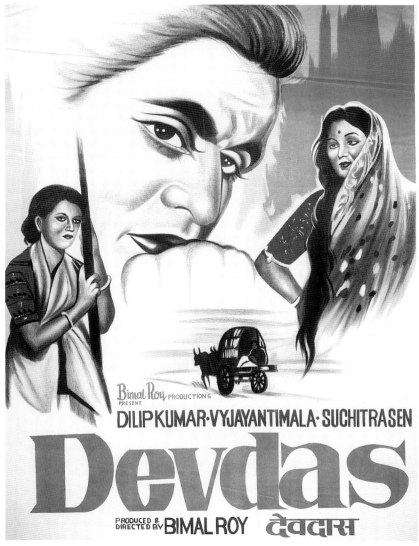

111 *Devdas*, 1955, poster.

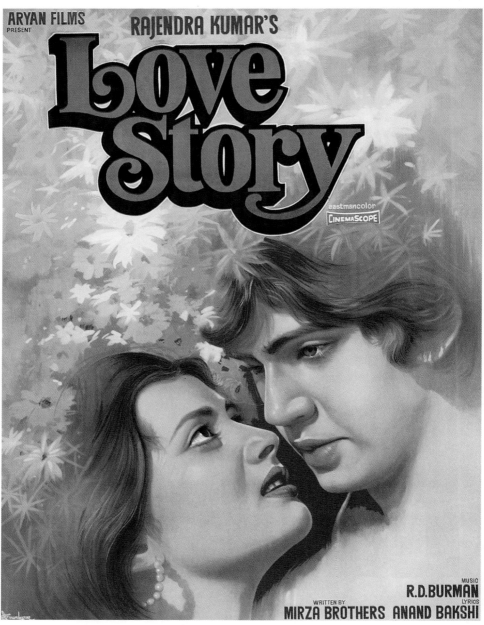

112 Diwakar Karkare, *Love Story*, 1985, poster.

113 *Umrao Jaan*, poster, 1981.

114 *Patthar ki Lakeer*, 1982, booklet cover.

painter Ravi Varma and his creation of an image representing the ideal figure of Indian womanhood is evident (see chapter Three). Thus, as seen in the poster for *Love Story* (illus. 112), *Uphaar* (directed by Sudhendu Roy, 1971) and *Devi* (directed by Madhusudan Rao V, 1970), among others, pale skin, elongated lotus-petal eyes and rosebud lips are embellished through overpainting to conform to the nationalist fair-skinned Aryan model of Indian beauty.[40]

115 Meera Prabhu, *Nehle peh Dehlaa*, 1976, poster.

In contrast, women depicted in Western costumes, including dresses, short skirts and bikinis, and often accompanied by other Western attributes such as short hair, are regarded as 'modern' in character with all the moral values associated with a modern or Western lifestyle. They are projected either as misguided young women enjoying the 'folly of youth', who eventually revert to their traditional roles, or as

116 *Satyam Shivam Sundaram*, 1978, poster.

vamps. Thus, on the booklet cover for *Patthar ki Lakeer* (1982), we see a young woman dressed in a bikini surrounded by male portraits of different ages, all of whom direct their gaze towards her body (illus. 114). The recent trend of dressing young film stars in Western designer clothes is also a signifier of modernity; here, however, despite the revealing nature of the costumes, the focus is not on female sexuality but on youth and romance. An extreme example of woman as vamp can be seen in the poster for *Nehle peh Dehlaa* (*One Up-manship*, directed by Raj Khosla, 1976; illus. 115). Here all that is seen is a pair of legs, clad in Western stockings and glimpsed through a revealing red skirt. The playing cards pushed into the tops of her stockings and the gun are all indicators of the illicit nature of her actions, which are associated with the West through the clothes she is depicted in. Representations of women in Western clothes, as in this case, are also often an overt expression of sexuality and are usually associated with Western immorality.

Sexuality, however, is not only seen in representations of 'modern' women, for it also appears in the posters for, among others, *Satyam Shivam Sundaram* (*Love, Truth and Beauty*, or *Love Sublime*, directed by Raj Kapoor, 1978; illus. 116), *Sargam* (*Musical Note*, directed by K. Vishwanath, 1979) and *Aasha* (directed by J. Om Prakash, 1980). While the depiction of the sexualized female form has been an integral part of classical Indian art, the perception of it has proved problematic in later years. Sculptural and painted images, from goddesses and celestial figures to *yakshis* (dancers) and *nayikas* (courtesans), have through the ages been depicted as sensuous and voluptuous women. Early criticism of these sexualized images with their 'inappropriate and vulgar' eroticism was counteracted by a post-Independence justification that focused instead on their aesthetic value, as well as their Indianness, which bestowed on them a spiritual and symbolic meaning. Hence the 'aesthetic and the symbolic function as key rhetorical devices in the imaging of this whole range of bare-bodied female figures, blurring the divide between the divine and the non-divine, between goddesses and earthly women'.[41] Arguments linking expressions of sexuality to the 'Indian tradition' were also used to justify representations of female forms as seen on particular film posters. An extreme example of an overtly sexual image can be seen in the poster for *Satyam Shivam Sundaram*. Here the rural costume is seen as a means of revealing a sexuality that is projected as a natural part of everyday rural life. The sexual imagery is reinforced by the poster design, which alludes to the classic religious imagery of Krishna and Radha and the story of Krishna as the divine lover who steals the clothes of the *gopis* (milkmaids) and watches from a nearby tree as they bathe in the river.

Images of dancers also highlight the sexuality of the female form. Here the costumes accentuate their breasts and hips, focusing attention on their bodies, but this display of sexuality is acceptable because it is integral to their dance performance and dance is regarded as a classical art form. However, where the dance costume is Western, such as

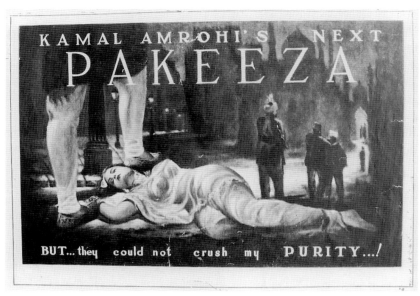

117 Back cover of booklet for *Daaera* (1953) showing an early advertisement for *Pakeezah*.

a cabaret costume, displays of sexuality are unacceptable. The equation of sexuality with tradition is epitomized in the figure of the courtesan. Two of the most important films in this genre are *Pakeezah* (*Pure Heart*, directed by Kamal Amrohi, 1972) and *Umrao Jaan* (directed by Muzaffar Ali, 1981). In the booklet for *Pakeezah* we are given an explanation of what these women stand for. Known as *tawaifs*, they are regarded as being of a much higher status than the Western term 'prostitute' allows for. The booklet projects them as representing a tradition and a form of cultural institution, and their existence is traced back to ancient India where they are mentioned in texts and were used as informers by the administrators, thus placing them 'at the centre of politics and culture for centuries and centuries'. 'As late as the early 19th century ... it was the *tawaifs* who knew the intricacies of culture and the delicacies of language and poetry. Usually ... they were more than well versed in Hindi, Urdu, Persian, Oudhi and Brij poetry ...'. The booklet emphasizes that she is not in the sexual market and that she is 'almost a one-man woman'. This underlying contradiction between the impurity of her actions and the purity of her soul is not only made apparent in the title but also in an early advertisement for the film,[42] which uses a particularly dramatic image to symbolize the exploitation of her body, while emphasizing her internal turmoil, through the caption 'But ... they could not crush my purity' (illus. 117). Thus, while the cultural significance of the courtesan is highlighted, her profession places her on the outskirts of society, making her a highly vulnerable figure. Visual representations of the courtesan on posters (illus. 113) and booklets depict her in her elaborate and heavily embroidered dance costume, fully adorned with jewellery from the ornaments in her hair to the rings on her fingers, and with her hands and feet stained with red *mehndi* (henna). Dressed in this way and set against the scenery of grand palace settings (*Umrao Jaan* is set within the nawabi culture of nineteenth-century Lucknow), the courtesan is associated with wealth, luxury and refined society. These images are therefore a reminder of a once glorious and cultured past and focus on the courtesan's body as a signifier of tradition rather than a signifier of immorality.

Sexuality has therefore always been a part of the aesthetic process that has defined female identity. However, in these depictions the mode of representation creates images that have been criticized for sexually objectifying the female body. Here, too, the images of Ravi Varma have played a defining role. His realist technique emphasized the physicality of the female form, it 'reworked the nature of female sexuality in art and offered artists a new way of playing on the sexual temptation of the half-clothed female figure ...'. The mass reproduction of his work led to distortions of his original paintings and resulted in a vulgarity defined by an excess of colour, a flattening of depth and crudely suggestive female figures, in which 'realism was played out mainly in a sense of volume, in a sensuous accentuation of body contours, and in a strategic emphasis on swelling breasts and hips beneath layers of drapery'.[43] It is these elements that were transferred to popular prints and film imagery. A consequence of the realism of these images and their proliferation through mass reproduction has been their increased accessibility to the male gaze that implies a sense of possession of the subject.[44] It is because of this that sexual objectification becomes the defining characteristic within these images.

Since the beginning of the 1990s, however, the oppositional structures and dramatic distinction in female character types are no longer manifested through the type of clothes worn. The move away from the *masala* films to those defined by family, romance and love has seen a shift away from scenes of overt sexuality and violence to scenes of affluence, characterized by nice homes, cars, fashionable clothes and consumer goods. These films present a safe, middle-class, family-orientated world where the ideals of Indian culture and tradition are evoked[45] and where affluence is projected as a legitimate force for the preservation of Indian culture, religion and tradition. Here the young middle-class women are free to wear sexy Western designer clothes without any implied judgement as to morality and, though these are replaced by more traditional clothes after marriage, the poster depictions tend to focus on the heroines in their Western clothes (see illus. 40). Thus the representation of women in modern Western clothing is no longer a projection of immorality but rather a projection of an 'aspired-to' middle-class Utopian lifestyle.

Through the images and techniques used, posters, booklets and other forms of advertising are thus able to convey both simple messages and more complex cultural meanings about the society in which they are produced. Yet it is also possible for these images to project other meanings when appropriated and manipulated by other agencies, and this aspect is next explored.

Changes of Meaning: Popular Culture and Fine Artists

The dynamic nature of the film industry and the imagery it produces has influenced a range of fine artists who have observed and reinterpreted it in their work. Artists' responses to this most prominent element of public culture vary from highly critical, as seen in the work of Annu Palakunnathu Matthew and Gulam Mohammed Sheikh, to the celebratory work of Maqbool Fida Husain and Doug Aitken. In all these instances, however, it is the ubiquitous nature of the medium that has provoked such emotive responses.

In a series of works entitled *Bollywood Satirised*, Annu Matthew explores the position of women in Indian society and addresses the issues of arranged marriages, the dowry system, discrimination based on skin colour and inter-racial relationships. The series is both a response to her own personal experience of life in India (she was born in England, raised in India and now lives in the USA) and to the fantasy world created by the film industry. Matthew appropriates the most archetypal images used in film posters, with all their inherent meanings, and through the use of computer technology and the technique of montage she alters and reassembles them, juxtaposing them with text to create new meaning and critical comment. Her work takes the form of a pastiche of the film poster: thus not only are the imagery, typography and scale of the poster being mimicked, but their ephemeral quality is also projected through the deliberate and strategic damaging of the finished work, by folding, creasing and ripping, and by pasting it onto external walls over layers of old and peeling posters. This pastiche provides a fitting means through which to pass judgement on the happy romantic world of the Indian cinema, particularly its creation of an Aryan ideal of Indian womanhood, an ideal that automatically implies an imperfect opposite – the dark-skinned woman. In a piece entitled *Fair and Lovely* (illus. 118) Matthew uses portraits of herself as a dark-skinned child set against images of fair-skinned film stars. These images are superimposed with text that reads 'Don't play in the sun ... you'll get dark and no one will marry you'. Similarly in *Kala Patti* the theme is echoed with the words 'As a woman, you can be dark and rich, or you can be fair and poor, but you can't be dark and poor and expect to get a good catch', thus highlighting the discriminatory views and value systems that Indian society imposes on its women. Here, as in much of Matthew's work, the subversion of meaning is achieved through the inclusion of substantial amounts of text.

Matthew's exploration of the subjugation of women also addresses the variety of extreme acts of violence against them. In *The Acid Thrower* (illus. 119) the artist highlights the plight of women who have been the victims of acid attacks, the desired effect being to disfigure their faces and bodies, making them undesirable to anyone else and outcasts to society. Matthew projects this brutality by using the imagery and technique typical of posters from the 1970s, a period known for the introduction of violence into the film formula (discussed in chapter Three). Thus she includes a large-scale male portrait with an overly aggressive expression rendered in an overpainted effect and surrounded by many smaller images, some of which are of a violent nature. The giant typography is also characteristic of the period and the message is further reinforced through the use of text. Matthew's work therefore serves to reflect the reality of an unjust society that exists behind the 'ideal moral universe' of the Indian film, and by using a product of the medium itself to achieve this she invests these images with new meanings and forces audiences to look at them anew.

The highly critical stance taken by Annu Matthew is echoed in a work by Gulam Mohammed Sheikh. In *City for Sale* (illus. 120) Sheikh explores the urban environment of the city of Baroda in which he lives. Completed between 1981 and 1984, the painting is a response to two factors: the release of the film *Silsila* and the communal riots that broke out across what is regarded as a 'city of culture'. For Sheikh these 'two events constituted the heights of vulgarity and violence: shameless profiteering from the public display of privacy and collective carnage'.[46] At the time Sheikh was commenting on how cinema had become central to Indian life and synonymous with culture. The magazines and newspapers were full of gossip about the alleged adulterous affair between Amitabh Bachchan and Rekha. *Silsila* reflected that triangle and even had Bachchan's wife, Jaya Bhaduri, return to the

118 Annu Palakunnathu Matthew, *Fair and Lovely* from the 'Bollywood Satirised' series, designjet computer print, 1998.

119 Annu Palakunnathu Matthew, *The Acid Thrower* from the 'Bollywood Satirised' series, luminage digital print, 2000.

120 Gulam Mohammed Sheikh, *City for Sale*, 1980–84, oil on canvas.
Victoria & Albert Museum, London.

screen to play the role of his wife. Scenes in the film appeared to fuel
the gossip columns, thereby encouraging people to see the film as well
as investing in the continued construction of the stars' identities. It
was this playing out of their private lives on the public screen and the
commercial gains made from it that Sheikh objected to. He therefore
made it the focus of his painting. At the centre of the large canvas he
has depicted the inside of a cinema, and showing on the cinema screen
is the climactic scene from the film in which the wife comes face to
face with her husband and his mistress. While the film itself did not
dwell on that particular scene, it still became famous and was
depicted on record covers and magazines.

Outside the cinema, in front of the screen, is a hoarding painter
who is caught in the process of completing a portrait of Rekha by filling in her eyes. Sheikh has intimated that the image is partly
biographical, in that he sees himself as the painter and that it also
alludes to the Jadu painters of Bengal.[47] These are said to have the
power of bestowing sight to the recently deceased, who are believed
to be wondering blind in the other world. The Jadu painters visit the
deceased relatives, taking with them incomplete paintings of human
images, which are then completed in front of the relatives by filling
in the eyes.[48] Here, the painting-in of Rekha's eyes can be regarded as
a metaphor for the opening of her eyes to the blindness of fame and to

the reality of the world beyond the film set: a ritual opening of the eyes that Sheikh, as the artist both outside and within the picture frame, has initiated. That this depiction of the cinema is surrounded by, and juxtaposed with, complexly structured images of the city and the riots highlights both the harsh realities of urban life and the shallow fantasy world of film.

The criticism offered by Sheikh and Matthew is counteracted by the work of Doug Aitken and M. F. Husain. Both artists use the medium of film to explore film. Both explore the world between film and reality, and the relationship between film and the audience. For Husain, one of India's most important contemporary artists, it is the ability of film to transform reality and create fantasy that fascinates him. Husain's involvement with the industry has been long, since on arriving in Bombay in the late 1930s he supplemented his income by painting cinema hoardings. The experience of painting on such a large scale and the skill required to express and communicate to mass audiences has remained with him. Through his film *Gaja Gamini* (2000) his desire is once again to communicate to the masses his vision of a union between art and the cinematic medium. Accordingly the film is a space 'where the sets were not sets in the regular sense ... but were art installations – where the artist interprets ideas, reality and illusion ... and where all the elements, including the actors and actresses and even the dialogues, become an intrinsic part of the work of art, filtered through the very personal and very unique artists vision ...'.[49] The film itself is an exploration of womanhood spanning a period of 5,000 years. Within this there are parallels with the work of Ravi Varma. While Varma searched for and created an ideal figure of Indian womanhood, Husain's vision was more universal. He sees the film as a means of exploring woman as metaphor and doing this through the presentation of many archetypal women who are individual figures but are also encompassed within one ideal woman. Thus the actress Madhuri Dixit is the one who transforms herself into many women but is ultimately epitomized as the 'one eternal enigmatic woman who keeps her place in the world of men'.[50] Husain's vision is inspired by his discovery of Madhuri. His fascination with her, reported extensively in the press, resulted in a series of paintings, which he then had reproduced as prints to make them accessible to a wider public (although as limited edition fine art prints they are not as accessible as Varma's oleographs). For Husain, therefore, the medium of film enables mass accessibility to his creation of womanhood and his belief in the union of art and cinema.

The ability of film to communicate to the masses is also explored by Doug Aitken. He sees the Bombay film industry as 'the place where

"into the sun" ♦ **doug aitken**

7 october to 12 november 1999

private view wednesday 6 october 1999

victoria miro gallery 21 cork street london w1x 1hb

tel: 0171 734 5082 fax: 0171 494 1787 e-mail: vicmir@dircon.co.uk

121 Poster for the installation "into the sun" by Doug Aitken at the Victoria Miro Gallery, London, 1999.

perfect communication between film and the audience is achieved'.[51] The sheer scale and output of the industry, the way in which film permeates all aspects of everyday life, and particularly the way in which the medium feeds the desires and fantasies of millions of people, is a fascinating phenomenon to observe. While Husain has created a fantasy, Aitken, who unlike Husain is an outsider looking in, is interested in the components that manufacture the fantasy and the way in which the audience is totally immersed in that world. Aitken's film installation *"into the sun"* is itself constructed from those components (illus. 121). The film is projected against all four walls of a room. These are covered in white canvas to give the effect of a film backdrop or stage set,[52] while the floor is covered with Indian sand to add to the stage set or makeshift atmosphere. Aitken's film is constructed from hundreds of stills showing publicity shots, the stars, the extras, the sets, advertising posters and crowds watching the making of a film, which are then re-filmed into a continuous reel, the different speeds of filming resulting in a flickering screen that imparts a dreamlike or magical quality to the show. This is accompanied by a soundtrack consisting of film music, street sounds, traffic and crowd noises. With this installation Aitken has created an experience in which viewers are totally immersed. From the sand underneath their feet, to the sound and vision that encloses them, and through to the allusion of fantasy created by the flickering screen, the experience echoes the all-encompassing nature of the film industry. His work, like that of the other artists, is therefore a reflection of the vibrancy of the cinematic medium, its transformative qualities, dynamic imagery, effects on society, complexity and its power.

Conclusion

From its very inception, Hindi film and its associated visual culture has been a hybrid product, adapting, incorporating and responding to a diverse range of influences. The most recent development, discussed in the preceding chapters, is the move away from films dominated by violence and themes of revenge to those with themes of family, love and romance, set among the élite groups. Visually this change is reflected in the increasingly sophisticated 'look' of the film, which uses modern locations often associated with consumerist lifestyles, such as shopping malls, clubs and loft-style apartments, and by integrating Western and Indian designer clothes, which are emphasized in new forms of slick, stylish, Western-inspired advertising.

As this book shows, the visual culture of Hindi film responds to and reflects changes in economic, political, social and ideological structures in contemporary society. This is true of the recent changes, which mark a significant shift in those structures. It is in the process of globalization that we are able to locate those structural shifts. Globalization has 'shrunk the distance between élites, shifted key relations between producers and consumers, broken many links between labour and family, obscured the lines between temporary locales and imaginary national attachments',[1] and as such has been seen as a homogenizing force where cultures are subsumed by 'Americanization' or 'McDonaldization'. However, this definition is limiting and simplistic. Rather, it needs to be seen as a series of complex, overlapping, disjunctive, global cultural flows of people, information, technology, finance, and ideology.[2] These cultural flows, their interactions and relationships help us to understand the underlying processes behind the production of Hindi film today.

While the interconnection between these cultural flows makes them collectively important in the film-making process, it is the flows of information that have the greatest bearing on the film's visual culture. Disseminated through newspapers, magazines, cable and satellite television, cinema and the Internet, audiences around the globe receive and experience a large, constant, complex and interconnected supply of images from around the globe. Here the 'world of commodities and the world of news and politics are profoundly mixed'.[3] It is these globally mobile images that inform those who are now making Hindi films. The past decade has thus seen the emergence of a younger generation of directors, writers, musicians, choreographers, art directors, editors, stylists, distributors and publicists who have been 'raised on Hollywood but firmly grounded in Bollywood',[4] resulting in films that are a 'clever cocktail of *desi* (local) values draped in Yankee slickness'.[5] To viewers these films project ultramodern affluent lifestyles filled with glamour and excitement. This is a lifestyle where gender rules are relaxed, women have greater freedom, and where young people live in a society in which boys and girls mix freely and frequent bars and clubs. It is a consumerist lifestyle enjoyed by the middle or upper-middle classes,[6] a new social group rich in economic capital and with a new spending power, especially among the young. This class has different patterns of consumption and leisure from the older middle classes and forms an important part of those attending film showings, as well as engaging with a wider range of media associated with the cinema, such as film magazines, satellite and cable channels and Internet sites. However, while films project this lifestyle (one that on a global level is only shared by the few and is unobtainable to most, but is desirable and aspired to by many), they still maintain their distinct Hindi film structure through their continued use of the song and dance sequences and their projection of traditional cultural and religious values. It is this unique combination that has resulted in the success of Hindi film with a new audience; that of the Asian diaspora.[7]

Over the last ten years Hindi films have been attracting ever larger audiences, particularly from the growing diasporic communities in the West. During the 1960s and '70s Britain saw the screening of Hindi films on Sunday mornings and at 'off-peak' times.[8] This was displaced by the arrival of the home video in the 1980s, which also saw a reduction in Western audiences attending cinemas during this period. The Asian video market went into decline in the 1990s on account of the introduction of Asian cable and satellite television channels and the practice of 'video-holdback'. Simultaneously, during this period Western audiences, including those in the UK, began to return to the cinemas due in part to the rise of new multiplex cinemas. This in turn left many smaller cinemas redundant and those in areas with a high Asian population were taken over by Indian film distributors. Indian film makers have found that one of their most important markets is now overseas, less in terms of numbers than in the actual financial returns, since the low exchange value of the Indian rupee means that a single ticket can cost more than ten times the cost of a ticket in India. There is also the additional benefit to the makers of earning foreign exchange to finance further overseas work. Some of the film makers have consciously attempted to make films that appeal to this diasporic market, by celebrating a notion of Indianness that is not dependent on being an Indian citizen but on upholding 'Indian values'. Subhash Ghai's *Pardes* (*Overseas*, 1998), with its songs such as 'I love my India', celebrates the 'purity' of Indian women, showing the West to be a source of possible corruption. The diasporic Indian, or NRI (non-resident Indian), has now become a stock feature in many films, no longer a young man who returns 'corrupted' but ready to be purified by the love of an innocent Indian woman, but just as a character who has the means to travel and embodies globalization. In *Dilwale Dulhania Le Jayenge* (*The Brave Heart Will Take the Bride*, directed by Aditya Chopra, 1995) the NRI hero is more determined to uphold traditional Indian values than his elders or the local Punjabi men. Thus Indian cinema has gone through a period of resurgence and Hindi film has re-established itself not only with the older diasporic audiences but more importantly with the next generation.

With this younger age group, the style of the film has much to do with its success; hence the 'characters are modern, not filmi. Anything filmi is out, anyone filmi is out.'[9] The 'filmi' style, which defined the visual culture of the Hindi film up to the 1990s (and which has been the focus of this book), is a thing of the past and is considered to be the very antithesis of the new 'look'. It is the new globally defined visual culture that has played a large part in the success of these films. With their new slick and sophisticated look they have a greater appeal than the films of the past and reflect a world with which this group is more familiar; for their part they lead the consumerist lifestyle seen in the films, acquire similar clothes and aspire to inhabit similar bars and clubs, and they identify with the new heroes and heroines with their young toned bodies. It is an appeal based on a globally shared visual culture that projects affluence and modernity.

While this global visual culture has succeeded in engaging the diasporic audience, there is a certain irony that, as 'filmi style' is being discarded by the Hindi film industry, this is the means by which it is finally gaining the recognition it has long sought in the West. Since around 2000 'Bollywood' has become a buzz word in the West, recognized and celebrated as denoting the flamboyant attractions of the Hindi movie. A form of hybrid music has entered the record charts and film images are projected on walls in clubs across the UK. The song and dance sequences, the melodramatic style and the opulent costumes are celebrated and parodied on television shows such as prime time's 'Goodness Gracious Me!'. Despite the increased familiarity with 'Bollywood', however, the films themselves are finding it hard to reach out beyond the South Asian diasporic audience. An exception has been

Lagaan (*Once upon a Time in India*, directed by Ashutosh Gowariker, 2001), which has succeeded in attracting Western audiences. This has been attributed to the fact that through its projection of the Raj it has a Western story line, allowing audiences an easy access point into Hindi film. The film still maintained the distinct style and attractions of the Hindi film, including the star and the song and dance routines, while incorporating new attractions such as the deployment of a cricket match as spectacle. In a bid to capitalize on this Western and diasporic interest, the film *Asoka* (directed by Santosh Shivan, 2001) has just received an unprecedented degree of marketing in the UK. It has been well reviewed by the mainstream press and shown in central London cinemas. Its posters can be seen on public transport across London and advertisements have been placed in mainstream newspapers and magazines. It did not, however, fare well at the box office. Thus the visual culture of Hindi film is becoming (and in the year 2002 is set to become)[10] ever more visible, and it is its unique nature, its ability to incorporate both global influences and maintain its distinct Indian style, that appeals to both local and global audiences.

References

Introduction

1 Satyajit Ray, *Our Films, Their Films* (New Delhi, 1976), p. 19.
2 *Ibid.*, p. 23.
3 See the Introduction to Rachel Dwyer and Christopher Pinney, eds, *Pleasure and the Nation: The History, Politics and Consumption of Public Culture in India* (New Delhi, 2000).
4 See Rosie Thomas, 'Indian Cinema: Pleasure and Popularity' in *Screen*, XXVI/3–4 (1985), pp. 116–32. While Thomas and others argue that the specific form of Indian cinema may be attributed to its origins in the folk/oral traditions of India, M. Madhava Prasad argues that this 'culturally specific form' is determined by the political structure and capitalist industry of the society in which it is produced and marketed (*Ideology of the Hindi Film*, New Delhi, 1998, pp. 15–16).
5 See W. Dissanayake and M. Sahai, *Sholay: A Cultural Reading* (New Delhi, 1992).
6 Ravi Vasudevan, 'The Politics of Cultural Address in a "Transitional" Cinema: A Case Study of Popular Indian Cinema', in *Reinventing Film Studies*, ed. C. Gledhill and L. Williams (London, 2000), p.133.
7 These include Erik Barnouw and S. Krishnaswamy, *Indian Film* (Oxford, 1980) and B. D. Garga, *So Many Cinemas* (Mumbai, 1996).
8 Ashish Rajadhyaksha and Paul Willemen, *Encyclopaedia of Indian Cinema* (Oxford, 1999).
9 These include Sumita S. Chakravarty, *National Identity in Indian Popular Cinema 1947–1987* (New Delhi, 1996); see also M. Madhava Prasad, *op. cit.*, and Yves Thoraval, *Les cinémas de l'Inde* (Paris, 1998).

1 Indian Cinema

Some parts of this chapter draw on Rachel Dwyer, *All You Want is Money, All You Need is Love* (London, 2000) chapter 4.

1 The key works on the history of Indian cinema are Erik Barnouw and S. Krishnaswamy, *Indian Film*, 2nd edn (New York, 1980); Ashish Rajadhyaksha's articles 'Indian Cinema: Origins to Independence' and 'India: Filming the Nation' in *The Oxford History of World Cinema*, ed. G. Nowell-Smith (Oxford, 1996), pp. 398–409, 678–89; and Ashish Rajadhyaksha and Paul Willemen, *An Encyclopaedia of Indian Cinema*, 2nd edn (Oxford, 1999).
2 On Phalke's work and his background see Ashish Rajadhyaksha, 'The Phalke Era: Conflict of Traditional Form and Modern Technology', in *Interrogating Modernity: Culture and Colonialism in India*, ed. T. Niranjana *et al.* (Calcutta, 1993), pp. 47–82.
3 Many of the film companies, despite their *swadeshi* or nationalist ideologies, used highly orientalized names. See Barnouw and Krishnaswamy, *Indian Film*, pp. 36–7.
4 Partha Chatterjee, *Nationalist Thought and the Colonial World: A Derivative Discourse?* (London, 1986).
5 Rajadhyaksha, 'The Phalke Era'.
6 Rajadhyaksha, 'The Phalke Era'.

7   On this theatre see Anuradha Kapur, 'The Representation of Gods and
    Heroes: Parsi Mythological Drama of the Early Twentieth Century', in
    Journal of Arts and Ideas, 23–4 (1993), pp. 85–107, and Kathryn Hansen,
    Grounds for Play: The Nautanki Theatre of North India (Berkeley, 1992) and
    her 'The *Inder Sabha* Phenomenon: Public Theatre and Consumption in
    Greater India (1953–1956)', in *Pleasure and the Nation: The History,
    Consumption and Politics of Public Culture in India*, ed. R. Dwyer and
    C. Pinney (New Delhi, 2000), pp. 76–114.

8   For more on the visuality of theatre and the relationship between cinema and
    the other new industrial arts see chapter Two below.

9   The personnel were not all Parsis, but included many Muslims and Anglo-
    Indians (Hansen, *Grounds for Play*, p. 80).

10 For an autobiographical account of the Bengali theatre see Binodini Dasi,
    My Story and *My Life as an Actress*, ed. and trans. R. Bhattacharya (New
    Delhi, 1998).

11 See Kapur, 'The Representation of Gods and Heroes'.

12 Yves Thoraval, *Les cinémas de l'Inde* (Paris, 1998), p. 21.

13 The Germans who worked with Bombay Talkies, Franz Osten and Joseph
    Wirschung, were not the only Europeans working in the Indian film industry.
    Other foreigners included the American Ellis R. Duncan and the Australian
    'Fearless Nadia'.

14 Film production centred on Bombay, Poona and Calcutta. Tamil films were
    not made in Madras until 1935.

15 Vasudevan, 'The Politics of Cultural Address in a "Transitional" Cinema:
    A Case Study of Popular Indian Cinema', in *Reinventing Film Studies*, ed.
    C. Gledhill and L. Williams (London, 2000), p. 133.

16 Kesavan takes this term from Marshall Hodgson's *Venture of Islam*, saying it
    'would refer not directly to the religion, Islam, itself, but to the social and
    cultural complex historically associated with Islam and the Muslims, both
    among Muslims themselves and even when found among non-Muslims'
    (Mukul Kesavan, 'Urdu, Awadh and the tawaif: The Islamicate Roots of Hindi
    Cinema', in *Forging Identities: Gender, Communities and the State*, ed.
    Z. Hassan (New Delhi, 1994), p. 246).

17 State governments also taxed the film industry, although some assisted film
    makers, such as the Government of West Bengal, which helped Satyajit Ray.

18 Barnouw and Krishnaswamy, *Indian Film*, pp. 207–14.

19 See below.

20 Madhava Prasad, *Ideology of the Hindi Film: A Historical Construction*
    (New Delhi, 1998).

21 *Ibid.*, p.118. He discusses these at length in chapters 8, 7 and 6 respectively.

22 There are several professional comedians whose presence in films offers a
    point of identification for the viewer (*ibid.*, p. 73).

23 See Rachel Dwyer, *All You Want is Money, All You Need is Love: Sex and
    Romance in Modern India* (London, 2000).

24 On the effects of liberalization see Dwyer, *All You Want is Money*, chapter 4,
    and Prasad, *Ideology of the Hindi Film*, chapter 9.

25 Prasad, *Ideology of the Hindi Film*.

26 *Ibid.*, p. 30.

27 *Ibid.*, pp. 31–2.

28 *Ibid.*, p. 32.

29 Yash Raj Films took insurance from the United India Insurance Co. for
    Mohabbatein.

30 On *rasa* theory, see Rachel Dwyer, *Yash Chopra* (London, 2002), pp. 66–70.

31 See Vasudevan, 'The Politics of Cultural Address in a "Transitional"
    Cinema', pp. 134–6.

32 Ien Ang, *Watching Dallas: Soap Opera and the Melodramatic Imagination* (London, 1985), p. 61. The classic work on melodrama is Peter Brooks, *The Melodramatic Imagination: Balzac, Henry James, Melodrama and the Mode of Excess* (New Haven, 1976, 2nd edn 1985).

33 Ang, *Watching Dallas*, pp. 61–8, is an excellent summary and analysis of the forms and functions of melodrama.

34 Steve Neale, 'Melodrama and Tears', *Screen*, xxvi/6 (1986), pp. 6–22.

35 Prasad, *Ideology of the Hindi Film*, p. 71.

36 There are a number of websites dedicated to Hindi film dialogues, several of them 'humorous'.

37 Kidar Sharma said of New Theatres' *Devdas*, 'This isn't dialogue, this is the way we talk' (quoted in Barnouw and Krishnaswamy, *Indian Film*, p. 80).

38 Manil Suri, *The Death of Vishnu* (London, 2001).

39 Quoted in Richard Dyer, *Stars*, 2nd edn with a supplementary chapter by Paul McDonald (London, 1998).

40 Vasudevan, 'The Politics of Cultural Address in a "Transitional" Cinema', p.131.

41 Tom Gunning, 'The Cinema of Attraction: Early Film, its Spectator and the Avant-garde,' *Wide Angle*, viii/3–4 (1986).

42 Tom Gunning, 'An Aesthetic of Astonishment: Early Film and the (In)credulous Spectator', in *Viewing Positions: Ways of Seeing Film*, ed. L. Williams (New Brunswick, 1997), p. 131, n. 13.

43 Vasudevan, 'The Politics of Cultural Address in a "Transitional" Cinema', p.133.

44 In the mythological genre it also included the presentation of miracles as spectacle, as noted in mythological plays by Anuradha Kapur, 'The Representation of Gods and Heroes'.

45 See Dwyer, *All You Want is Money*, chapter 4, for a longer discussion of the problematic status of the Hindi film.

46 Prasad, *Ideology of the Hindi Film*, chapter 2, sees this loose structure of the film as a result of the conditions of production.

47 Richard Dyer, *Stars* (London, 1979).

48 Dyer, *Stars*, pp. 34–7.

49 See also Christine Gledhill, 'Signs of melodrama', in *Stardom: Industry of Desire*, ed. C. Gledhill (London, 1991), p. 214.

50 Gledhill, *Stardom*, p. 215.

51 Murray Smith, *Engaging Characters: Fiction, Emotion and the Cinema* (Oxford, 1995), pp. 193–4.

52 The pleasure of hearing is rarely discussed. In the Indian cinema the most prominent element of the sound is the music, which is part of the spectacle in the film but has an importance existence outside the cinematic experience. Recordings of dialogues are also found, the most famous being that of *Sholay* (now available on CD). A further example is that of the voice of Amitabh Bachchan acting, reciting poetry and even singing some of his own songs.

53 Jackie Stacey, *Star Gazing: Hollywood Cinema and Female Spectatorship* (London, 1993), pp. 130–38.

54 Sara Dickey, *Cinema and the Urban Poor in South India* (Cambridge, 1993); 'Opposing Faces: Film Star Fan Clubs and the Construction of Class Identities in South India', in *Pleasure and the Nation: The History, Consumption and Politics of Public Culture in India*, ed. R. Dwyer and C. Pinney (New Delhi, 2000), pp. 212–46; M. S. S. Pandian, *The Image Trap* (Delhi, 1992) and S. V. Srinivas, 'Devotion and Defiance in Fan Activity', *Journal of Arts and Ideas*, 29 (1996), pp. 66–83.

55 See Lawrence Babb, 'Glancing: Visual Interaction in Hinduism', *Journal of Anthropological Research*, xxxvii/4 (1981), pp. 387–401, and Diana Eck,

Darsan: Seeing the Divine Image in India (Chambersburg, PA, 1985).

56 Vasudevan, 'The Politics of Cultural Address in a "Transitional" Cinema'.
57 Behroze Gandhy and Rosie Thomas, 'Three Indian Film Stars', in *Stardom: Industry of Desire*, ed. C. Gledhill (London, 1991), pp. 107–31.
58 See Dwyer, *All You Want is Money*, chapter 6.
59 Kishore Valicha, *The Moving Image: A Study of Indian Cinema* (London, 1988).
60 Prasad, *Ideology of the Hindi Film*, chapter 6.
61 *Ibid.*, p. 271.
62 Nasreen Munni Kabir, *Talking Films: Conversations on Hindi Cinema with Javed Akhtar* (Delhi, 1999), p. 75.
63 Asha Kasbekar, 'Hidden Pleasures: Negotiating the Myth of the Female Ideal in Popular Hindi Cinema', in *Pleasure and the Nation*, ed. R. Dwyer and C. Pinney, pp. 286–308.
64 Sean Cubbitt, 'Phalke, Méliès and Special Effects Today', p. 4 [unpublished paper].
65 Cubbitt, p. 5.
66 I believe Ashish Rajadhyaksha is researching this topic, building on his earlier work.

2 Film Style: Settings and Costume

1 These are the categories used in the standard work on film art, David Bordwell and Kristin Thompson, *Film Art: An Introduction*, 5th edn (New York, 1997).
2 Each of these aspects of film style involves a huge number of specialized personnel, such as the cameraman, cinematographer, camera operator, grip, gaffer and sound people as well as director.
3 Notably Ravi Vasudevan, 'Shifting Codes, Dissolving Identities: The Hindi Social Film of the 1950s as Popular Culture', *Journal of Arts and Ideas*, 23-4 (1993), pp. 51–79 (plus appendix), and 'Sexuality and the Film Apparatus: Continuity, Non-continuity and Discontinuity in Bombay Cinema', in *A Question of Silence? The Sexual Economies of Modern India*, ed. M. John and J. Nair (New Delhi, 1998), pp. 192–215.
4 David Bordwell, *On the History of Film Style* (London, 1997).
5 See chapter One above on the relationship between Hindi and Indian cinema.
6 André Bazin dates Hollywood style as established in 1939 in his *What is Cinema?*, trans. H. Gray, 2 vols (Berkeley, 1992), I, p. 29.
7 Tapti Guha-Thakurta, 'The Ideology of the "Aesthetic": The Purging of Visual Tastes and the Campaign for a New Indian Art in Late Nineteenth/Early Twentieth Century Bengal', *Studies in History*, n.s. VIII/2 (1992), pp. 237–81 and *The Making of a New 'Indian' Art: Artists, Aesthetics and Nationalism in Bengal, c. 1850–1920* (Cambridge, 1992).
8 Christopher Pinney, *Camera Indica: The Social Life of Indian Photographs* (London, 1997) and Vidia Dehejia, ed., *India through the Lens: Photography 1840–1911* (Washington, DC, 2000).
9 Kajri Jain, 'Gods in the Bazaar', *South Asia*, XXI/1 (1998), pp. 91–108; Christopher Pinney, 'The Nation (Un)pictured? Chromolithography and 'Popular' Politics in India, 1878–1995', in *Critical Inquiry*, XXIII (1997), pp. 834–67, and Patricia Uberoi, 'Feminine Identity and National Ethos in Indian Calendar Art,' *Economic and Political Weekly*, XXV/17 (1990), pp. WS41–8.
10 Arjun Appadurai and Carol Breckenridge, 'Museums are Good to Think: Heritage on View in India,' in *Museums and Communications: The Politics of Public Culture*, ed. I. Karp *et al.* (Washington, DC, 1992), p. 52.

11 Christopher Pinney, 'Hindu Chromolithographs in their "Inter-ocular" Field', p.2 [unpublished paper]

12 See chapter One for more on theatre.

13 Pinney, 'Hindu Chromolithographs'.

14 Even the titles of many of Ravi Verma's chromolithographs were the same as those of many of the early films (*ibid.*).

15 Vasudevan, 'Sexuality and the Film Apparatus', and 'The Politics of Cultural Address in a "Transitional" Cinema: A Case Study of Popular Indian Cinema', in *Reinventing Film Studies*, ed. C. Gledhill and L. Williams (London, 2000), pp. 130–64.

16 Ashish Rajadhayksha, 'The Phalke Era: Conflict of Traditional Form and Modern Technology', in *Interrogating Modernity: Culture and Colonialism in India*, ed. T. Niranjana *et al.* (Calcutta, 1993), p. 54.

17 Geeta Kapur, 'Revelation and Doubt: *Sant Tukaram* and *Devi*,' in *Interrogating Modernity: Culture and Colonialism in India*, ed. T. Niranjana *et al.* (Calcutta, 1993), p. 23.

18 *Ibid.*, p. 20.

19 *Ibid.*, p. 20.

20 *Ibid.*, p. 23.

21 Roland Barthes, *Image, Music, Text*, essays selected and trans. S. Heath (London, 1977), p. 70.

22 Peter Brooks, *The Melodramatic Imagination: Balzac, Henry James, Melodrama and the Mode of Excess*, 2nd edn (New Haven, 1985), p. 62.

23 Madhava Prasad, *Ideology of the Hindi Film: A Historical Construction* (New Delhi, 1998), pp. 76–7, which draws on Lawrence Babb, 'Glancing: Visual Interaction in Hinduism', *Journal of Anthropological Research*, XXXVII/4 (1981), pp. 387–401, and Diana Eck, *Darsan: Seeing the Divine Image in India* (Chambersburg, PA, 1985). See also Vasudevan, 'The Politics of Cultural Address in a "Transitional" Cinema', pp. 139-47.

24 Vasudevan, 'The Politics of Cultural Address in a "Transitional" Cinema', p. 140.

25 Vasudevan, 'Shifting Codes, Dissolving Identities', *passim*, and 'The Politics of Cultural Address in a "Transitional" Cinema', pp. 147–50.

26 Vasudevan, 'The Politics of Cultural Address in a "Transitional" Cinema', pp.147–8.

27 Anuradha Kapur, 'The Representation of Gods and Heroes: Parsi Mythological Drama of the Early Twentieth Century,' *Journal of Arts and Ideas*, 23–4 (1993), pp. 85–107.

28 One such analysis is of a song filmed in a theatre in *Kismet* (*Fate*, directed by Gyan Mukherjee, 1943), which combines the iconic, the realistic, images of theatre, chromolithography and set design in the context of a depiction of Indian nationalism. See Ravi Vasudevan, 'The Cultural Space of a Film Narrative: Interpreting *Kismet* (Bombay Talkies 1943)', *Indian Economic and Social History Review*, XXVIII/2 (1991), pp.171–85.

29 For more on this phenomenon see below.

30 Ashish Rajadhyaksha and Paul Willemen, *An Encyclopaedia of Indian Cinema*, 2nd edn (Oxford, 1999), pp. 386–7.

31 Interview with Yash Chopra.

32 Art design and costume design are two of the few areas, other than acting, in which women have achieved major success in Hindi cinema. Roy acknowledges that she managed to get a break by working with her father, himself a famous art director.

33 For example, Sharmishta Roy says that for *Mohabbatein* (*Loves*, dir. Aditya Chopra, 2000) Narayan Shankar's character was cold and remote, so they built him a huge set to dwarf him and used stone to give a cold look.

34 See George Michell and Antonio Martinelli, *The Royal Palaces of India* (London, 1994).

35 These styles can be seen in museums that have rebuilt these houses, such as Dakshinachitra near Madras.

36 See Robert Skelton, *Rājasthānī Temple Hangings of the Krishna Cult, from the Collection of Karl Mann, New York* (New York, 1973) and Amit Ambalal, *Krishna as Shrinathji: Rajasthani Paintings from Nathdvara* (Ahmadabad, 1987).

37 See Rachel Dwyer, *All You Want is Money, All You Need is Love: Sex and Romance in Modern India* (London, 2000), chapter 2.

38 See *ibid.*, chapter 3.

39 See *ibid.*, chapter 2 for a discussion of Eva Illouz's definition of postmodern love, where love and capitalism are bound together by consumption and the mass media (Eva Illouz, *Consuming the Romantic Utopia: Love and the Cultural Contradictions of Capitalism*, Berkeley, 1997).

40 'Among so many architectural cads and pretentious bounders, it is the only gentleman. In Bombay, it seems as good as the Parthenon' (Aldous Huxley, *Jesting Pilate* (New York, 1926), p.18).

41 Bhattacharya in Binodini Dasi, *My Story* and *My Life as an Actress*, ed. and trans. R. Bhattacharya (New Delhi, 1998), p. 171.

42 Rajadhyaksha, 'The Phalke Era', pp. 68–9 on the backdrop painted from a photograph of Bombay's Princess Street.

43 Rajadhyaksha, 'The Phalke Era' traces Phalke's multimedia training.

44 Rajadhyaksha, 'The Phalke Era'.

45 See chapter One above for a discussion of this term, following Mukul Kesavan, 'Urdu, Awadh and the tawaif: The Islamicate Roots of Hindi Cinema', in *Forging Identities: Gender, Communities and the State*, ed. Z. Hassan (New Delhi, 1994), pp. 244–57.

46 On this style in the silent period, see Kaushik Bhaumik, 'The Bazaar, the Dancing Girl and the Home: Some Configurations of Female Stardom in the Early Bombay Cinema', unpublished paper, given at 'Stars beyond the Hollywood Firmament', University of Warwick, 19 May 2001.

47 Interview with A. V. Damle, son of V. Damle, 2001.

48 Interview with Shaukat Khan, son of Mehboob, 2001.

49 See Ashish Rajadhyaksha, 'India: Filming the Nation', in *The Oxford History of World Cinema*, ed. G. Nowell-Smith (Oxford, 1996), pp. 679–81.

50 See below.

51 See Rachel Dwyer, 'The Erotics of the Wet Sari in Hindi Films', *South Asia*, XXIII/2 (June 2000), pp. 143–59.

52 See Dwyer, *All You Want is Money*, chapter 3.

53 Gary D. Sampson, 'Photographer of the Picturesque: Samuel Bourne', in *India through the Lens: Photography 1840-1911*, ed. V. Dehejia (Washington, DC, 2000). See also other papers in this volume.

54 Marshall Berman, *All That is Solid Melts into Air: The Experience of Modernity* (London, 1983).

55 See Ashis Nandy, 'Invitation to an Antique Death: The Journey of Pramathesh Barua as the Origin of the Terribly Effeminate, Maudlin, Self-destructive Heroes of Indian Cinema', in *Pleasure and the Nation: The History, Consumption and Politics of Public Culture in India*, ed. R. Dwyer and C. Pinney (New Delhi, 2000), pp. 139–60.

56 Ashis Nandy, *The Secret Politics of Our Desires: Innocence, Culpability and Popular Cinema* (London, 1998).

57 I have been told of a great club life in Bombay in the 1970s, with transvestite dancers and live bands, frequented by diplomats and others, but have not seen much more than the average global 'disco' or club in the 1990s.

58 See Rachel Dwyer, 'Representing the Muslim: The 'Courtesan Film' in Indian Popular Cinema,' in *Imagining the Other: Representations of Jews, Muslims and Christians in the Media,* ed. T. Parfitt (London, forthcoming.)

59 In particular those of Richard Strauss. See Tim Ashley, 'Flights of Fancy', *The Guardian* (18 January 2001), G2, pp. 12–13.

60 See *Awāra* (*The Vagabond*, 1951) below. This idea of a link between heaven and earth is seen in the Buddhist carvings at Sanchi, dating from the second century BC.

61 Nandy calls Devdas the 'terribly effeminate, maudlin hero' (Nandy, 'Invitation to an Antique Death').

62 Raj Kumar Barjatya of Rajshri Films, when showing me clips and screen tests from their archive, saved his favourite film to the end. This was the *abhisheka* or bathing with liquids of the statue of the Jain saint Gomateshwara at Shravanbelgola (April 2000).

63 For *Pardesi* (*Foreigner*, directed by K. A. Abbas and Vassili M. Pronin, 1957), *Kagaz ke phool* (*Paper Flowers*, directed by Guru Dutt, 1959) and *Jis desh men Ganga behti hai* (*The Country in Which the Ganges Flows*, directed by Raj Kapoor, 1960).

64 For an analysis of this film see Gayatri Chatterjee, *Awāra* (New Delhi, 1992).

65 I carried out an extensive period of fieldwork on this film so it has an additional personal appeal. Roy has subsequently won acclaim for her sets for *Kuch kuch hota hai* (*Something Happens*, directed by Karan Johar, 1998) and *Taal* (*Rhythm*, directed by Subhash Ghai, 1999), among others.

66 Rajadhyaksha and Willemen, *Encyclopaedia of Indian Cinema*, p. 321.

67 See Chatterjee, *Awāra*, pp. 99–107 for an analysis of this scene.

68 Rajadhyaksha, 'The Phalke Era'.

69 Hindi films have highly dubious if not overtly racist ways of portraying 'Others', whether regional or non-Hindu people in India, Africans or others.

70 See Lawrence Cohen, 'The Pleasures of Castration: The Postoperative Status of hijras, jankhas and Academics', in *Sexual Nature, Sexual Culture*, ed. P. Abramson and S. D. Pinkerton (Chicago, 1995), p. 292.

71 Concerning a major family dispute when a village woman wanted to wear a cardigan, see Emma Tarlo, *Clothing Matters: Dress and Identity in India* (London, 1996).

72 Laura Mulvey, 'Visual Pleasure and Narrative Cinema', *Screen*, XVI/3 (1975), pp. 6–18.

73 This respectability was demonstrated in a *cause célèbre* in Bombay in the early 1990s, when two women dressed in saris were refused entrance to a nightclub on the grounds of dress, in that it would make people feel uncomfortable. For details see Ania Loomba, 'The Long and Saggy Sari', in *Women: A Cultural Review*, special issue of *Independent India* (guest editor A. Roy), VIII/3 (Autumn 1997), pp. 278–92

74 See Rachel Dwyer, 'Bombay ishtyle', in *Fashion Cultures: Theories, Explorations and Analysis*, ed. S. Bruzzi and P. Church Gibson (London, 2000), pp. 178–90.

75 Patrick Olivelle, 'Hair and Society: Social Significance of Hair in South Asian Traditions', in *Hair: Its Power and Meaning in Asian Cultures*, ed. A. Hiltebeitel and B. D. Miller (New York, 1998), pp.11–49.

76 Patricia Uberoi, 'Dharma and Desire, Freedom and Destiny: Rescripting the Man-Woman Relationship in Popular Hindi Cinema', in *Embodiment: Essays on Gender and Identity*, ed. M. Thapar (Delhi, 1997), pp.145–71.

77 As early as 1939 clothes from Indian films were being copied (Barnouw and Krishnaswamy, *Indian Film*, p. 85).

78 See Jackie Stacey, *Star Gazing: Hollywood Cinema and Female Spectatorship* (London, 1993).

79 The (white) female backing singer supporting the singer M (Robin Scott), who had a big hit in the UK with the song 'Pop muzik' in 1979, wore a sari for her appearance on BBC1's 'Top of the Pops'.

3 The Art of Advertising

1   Vikram Doctor and Anvar Alikhan, 'Kyon na aazmaye', *India Magazine* [Bombay] (December 1996), p. 47.
2   Jithubhai Metha, 'The Film Industry, Press and Publicity', *Filmfare* [Bombay] (17 August 1956), p. 55.
3   Erik Barnouw and S. Krishnaswamy, *Indian Film*, 2nd edn (New York, 1980), p. 21.
4   B. D. Garga, *So Many Cinemas* (Mumbai, 1996), p. 21.
5   Interview with D.G. Pradhan, Bombay, 28 November 1998.
6   See handbill for *Nala and Damayanti*, illustrated in Garga, *So Many Cinemas*, p. 28.
7   From an interview given to the author by Sahdev Ghei, Business Executive in charge of advertising at Yash Raj Films, Bombay, 15 February 2001.
8   Tapati Guha-Thakurta, 'Raja Ravi Varma and the Project of a New National Art', in *Raja Ravi Varma*, ed. R.C. Sharma (New Delhi, 1993), p. 45.
9   Tapati Guha-Thakurta, *The Making of a New 'Indian' Art* (Cambridge, 1992), p. 110.
10 A series of fifty prints from this press were purchased for the V&A Museum, London, in 1893.
11 Guha-Thakurta, *Making of a New 'Indian' Art*, pp. 78–117 and Partha Mitter, *Art and Nationalism in Colonial India 1850–1922* (Cambridge, 1994), pp. 173–8.
12 Juhi Saklani, 'The Magic Lantern Man', *India Magazine* [Bombay] (March 1998), pp. 7–13.
13 Booklet for *Setu-Bandhan*, property of the National Film Archive of India, p. 12.
14 For image see Partha Mitter, *Art and Nationalism in Colonial India*, p. 183.
15 See Anuradha Kapur, 'Deity to Crusader: The Changing Iconography of Ram', in *Hindus and Others: The Question of Identity in India Today* (Delhi, 1993).
16 Patricia Uberoi, 'Feminine Identity and the National Ethos in Indian Calendar Art', *Economic and Political Weekly*, 25 (17) (28 April 1990), WS41–WS47.
17 *Ibid.*, WS44.
18 *Ibid.*
19 Ashish Rajadhyaksha and Paul Willemen, *An Encyclopaedia of Indian Cinema*, (London, 1999), p. 246.
20 Garga, *So Many Cinemas*, p. 32.
21 *Ibid.*, p. 31.
22 Partha Mitter, 'Artistic Responses to Colonialism in India: An Overview', in *The Raj, India and the British 1600–1947*, ed. C.A. Bayly (London, 1990), pp. 361–8.
23 W. E. Gladstone Solomon, *The Bombay Revival of Indian Art*, (n.d.) p. 79.
24 Garga, *So Many Cinemas*, pp. 32–3.
25 Advertised in *Filmfare* [Bombay] (18 March 1955).
26 In the Wadia family collection.
27 Booklet for *The Court Dancer*, property of the National Film Archive of India, p. 2.
28 Burton Stein, *A History of India* (Oxford, 1998), pp. 303–4.
29 Metha, 'The Film Industry, Press and Publicity', p. 55.

30 For a good introduction to the style see Bevis Hiller and Stephen Escritt, *Art Deco Style* (London, 1997).

31 Jon Alff, 'Temples of Light: Bombay's Art Deco Cinemas and the Birth of the Modern Myth', in *Bombay to Mumbai*, ed. Pauline Rohatgi *et al.* (Mumbai, 1997) pp. 250–57.

32 Illustrated in Garga, *So Many Cinemas*, p. 92.

33 Friedrich Friedl, Nicolaus Ott and Bernard Stein, *Typography: When, Who, How* (Cologne, 1998), p. 164.

34 Hiller and Escritt, *Art Deco Style*, p. 122.

35 In 1926–7 15 per cent of the feature films released in India were Indian and 85 per cent were foreign, mostly American (Barnouw and Krishnaswamy, *Indian Film*, p. 42).

36 Doctor and Alikhan, 'Kyon na aazmaye', p. 53.

37 Hiller and Escritt, *Art Deco Style*, p. 206.

38 *Ibid.*

39 The style was also evident on contemporary book covers and illustrations and may have represented an agitprop aesthetic for the Communist Party of India. (I am grateful to Christopher Pinney for this suggestion.)

40 Christiane Brosius, 'India Personified in Hindutva Iconography', in *India Magazine* [Bombay] (November 1997), pp. 23–8.

41 Rajadhyaksha and Willemen, *Encyclopaedia of Indian Cinema*, p. 305.

42 For images see Pranabranjan Ray, *Somnath Hore*, Lalit Kala Akademi series of Monographs (New Delhi, n.d.).

43 For images see Amit Mukhopadhyay, 'Chittaprasad: Humanist and Patriot', *Art Heritage* [New Delhi], no. 5 (1985–6).

44 Rajadhyaksha and Willemen, *Encyclopaedia of Indian Cinema*, p. 285.

45 Sumita S. Chakravarty, *National Identity in Indian Popular Cinema 1947–1987* (New Delhi, 1996), p. 160.

46 *Ibid.*, p. 166.

47 Illustrated in P. K. Nair, 'The Evolution of Film in India, Seen through Posters', *Affiche, The International Poster Magazine*, no. 8 (December 1993), p. 54.

48 Barnouw and Krishnaswamy, *Indian Film*, p. 173.

49 Rajadhyaksha and Willemen, *Encyclopaedia of Indian Cinema*, p. 310.

50 Barnouw and Krishnaswamy, *Indian Film*, p. 174.

51 Stephen Rebello and Richard Allen, *Reel Art* (New York, 1988), p. 41.

52 I have only been able to locate one other such pressbook for the film *Aurat*.

53 Interview with Shaukat Khan of Mehboob Studios, Bombay, February 2001.

54 Cine Society, India, *J. B. H. Wadia*, retrospective booklet (Bombay, 1987).

55 Chakravarty, *National Identity in Indian Popular Cinema*, pp. 59–61.

56 In the V&A collection.

57 Rajadhyaksha and Willemen, *Encyclopaedia of Indian Cinema*, pp. 335.

58 Rosie Thomas, 'Sanctity and Scandal: The Mythologization of Mother India', *Quarterly Review of Film and Video*, 11/3 (1989), p. 23.

59 Chakravarty, *National Identity in Indian Popular Cinema*, p. 152.

60 Although the images are unsigned and the credits do not list his name, Mehboob's son Shaukat Khan, who now runs the studios, recalls Meganee and his work. Interviewed by the author, Bombay, February 2001.

61 See Geeta Kapur, *Contemporary Indian Artists* (New Delhi, 1978).

62 *Mother India* souvenir booklet (Bombay, 1957), p. 1.

63 *Ibid.*, p. 9.

64 Chakravarty, *National Identity in Indian Popular Cinema*, p. 218.

65 Rajadhyaksha and Willemen, *Encyclopaedia of Indian Cinema*, p. 392.

66 Ted Owen and Denis Dickson, *High Art: A History of the Psychedelic Poster* (London, 1999), pp. 3–15.

67 See W. Dissanayake and M. Sahai, *Sholay: A Cultural Reading* (New Delhi, 1992) and S. Basy *et al.* in 'Cinema and Society: A Search for Meaning in a New Genre', *India International Centre Quarterly*, VIII/1 (1981), pp. 57–76. Also see Iqbal Masud, 'The Seventies:Ways of Escape', *Cinema in India* [Bombay] (January–April 1988), pp. 24–7.

68 Information on the original Indian campaign provided by Mr Sascha Sippy of the Sippy family.

69 See Patricia Uberoi, 'Imagining the Family: an Ethnography of Viewing *Hum Aapke Hain Koun ...!*' in *Pleasure and the Nation*, ed. Rachel Dwyer and Christopher Pinney (New Delhi, 2001).

70 Anupama Chopra and Nandita Chowdhury, 'The New Bollywood Brigade', *India Today International* (June 28 1999), p. 43.

71 Interview with Rahul Nanda, Bombay, 24 November 1998.

72 Interview with Yash Chopra, Bombay, 15 February 2001.

73 Interview with Rahul Nanda, Bombay, 24 November 1998.

74 Interview with Rajesh Vaidya, Bombay, 16 February 2001. There may in fact be more than four firms in Bombay, but Rajesh was stressing the extent of the decline in studios. According to him hoarding painters enjoyed a peak in production in the 1970s with over forty studios in existence.

75 The process as recounted by Rajesh is as follows: He is provided with photographic stills or film booklets from which he selects the most important images and uses them to make a rough layout of the hoarding design. The canvas is then prepared, it is painted in white and the design is transferred onto the canvas using grid lines to enable accurate enlargement. This is then painted over. The whole process takes a maximum of three to four days as they are given commissions by the distributors of the film at the beginning of the week and the hoarding has to be in place on top of the cinema front by the end of the week.

76 Iwona Blazwick, ed., *Century City: Art and Culture in the Modern Metropolis*, exh. cat., Tate Modern (London, 2001).

77 All information from an interview given to the author by Sahdev Ghei, Business Executive in charge of advertising at Yash Raj Films, Bombay, 15 February 2001.

4 Advertising and the Communication of Meaning

1 Ernst Gombrich, *The Image and the Eye* (Oxford, 1982), p. 289.

2 Perminda Jacob, 'Film and Political Advertisements of South India: Urban Spectacle, Popular Culture, Third World Industry', PhD thesis, University of California, 1994. Jacob in her analysis of film hoardings uses the methodology put forward by Roland Barthes in *Image–Music–Text*, trans. Stephen Heath (London, 1977). Here, an advertisement is seen to incorporate three types of messages – linguistic, denoted and connoted. A denoted message is one that is objective and overt and a connoted message is subjective and implied. Jacob argues that Indian film hoardings are entirely coded and that the linguistic and denoted meanings are superseded by the connoted message, which is culturally specific.

3 Richard Brilliant, *Portraiture* (London, 1991), p. 9.

4 *Ibid.*, p. 10.

5 Richard Dyer, *Heavenly Bodies: Film Stars and Society* (London, 1993), pp. 2–3. John Ellis calls this the 'narrative image'; see John Ellis, *Visible Fictions* (London, 1982), pp. 91–108.

6 Vijay Mishra *et al.*, 'The Actor as Parallel Text in Bombay Cinema', *Quarterly Review of Film and Video*, 11/3 (1989), p. 55.

7 Brilliant, *Portraiture*, p. 56. The concurrence of these three factors is

discussed in relation to a daguerreotype of Daniel Webster, which is seen to project his role as an icon of American political history.

8 Mishra, *et al.*, 'The Actor as Parallel Text in Bombay Cinema', p. 56.
9 *Ibid.*, p. 55.
10 Stephen Rebello, 'The 007 Files: Selling Bond', *Cinefantastique*, XIX/5 (July 1989), p. 30.
11 Sumita Chakravarty, *National Identity in Indian Popular Cinema, 1947–1987* (New Delhi, 1996), p. 229.
12 Brilliant, *Portraiture*, p. 12. Brilliant suggests that 'social roles, however enacted, are like masks or disguises, carefully assumed by individuals in order to locate themselves in a society conditioned to recognise and identify these forms of representation in practise and in art.' So unlike other forms of portraiture, the poster artist does not aim to convey the true character of the sitter.
13 Geeta Kapur, 'Mythic Material in Indian Cinema', *Journal of Arts and Ideas*, 14–15 (1987), p. 82.
14 Joanna Woodall, *Portraiture, Facing the Subject* (Manchester, 1997), p. 3.
15 Ernst van Alphen, 'The Portrait's Dispersal: Concepts of Representation and Subjectivity in Contemporary Portraiture', in *ibid.*, p. 240.
16 Tapati Guha-Thakurta, *The Making of a New 'Indian' Art: Artists, Aesthetics and Nationalism in Bengal, c. 1850–1920* (Cambridge, 1992), pp. 45-78.
17 Kapur, 'Mythic Material in Indian Cinema', p. 84.
18 Brilliant, *Portraiture*, p. 27.
19 The photographer Samuel Bourne, who travelled to India in 1862, comments that *cartes-de-visite* were as popular in India as they were in England (*British Journal of Photography*, July 1863, p. 269). For more information see Audrey Linkman, *The Victorians: Photographic Portraits* (London, 1993), pp. 61–83.
20 Judith Mara Gutman, *Through Indian Eyes: 19th and 20th Century Photography from India* (New York, 1982), pp. 103–33 and Christopher Pinney, *Camera Indica: The Social Life of Indian Photographs* (London, 1997), pp. 72–108.
21 Gutman, *Through Indian Eyes*, pp. 108–10.
22 Pinney, *Camera Indica*, p. 140.
23 Interview with the author, Pune, November 1998.
24 For more detailed discussion see Woodall, *Portraiture, Facing the Subject*, and Brilliant, *Portraiture.*
25 Stephen Haggard, 'Mass Media and the Visual Arts in Twentieth Century South Asia: Indian Film Posters 1947–Present', *South Asia Research*, VIII/2 (May 1988), p. 87. 'Secular darsan' is used by Haggard as a term to emphasize that within a poster design there is no sense of any interpersonal communication between the people portrayed, only between the viewer and the primary subject.
26 Danny Leigh, 'The Awful Truth', *The Guardian* (1 August 1998), The Guide, pp. 16–19. Leigh gives a breakdown of the construction of a typical Hollywood film poster.
27 Rosalind Krauss, 'The Photographic Conditions of Surrealism', *The Originality of the Avant-Garde and Other Modernist Myths* (Cambridge, MA, 1985), pp. 87–118.
28 Mary Beth Haralovich, 'Advertising Heterosexuality: Changing Courtships in Film Posters of the Thirties and Forties', *Screen*, XXIII/2 (July–August 1982), p. 52.
29 Jacob, *Film and Political Advertisements of South India*, p. 194.
30 Leigh, 'The Awful Truth', pp. 16–17.
31 Haggard, 'Mass Media and the Visual Arts in Twentieth Century South Asia', pp. 87–8, and Jacob, *Film and Political Advertisements of South India*,

pp. 182–6, argue that the representation of emotion is linked to the Rasa theory derived from the ancient Sanskrit *Natyashastra* text, whereby images representing the nine *rasas* or emotions (laughter, sorrow, anger, fear, disgust, astonishment, peace, eroticism and heroism) give the general 'flavour' or mood of the film.

32 For more information see Sudhir Kakar, 'The Ties that Bind: Family Relationships in the Mythology of Hindi Cinema', *India International Centre Quarterly*, VIII/1 (1981), pp. 11–22. Also Ashis Nandy, 'An Intelligent Critic's Guide to the Indian Cinema', *The Savage Freud and Other Essays on Possible and Retrievable Selves* (Delhi, 1995) pp. 196–236.

33 Kakar, 'The Ties that Bind', p. 15.

34 *Ibid.*, p. 17.

35 This was a written response to a question by the author asking about the artist's intention in this poster design. Letter from the artist, 5 August 1998.

36 Haggard in 'Mass Media and the Visual Arts in Twentieth Century South Asia', pp. 81–2, argues that there is a symbolic use of colour in certain posters and cites an example of male characters who are coloured in blue to signify the Hindu god Krishna. Jacob, *Film and Political Advertisements of South India*, p. 233, argues against Haggard's hypothesis.

37 Rosie Thomas, 'Sanctity and Scandal: The Mythologization of Mother India', *Quarterly Review of Film and Video*, 11/3 (1989), p. 11. Also see Patricia Uberoi, 'Feminine Identity and the National Ethos in Indian Calendar Art', *Economic and Political Weekly* (28 April 1990), WS42–WS43.

38 Uma Chakravarti, 'What Ever Happened to the Vedic Dasi?: Orientalism, Nationalism, and a Script for the Past', in *Recasting Women*, ed. Kumkum Sangari and Sudesh Vaid (New Brunswick, NJ, 1990), pp. 27–87.

39 Jacob, *Film and Political Advertisements of South India*, p. 238

40 Geeta Kapur, 'Representational Dilemmas of a Nineteenth-century Painter: Raja Ravi Varma', *When was Modernism* (New Delhi, 2000), p. 163. Kapur argues that although Varma was said to travel across India painting women, most of his travels were concentrated in the northern states and therefore the bulk of his images displayed Aryan facial characteristics instead of being truly pan-Indian.

41 Tapati Guha-Thakurta, 'Clothing the Goddess: The Modern Contest over Representations of the Devi', in *Devi, the Great Goddess: Female Divinity in South Asian Art*, ed. Vidhya Dehejia, exh. cat., Arthur M. Sackler Gallery (Washington, DC, 1999), pp.157–77.

42 The advertisement appeared on the back cover of the booklet for the film *Daaera*, which the National Film Archive of India, Pune, has dated to 1953. This seems unlikely, however, since the publicity booklet for *Pakeezah* says that the story itself was not written until 1956. It is more likely to be dated around 1961, when filming first began.

43 Guha-Thakurta, 'Clothing the Goddess', p. 174.

44 John Berger, *Ways of Seeing* (London, 1972), pp.140–41, and also Walter Benjamin, 'The Work of Art in the Age of Mechanical Reproduction', *Illuminations* (London, 1973).

45 Patricia Uberoi, 'Imagining the Family: an Ethnography of Viewing *Hum Aapke Hain Koun ...!*', in *Pleasure and the Nation*, ed. Rachel Dwyer and Christopher Pinney (New Delhi, 2001), pp. 319–21.

46 Gulam Sheikh, *Celebrity Magazine* (December 1984), p. 80.

47 In an interview between the artist and Robert Skelton, transcript kept at the Victoria & Albert Museum, London.

48 Mildred Archer, 'Jadupatua Paintings', *Indian Popular Painting* (London, 1977), p. 16.

49 Anil Relia, 'A Living Canvas', *The Genesis of Gaja Gamini* (Ahmedabad,

2000), p. 42.

50 Geeti Sen, 'Gaja Gamini: The Act of Transformation', *Ibid.*, p. 176.

51 Heidi Zuckerman Jacobson and Phyllis Wattis, *Into the Sun*, University Art Museum, Berkeley, Matrix Exhibit 185, www.bampfa.berkeley.edu/matrix/185 (2000), p. 3.

52 This installation of *"into the sun"* was shown at the Victoria Miro Gallery, London, 7 October – 12 November 1999; its structure may be changed when exhibited elsewhere.

Conclusion

1 Arjun Appadurai, *Modernity at Large: Cultural Dimensions of Globalisation* (Minnesota, 1996), p. 9.

2 Appadurai uses the terms ethnoscapes, mediascapes, technoscapes, financescapes and ideoscapes, p.33.

3 Arjan Appadurai, *Modernity at Large*, p. 35.

4 Anupama Chopra and Nandita Chowdhury, 'The New Bollywood Brigade', *India Today International* (28 June 1999), p. 43.

5 *Ibid.*

6 See Rachel Dwyer, *All You Want is Money, All You Need is Love: Sex and Romance in Modern India* (London, 2000).

7 Appadurai sees this group as part of the global flow of people, the ethnoscapes

8 See Rachel Dwyer, '"Indian Values" and the Diaspora: Yash Chopra's Film of the 1990s', *West Coast Line* (Autumn 2000), pp. 6–27.

9 Anupama Chopra and Nandita Chowdhury, 'The New Bollywood Brigade', p. 43.

10 There are many projects planned for 2002. Selfridges, the department store, is to dedicate a month to 'Bollywood' with fashion shows, music and set constructions. The British Film Industry is organizing a major Asian film festival called ImagineAsia, in which Hindi film will play a part. A major exhibition of film posters and hoardings will take place at the Victoria and Albert Museum, London, and smaller exhibitions of film ephemera are being organized across the country to show in such venues as Cartwright Hall, Bradford, and the Watershed in Bristol.

Select Bibliography

Barnouw, Erik, and S. Krishnaswamy, *Indian Film*, 2nd edn (New York, 1980)

Bordwell, David, *On the History of Film Style* (London, 1997)

——, and Kristin Thompson, *Film Art: An Introduction*, 5th edn (New York, 1997)

Bruzzi, Stella, *Undressing Cinema: Clothing and Identity in the Movies* (London, 1997)

Chakravarty, Sumita S., *National Identity in Indian Popular Cinema 1947–1987* (New Delhi, 1996)

Dwyer, Rachel, *All You Want is Money, All You Need is Love: Sex and Romance in Modern India* (London, 2000)

——, and Christopher Pinney, eds, *Pleasure and the Nation: The History, Consumption and Politics of Public Culture in India* (New Delhi, 2000)

Kapur, Anuradha, 'The Representation of Gods and Heroes: Parsi Mythological Drama of the Early Twentieth Century', *Journal of Arts and Ideas*, 23–4 (1993), pp. 85–107

Prasad, Madhava, *Ideology of the Hindi Film: A Historical Construction* (New Delhi, 1998)

Rajadhayksha, Ashish, 'The Phalke Era: Conflict of Traditional Form and Modern Technology', in *Interrogating Modernity: Culture and Colonialism in India*, ed. T. Niranjana *et al.* (Calcutta, 1993), pp. 47–82

——, 'Indian Cinema: Origins to Independence', 'India: Filming the Nation', in *The Oxford History of World Cinema*, ed. G. Nowell-Smith (Oxford, 1996), pp. 398–409, 678–89

——, and Paul Willemen, *An Encyclopaedia of Indian Cinema*, 2nd edn (London, 1999)

Vasudevan, Ravi, 'The Politics of Cultural Address in a "Transitional" Cinema: A Case Study of Popular Indian Cinema', in *Reinventing Film Studies*, ed. C. Gledhill and L. Williams (London, 2000), pp. 130–64

Acknowledgements

Rachel: To my friends and colleagues in India who provided me with warm hospitality and sound advice at so many levels: in Bombay, Shaad Ali, Apurva Asrani, Pamela and Yash Chopra, the late Michel D'Costa, Shobha Dé, Imtiaz, Anil and Ayesha Dharker, Reima and Owais Husain, Udita Jhunjhunwala, Saras and Girish Karnad, Rahul Khanna, Pravesh Kumar, Jerry Pinto, Maithili Rao, Amrut, Rekhi, and Sonal Shah, Shaanu and Sameer Sharma; in Delhi, Meera and Muzaffar Ali, Rashmi and Rohit Khattar, Palash Mehrotra, Uma and Ashis Nandy, Ranjana Sengupta, Patricia Uberoi, and Ravi Vasudevan; in Poona, Mohan Agashe and Gayatri Chatterjee; in Bangalore, Saras Karnad and Madhava Prasad; in Hyderabad, Elahe Hiptoola, Meenakshi and Sujit Mukherjee; in Chennai, Latha and Rajiv Menon.

To my colleagues for their support and encouragement: Daud Ali, Dipesh Chakrabarty, Faisal Devji, Ron Inden, Sudipta Kaviraj, Uday Singh Mehta, Francesca Orsini, Chris Pinney, Peter Robb.

To former and present students of Indian cinema at SOAS who have witnessed much of this work in progress. Many ideas in this book have taken shape during discussions with research students. Among these, Anna Morcom's research on Hindi film music, Kaushik Bhaumik's work on the silent cinema and Urvi Mukhopadhyay's work on the historical film have been of great importance to my way of thinking about these issues.

To the SOAS Research Committee and the British Academy for funding my fieldwork. To Paul Fox and Glenn Ratcliffe for photographing material.

Thanks to Routledge for giving permission to draw on an earlier version of the fashion section of chapter Three, which was published as 'Bombay ishtyle', in *Fashion Cultures: Theories, Explorations and Analysis*, ed. Stella Bruzzi and Pamela Church Gibson (London, 2000), pp. 178–190.

To my family and friends, especially, again, always, Michael.

Divia: To those at the V&A who have supported me in this project: Deborah Swallow, Paul Greenhalgh, John Guy, Mary Butler and Ken Jackson and Graham Brandon for photographing the material. My friends and colleagues for their constant encouragement and support: Nick Barnard, Aanal Chandaria, Ben Curran, Fiona Leslie, Miranda Percival, Sophie Gordon and particularly Sudeshna Guha, Graham Parlett and Shashi Sen for their invaluable assistance and critical advice.

To The Nehru Trust and the Museums and Galleries Commission for funding my research trips to India.

To those in India who have extended their hospitality and made my visits both enjoyable and productive: Radhika Goyal, Kristine Michael, Niyatee Shinde, Kavita Singh and Vinci Wadia.

To Edward Johnson, whose original collection of film posters formed the basis of the V&A collection, and to the artists who provided the inspiration for my work: D.G. Pradhan, Diwakar Karekare, Rahul Nanda, Rajesh Vaidya and those at Balkrishna Arts. To the Victoria Miro Gallery, Annu Palakunnathu Matthew and Gulam Mohammed Sheikh for use of their images.

Above all I would like to thank my family, and particularly my mother, for their support.

Our collective thanks: To Arti Karkhanis and Lakshmi Iyer of the National Film Archive of India, Pune.

To the producers who kindly provided us with material, free of charge, and permission to use it. Some producers were extraordinarily helpful, notably K. K. Barjatya (Rajshri Films), Vidhu Vinod Chopra, Yash Chopra (Yash Raj Films), Mr and Mrs A. Damle (Prabhat Films), Subhash Ghai (Mukta Arts), Karan Johar (Dharma Productions), Randhir Kapoor (R.K. Films), Shaukat Khan (Mehboob Films), Gulshan Rai (Trimurti Films), Shakti Samanta (Shakti Films), Kiran Shantaram (V. Shantaram Productions), Sascha Sippy (Sippy Films), Shekhar Verma (Verma Corporation Ltd).

Photographic Acknowledgements

The authors and publishers wish to express their thanks to the sources below of illustrative material and/or permission to reproduce it:

Courtesy Muzaffar Ali: 22, 37, 113; courtesy B.R. Films: 15, 27; Courtesy A. Damle: 9; courtesy Dharma Productions: 33; courtesy Raj Kamal Studios: 7; courtesy Annu Palakunnathu Matthew: 118, 119; courtesy Mehboob Productions Pvt Ltd: 12, 13, 24, 78, 86, 87, 89, 94, 95, 96; courtesy Mukta Arts Pvt. Ltd: 8, 18, 36; National Film Archive of India, Pune: 1, 2, 3, 4, 6, 9, 10, 14, 16, 19, 22, 24, 25, 26, 28, 30, 31, 34, 37, 42, 43, 45, 46,47, 48, 49, 50, 51, 52, 53, 57, 58, 59, 60, 61, 62, 63, 64, 65, 66, 67, 68, 72, 73, 79, 80, 84, 85, 90, 95, 117; courtesy Divia Patel: 100, 105; courtesy Rajshri Productions (P) Ltd: 39; courtesy R.K. Films: 4, 11, 28, 34, 54, 88, 91, 92, 93, 99, 116; courtesy Shakti Films: 17, 23; courtesy Gulam Mohammed Sheikh: 120; courtesy Sholay Media & Entertainment/G.P. Sippy: 101, 102; courtesy Trimurti Films Pvt. Ltd: 7, 106, 108, 109, 110; V&A Picture Library: 41, 44, 45, 46, 47, 49, 50, 51, 52, 54, 55, 56, 58, 59, 62, 65, 66, 67, 69, 70, 71, 72, 74, 75, 76, 77, 78, 79, 80, 81, 82, 83, 85, 86, 87, 88, 89, 90, 91, 92, 93, 94, 95, 96, 97, 98, 99, 100, 101, 102, 103, 104, 106, 107, 108, 109, 110, 111, 112, 113, 114, 115, 116, 120, 121; courtesy Verma Corporation Ltd: 20, 21, 35; Victoria and Albert Museum, London: 44 (IS.59-1978), 54 (IS.42-2001), 75 (IS. 110-1986), 76 (IS. 53-1987), 77 (IS. 113-1992), 78 (IS. 8-2001), 81 (IS. 181-1992), 82 (IS. 91-1986), 83 (IS. 108-1986), 86 (IS.13-1992), 87 (IS.10-2001), 88 (IS.28-2001), 89 (IS.7-2001), 91 (IS.27-2001), 92 (IS.29-2001), 93 (IS.107-1986), 94 (IS.158-1992), 96 (IS.9-2001), 97 (IS.97-1986), 98 (IS.88-1992), 99 (IS.33-2001), 101 (IS.190-1992), 102 (IS.80-1987), 103 (IS.101-1986), 104 (IS.105-1988), 106 (IS. 264-1992), 107 (IS.98-1986), 108 (IS.96-1988), 109 (IS.95a-1988), 110 (IS.95-1988), 111 (IS.94-1988), 112 (IS.291-1992), 113 (IS.200-1992), 114 (IS.166-1992), 115 (IS.128-1988), 116 (IS.75-1987), 120 (IS.15-1986); courtesy Victoria Miro Gallery, London: 121; courtesy Yash Raj Films Pvt Ltd: 5, 29, 32, 33, 38, 40, 104.

Index

Numerals in *italics* refer to illustrations.